A SOCIOLOGY OF MENTAL ILLNESS

A SOCIOLOGY OF MENTAL ILLNESS

Mark Tausig
University of Akron

Janet Michello
*LaGuardia Community College
of the City University of New York*

Sree Subedi
Miami University

PRENTICE HALL, UPPER SADDLE RIVER, NEW JERSEY 07458

Library of Congress Cataloging-in-Publication Data

TAUSIG, MARK.
   A sociology of mental illness/Mark Tausig, Janet Michello, Sree Subedi.
     p. cm.
   Includes bibliographical references and index.
   ISBN 0-13-459637-4
   1. Social psychiatry. 2. Mental illness—Social aspects.
   3. Mentally ill—Social conditions. I. Michello, Janet.
   II. Subedi, Sree. III. Title.
   RC455.T28 1999
   616.89—dc21
                                              98-42451
                                            CIP

Editorial director: Charlyce Jones Owen
Editor in chief: Nancy Roberts
Senior acquisitions editor: John Chillingworth
Managing editor: Sharon Chambliss
Marketing manager: Christopher DeJohn
Editorial/production supervision: Kari Callaghan Mazzola
Electronic page makeup: Kari Callaghan Mazzola
Electronic art creation: John P. Mazzola
Interior design: John P. Mazzola
Cover director: Jayne Conte
Cover design: Bruce Kenselaar
Buyer: Mary Ann Gloriande

This book was set in 10/12 New Century Schoolbook by Big Sky Composition
and was printed and bound by Courier Companies, Inc.
The cover was printed by Phoenix Color Corp.

Printed in the United States of America
10 9 8 7 6 5 4 3 2 1

ISBN 0-13-459637-4

PRENTICE-HALL INTERNATIONAL (UK) LIMITED, *London*
PRENTICE-HALL OF AUSTRALIA PTY. LIMITED, *Sydney*
PRENTICE-HALL CANADA INC., *Toronto*
PRENTICE-HALL HISPANOAMERICANA, S.A., *Mexico*
PRENTICE-HALL OF INDIA PRIVATE LIMITED, *New Delhi*
PRENTICE-HALL OF JAPAN, INC., *Tokyo*
SIMON & SCHUSTER ASIA PTE. LTD., *Singapore*
EDITORA PRENTICE-HALL DO BRASIL, LTDA., *Rio de Janeiro*

CONTENTS

PART I: SOCIAL CAUSES OF MENTAL ILLNESS

Chapter 8
The Intersection of Statuses and Roles   86

Part II: Social Reactions to Mental Illness

Chapter 9
Labeling Deviant Behavior as Mental Illness   103

PREFACE

If Alice, caught in Wonderland, ran as fast as she could just to stay in the same place, then many of us feel we are losing ground in our own fast-paced wonderland. Stress is everywhere. No one has enough time. No one has enough money. No one is sure if they will keep their job. There are drugs, crime, AIDS, divorce, suicide, pollution, and threats of war. We worry for ourselves and our children. It is no wonder, in our wonderland, that being "stressed out" or "burned out" are commonly understood expressions and commonly observed reactions to modern life. Life can drive us crazy. Reliable estimates suggest that an adult has a fifty-fifty chance of experiencing a mental illness in his or her lifetime.

But everyone's chance is not the same. Rather, the frequency of mental illness varies by such factors as gender, socioeconomic status, marital status, and work status. While some would explain these differences as due to biological predispositions, sociologists wonder if these social factors themselves might cause people to feel distressed or to become mentally ill. Sociologists have long recognized that the organization of society affects the life chances of its members. The sociology of mental illness suggests that the organization of society also affects the mental health of its members. Economic hardship arising from lower class membership, for example, can be demoralizing, and it doesn't take much imagination to think that poverty might cause distress. This perspective often implicates the day-to-day experiences of individuals that are related to their membership in one social stratum or another as direct causes of disorder.

In the past thirty years, a distinctive sociological perspective on the meaning, origins, and treatment of mental illness has emerged to address these concerns. The perspective is intended to explain how we get stressed out by considering how the organization of social life affects our psychological states. This impressive body of knowledge adds important insights into human behavior and into collective responses to certain forms of social behavior. Each of us has taught courses in our respective college or university utilizing a sociological approach for understanding mental illness and we felt it was time to create a new summary of this research. We do not claim that our book represents a complete summary of such research, nor that all scholars would agree with our interpretation and organization of the material. Hence, this book is *a* sociology of mental illness, not *the* sociology of mental illness.

The modern world (our wonderland) is a vastly complex place. It is also full of contradictions stemming from that complexity. For instance, contemporary societies create opportunities for people to realize their dreams. There seems to be no end to the things people can do to make a living and to the chances for people to be who they want to be. But this limitless freedom is an illusion. Complex systems require high degrees of control in order to function well; they put limits, therefore, on what people can actually do. Norms of acceptable behavior serve important limiting functions, hence the contradiction that we sometimes experience between personal autonomy and social constraint. This is what Sigmund Freud called "civilization and its discontents."

Whatever its origins, mental illness can be described as behavior and thought patterns that are not normative and that require control or constraint because of their potential to disrupt individual and collective arrangements. We would mostly agree that mental illness can have negative effects on individual life chances, disrupt families, and, in some instances, threaten the general community and the continuity of social systems. One means for constraining undesirable behavior is to punish it. Another means is to "treat" it.

A casual review of the listing of official diagnostic categories currently used by professional mental health practitioners to treat mental illness is enough to suggest that much of what is considered to be mental illness also represents violations of social norms of behavior. Hence, sociologists view mental illness as a way to categorize forms of behavioral deviance for the purpose of controlling them. This perspective emphasizes the idea that mental illness is a social construction or idea. It allows us to regard mental illness and its treatment from a sociological perspective as part of a system for the social control of deviance.

Our teaching experience has also made us realize that students do not easily accept the notion that mental illness can have social causes. Although we agree with some of our colleagues that social causes may actually be more important for explaining mental illness than other factors such as genetics and cognitive errors, we will not make this claim. Rather, our intent is to demonstrate the basis for such a claim and let the readers decide (if they feel the need to do so).

If one in two adults will experience symptoms of mental illness during his or her lifetime (and this proportion goes up every time the definitions of mental illness expand), then it seems important to understand how this situation arises and how we deal with it. Alice, after all, was threatened with beheading. In our wonderland we may keep our heads but lose our minds.

Mark Tausig
Janet Michello
Sree Subedi

INTRODUCTION:
SOCIAL CAUSES AND CONSEQUENCES
OF MENTAL ILLNESS

What causes psychological distress? What happens to people with psychological problems? These are the fundamental questions that the sociological study of mental health and illness addresses. Sociologists answer the first of these basic questions by examining the relationship between the way social systems are organized and people's sense of well-being. They answer the second question by examining how persons become labeled as mentally ill, how others react to the labels, and how societies organize the treatment of persons with mental illness.

Over the last thirty years considerable research has been undertaken by sociologists to answer these questions. In our book we use this research to create a consistent narrative that represents the state of current sociological knowledge. The sociological approach to these problems differs from biological and psychological approaches and it makes distinctive and important contributions.

BIOLOGICAL AND PSYCHOLOGICAL PERSPECTIVES

What causes psychological distress? In contemporary American society, the usual explanations of what causes mental illness include the investigation of individual biological and psychological phenomena. We try to explain why a person becomes mentally ill by focusing on the specifics of that person's *inner* life. Is there a history of mental illness in the family? What was their childhood like?

Biological/genetic explanations for mental illness are based on the idea that mental illness is like other forms of illness. It represents a malfunction within the body that produces the signs and symptoms that we

1

typically associate with mental disorder. If the other parts of a person's body are subject to breakdown and disease, why should the brain be any different? There is considerable evidence that biological factors affect the state of one's psychological functioning and that genetic and biochemical anomalies are related to some forms of mental illness.

The psychological explanation of the causes of mental illness stems from the extraordinary work of Sigmund Freud at the end of the nineteenth and beginning of the twentieth centuries. His approach emphasized the relationship between early childhood experience and later psychopathology. A large variety of "psychodynamic" theories have been developed since Freud. To a greater or lesser extent all of these theories propose that mental illness arises from internal mental processes that reflect the interaction of the individual with his or her environment. There is also considerable evidence that such processes affect psychological functioning and that certain forms of mental illness are related to patterns of childhood and family interaction.

THE MEDICAL MODEL

The biological and psychological explanations for the causes of mental illness represent a "medical" model for explaining illness. This model is based on explanations for illness in which it is presumed that some identifiable cause, such as a germ, virus, or genetic flaw, leads directly to disease. The success of modern medical techniques in reversing, eliminating, or treating diseases using this model has encouraged experts in mental illness to adopt this general model as well. Thus, the current understanding of the origins of psychological disorder stem, in part, from the acceptance of a medical model of the cause of disease. Psychiatrists are, first, physicians who are trained to understand and use this medical model. Psychologists may not use biological explanations but they see the ultimate cause of disorder as an individualistic process that is consistent with a medical model.

For both psychologists (Freudian and others) and psychiatrists, mental illness is a clinical problem. Therapists are trained to relate their understanding of what causes mental illness to the specific life histories of the individuals who seek their help. This way of encountering mental illness (in the form of unique personal histories) contributes to the belief that the causes of mental illness stem from a person's particular physical and psychological makeup. Regularities in patient's experiences, symptoms, and responses to treatment allow psychiatrists and psychologists to reach some general conclusions about the causes of mental illness. Finding, for example, that there is a high prevalence of schizophrenia within families encourages a biogenetic causal explanation. Similarly, the discovery that persons who are diagnosed as antisocial personalities often report losing their father at an early age suggests that this loss may contribute to a failure to develop a mature, functional personality.

Medical authorities also have great prestige and influence in American society. To the average person, physicians are highly regarded and trustworthy. Therefore, the assertion that mental illness resembles other forms of illness carries great weight and influences the way in which we think about the causes and cures of mental illness. The medical model fits both biological and psychological explanations for the causes of mental illness and its use dominates the way persons are treated for identified psychological disorders.

The individualistic approach represented in these familiar explanations have limits, however. For instance, neither can explain why single, working mothers are more depressed than married, working mothers or why people with poor jobs are more depressed than those with good jobs. We do have an intuitive idea of how to explain these observations. We know that single mothers have to manage both paid work obligations and a household without help and that this is stressful. We know that a dull, repetitive job that offers no opportunity for creativity can be demoralizing. But neither explanation exactly fits a biological or psychological explanation for mental disorder.

THE SOCIOLOGICAL PERSPECTIVE

By contrast, sociologists make very different assumptions about the causes of disorder and responsibility for illness. Sociology is not a clinical science. It works with collective behavior that is attributed to the general organization of society. As such, it focuses less on individual experience and more on conditions that determine why so much experience is common to different people. Thus, sociologists suggest that unmarried, working mothers, because they are women, are channeled into "women's" jobs that have stressful characteristics and low pay, and that they retain responsibility for child-rearing and household management because of the traditional gendered division of labor. Unmarried, working women with young children can be overwhelmed with demands and they do not have the resources to deal with these demands. The result? They are comparatively more likely to be depressed. Similarly, sociologists understand that all jobs are not the same. Some jobs are more rewarding. They give people a chance to use their creativity, they pay well, and work conditions are pleasant. The chances of landing such a job differ as a function of race, gender, education, and family background. If people with bad jobs are more distressed than people with good jobs, part of the explanation has to do with why there are differences in job conditions and why there are differences in the chances of getting good jobs simply based on social background.

The sociological explanation suggests that the ways in which societies are organized, not just biological and psychological characteristics of individuals, must be considered as causal factors in mental illness. Sociologists do not argue that people should not be held responsible for their behavior because they are victims of "society," but they do suggest that social structure imposes restrictions on behavior as surely as biological inheritance and that the effects of social conditions on mental illness need to be understood, to explain both individual distress and how that distress might be related to larger forces.

Sociologists rely on evidence collected from random samples of people residing in the community rather than on clinical samples. The advantage of this technique is the ability it gives us to make generalizations about the relationship between conditions of people's lives and psychological distress. Its disadvantage is that it cannot provide the fine-grained detail of clinical information. The insights gained from this *epidemiological* method are, however, profound.

The epidemiological approach deals with the distribution of disorders in a defined population. In a social epidemiologic approach we deal with the distribution of disorder in terms of important social categories such as gender, occupation, race, age, and economic status. As we observe differences in the probability of finding persons with disorders in these different categories, we naturally also ask why they are observed. What is it about being female or poor, for instance, that makes it more likely that such persons have relatively higher rates of distress or disorder? These are sociological questions and their answers rely on the utilization of sociological theory. Starting from an epidemiologic approach leads us to ask more refined questions about the origins of distress and disorder and has lead to the development of some sophisticated answers.

We briefly outline below the central theoretical model that has been used by sociologists to explore these observations. In subsequent chapters we will elaborate the theory and summarize the empirical studies that have utilized this perspective. The approach can be labeled, "the sociological study of the stress process" (Pearlin 1989). The sociological study of the stress process is a structural approach that addresses the question of how the organization of social life affects the "emotional interiors of peoples lives" (Aneshensel et al. 1991) or, what causes psychological distress. There is a genuine sense in which we can say that social life causes mental disorder.

THE ORIGINS OF THE SOCIOLOGICAL STUDY OF THE STRESS PROCESS

The current understanding of the social causes of distress, ironically, emerged from medical studies of the relationship between stress and health. The medical model is a model of individual pathology, a disease model in which a biological defect or exposure to an infectious agent leads to illness. It is decidedly not a social model but, as we will see, its use by sociologists leads to a very clear statement of a sociological model.

None of us would be surprised to hear that stress causes people to "go nuts," "flip out" or "get depressed." In fact, we have become so used to this understanding that we think nothing of relating someone's temporary "disorder" to the fact that he/she "has been under a lot of stress lately."

In 1967 Drs. Thomas Holmes and Richard Rahe published a paper describing the "social readjustment" rating scale and presented data that suggested that the experience of social "life events" by an individual can lead to physical illness (Holmes and Rahe 1967). Holmes and Rahe argued that we generally live in a fairly sedate, balanced state—an equilibrium state—in which we are generally healthy and happy. However, in social life there are any number of "events" that can happen to a person that require "readjustment." That is, events are "life changes" and each event represents a certain number of "life change units." If one accumulates a relatively large number of life change units in a short period of time, the person may be unable to reestablish an equilibrium and this will ultimately cause a physiological breakdown that is experienced as illness.

This is very much a medical model of illness, in which bodily functioning is overwhelmed by the required readjustment and so bodily breakdown occurs. This explanation has its basis in an earlier argument that animals of all kinds, aroused without possibility of flight and unable to remove the source of arousal, will eventually reach a state of exhaustion that, in some instances, leads to death (Selye 1956). Holmes and Rahe's formulation is very much in keeping with this idea. More life change is the same as continuous arousal. Too much readjustment, like unabated arousal, leads to illness.

Unlike some other theories, however, Holmes and Rahe identified events of social living such as marriage, parenting, household changes, work changes, and personal changes rather than physical threats and assaults as the stimuli evoking a physiological response. They argued that readjustments of daily activity that result from occurrences in one's social life actually cause physiological stress in exactly the same way that the body responds to changes of temperature, for example. As such, this "socio-medical" model emphasizes the social antecedents of mental disorder, that is, how events in one's social life affect one's mental health.

This novel formulation was quickly expanded in several ways. The list of "stressful" life events was expanded, modified, and grouped in different fashions, and the health outcomes of experiencing stressful events was expanded to include psychological outcomes, especially depression. Over the next ten years there was an enormous volume of research demonstrating a relationship between the social readjustment rating scale and a host of illnesses including heart disease, stomach problems, and cancer. Sociologists too were eager users of this scale but they began to work with the data in slightly different ways.

For one thing, they noticed that not everyone who experienced many life events became ill. In fact, statistically speaking, life events themselves explained only a tiny portion of observed illness (Rabkin and Streuning 1976). Most people who experienced life events did not get sick and lots of people without any life events did get sick. So people started asking, why? Initially two ideas were suggested. First, some people have "support" or "social support" when facing crises. That is, people who experience life events, but who receive help from others to deal with the stressor, will not get sick. Second, it was also proposed that personality, particularly such psychological coping resources as self-esteem, mastery, or sense of personal control could offset the stressful effects of events. It was proposed that in the face of events, one's belief that he or she can deal with the readjustment required, reduced the likelihood that he or she would become ill from the experience of events (Dohrenwend and Dohrenwend 1981).

Whereas the original model was sociological in the sense that events often arise because of one's participation in social life, this new model added that one's social relationships may also affect the likelihood of being able to handle the event without becoming ill. Now we have a model in which there is an explanation for why everyone does not get sick when they experience events. Some people get social support or have the personal ego-strength to deal with the event(s) and some do not. Those who do not, get sick.

But this is still a medical model. It still assumes that some noxious stimuli (life event) behaves like an invading germ or virus to cause illness (even if the illness is often defined as depression or depressed mood). Social support and coping mechanisms act like antibodies or drugs to stimulate a positive reaction from the sufferer. Nevertheless, many sociologists eagerly embraced this enhanced socio-medical model and explored the effects of variations in the types and number of supporters and the exact causal ordering of relationships between events, support, and illness.

THE CURRENT SOCIOLOGICAL STUDY OF THE STRESS PROCESS

At the same time, however, people began to pay attention to the persistent findings that women appeared to be depressed more often than men, and that persons with better education and better jobs were less likely to be depressed. From a biological perspective this can be explained in one of two ways. First, women and less-well-educated people may be biologically less hardy and therefore more prone to illness. Second, women and less-well-educated people might experience more stressful life events and, therefore, be more prone to illness because they are more often exposed to stressful conditions. However, research does not support either idea. Although they may be exposed to different life events, men and women do not seem to be exposed to different numbers of events (Thoits 1987).

Sociologists suggest that we observe different rates of disorder by social characteristics because of the ways in which people experience life based on social characteristics and the different levels of resources, such as personal coping skills and social support, that people in different status levels have or can obtain. This is the description of the *sociological study of the stress process* that focuses on the mental health consequences of patterns of social organization (Pearlin 1989). Sociological theory explains how normative social arrangements generate conditions that cause people to become distressed.

We will argue that distress that is observed often arises not exclusively from events, but from differences in people's ability to deal with the everyday stresses and strains created by the social context and their position within it. In other words, we will recognize that the causes of distress can arise in the ordinary course of one's life as a direct result of the unequal distribution of life chances and resources. Sociologically, this distribution of opportunities and resources is defined by social structure.

Statuses and Roles as Causes of Distress

There are two components to the idea of social structure that we will use to explore how social context affects mental health. First, people can be arranged in social categories that reflect graduated access to some valued social resource such as money, prestige, or education (Blau 1978). Thus people can be categorized in terms of their income, from those who have a great deal to those who have very little or none. We suggest that persons with high income possess a resource that they can use to deal with situations that arise in their lives and, to the extent that money can buy happiness, rich people will be better able to buy happiness. Similarly, people who are better educated will probably also be better able to think of or discover alternate solutions to problems and, thus, be better able to confront these problems and avoid feelings of distress. Better educated people also get better jobs that pay better. Gender and race are also graduated statuses. Males have better access to resources such as well-paying jobs than do females, and there are fewer favorable employment and educational opportunities available to people of color. Variations in the possession of, or access to, valued resources affect one's ability to meet needs and deal with life experiences. Research shows that persons who are ranked at the lower levels in these social hierarchies are more likely to suffer from emotional distress. Hence position in these social structures is related to distress.

Second, we are also embedded in social structures defined by social roles that we are committed to enact, such as spouse, parent, and worker (or student). Roles define social obligations and consist of sets of norms that govern behavior. Roles and the combination of roles we play can be sources of strain (Pearlin 1983). Roles make demands on us to use our resources to fulfill expectations of those roles. Thus, parents are expected to clothe, feed, and socialize their children. But sometimes role demands can conflict or overload a person, such as when an unmarried woman works outside the home and is still expected to take care of housework and children. The specific roles one plays and the specific role combinations one has (e.g., spouse, parent, employee) determine, in part, the types of experiences one will have and, thus, the potential to encounter stressful situations (Menaghan 1989). Only employees can have troubles with their bosses or experience conflicts between work roles and domestic roles, for example. Roles can provide access to resources, such as income for workers and social support (hopefully) from one's spouse. At the same time roles and combinations of roles govern our daily activities and expose us to different kinds of situations, some of which may be stressful.

A principal contribution to a sociology of mental illness, then, is the explication of how status characteristics and social roles as components of social structure affect levels of distress—how they cause mental illness. The sociological perspective, however, can also be used to address questions about how people who are diagnosed as mentally ill are viewed by others (often stigmatically) and how treatment is organized.

SOCIAL REACTIONS TO MENTAL ILLNESS

A sociology of mental illness must also deal with societal reactions to mental illness. Whether one is persuaded that social factors can be used effectively to explain the causes of disorder, it is certainly true that there are individual and organizational reactions to those who are defined as mentally ill. The other major area that sociologists address is, "What happens to people with psychological problems?"

To pursue this question, we need to discuss the social processes that result in the identification of mental disorder (labeling, the relationship between public attitudes toward the mentally ill and professional diagnosis, the medicalization of deviance) as well as the formal social organizational methods that represent society's response to persons who are labeled as mentally ill (the mental health system).

THE LABELING OF DEVIANT BEHAVIOR AS MENTAL ILLNESS

Persons who experience distress or who act in bizarre or unusual ways are not uniformly defined as mentally ill, nor is all bizarre or unusual behavior evidence of mental illness. The recognition of "deviant" behavior as indicative of mental disorder is the outcome of a social process that depends on the reactions of others and on the labeling of the individual as mentally ill. Mental illness labels have significant consequences for the labeled person. The label shifts that person into a world of treatment that most of us will never experience but one that can have profound effects for persons who are directed into that world. The label marks people as different and bad, and there is a great deal of fear associated with our stereotypes of the mentally ill.

Perhaps the principal insight in this perspective is the notion that mental illness is in the eye of the beholder more than in the actions of an individual. If a tree falls in a forest and no one hears it, does the falling tree make a sound? If a person behaves in a very unorthodox way and no one observes it, is the behavior deviant? Does it indicate mental illness? It is the public labeling of behavior as deviant (mental illness) that provides the meaning of the behavior and that determines the consequences of such acts for the individual.

Labeling theory in its more formal statement suggests that the process of "becoming mentally ill" begins with the production of some form of deviant behavior by an individual, its recognition and identification as mental illness by others, and then individual incorporation of the label as a description of personal identity, leading, finally, to the production of more behavior consistent with the newly labeled identity (Scheff 1984).

In the realm of the school system, for example, a child's early lack of conforming behavior might be taken as evidence of a learning or behavioral disability. The child is labeled as "disabled," and placed in a special class in which deviant behavior is expected (but for which the classroom is especially equipped). The child is quite likely to continue to display this nonconforming behavior, or new nonconforming behavior because he or she *and* the school authorities *expect* to see this kind of behavior. The child has taken on the identity of *learning-disabled,* produces behavior that is consistent with that label, and thus confirms the original diagnosis.

If labeling can be seen as a cause of mental illness, we are also interested in the social consequences of labeling. As soon as the label is applied, people begin to react differently to the labeled person and the behavior they see coming from that person. These reactions are of two kinds. First, the person enters a deviant status in which they are held responsible for their deviance and for which they are stigmatized. This means that others interact with them in ways that are different from the way they interact with nonstigmatized persons. Such interaction may enhance the stigmatized person's feeling of isolation and exclusion. Second, we tend to see subsequent behavior as confirmation of the stigmatic label that, from the stigmatized person's perspective, means that they are trapped in their label. It is this latter feeling that leads to the production of further evidence of the accuracy of the label and the acquisition of a deviant identity. The only behavior for which the labeled person receives any social acknowledgment is behavior consistent with the public expectations for persons with that particular label. So part of the sociological approach is to recognize that societal reaction may have something to do with the identification of mental illness.

The labeling approach is highly sociological because it explains how *other* people's reactions to deviant behavior *cause* mental illness. In some forms, it goes so far as to question the existence of mental illness at all, seeing even the most severe forms of disturbance as socially produced (Szasz 1961). But what is important for us is the idea that, once again, individual biological and personality attributes are not the focus of investigation. Rather, a social construction of the meaning of deviant behavior (a label) governs reactions to individuals who receive this label.

THE RELATIONSHIP BETWEEN PUBLIC ATTITUDES AND PROFESSIONAL LABELS

The attitudes of the general public to mental disorder represent a crucial factor in legitimating how that disorder is defined and who is given authority to deal with it. The general public have stereotypical images of what constitutes mental illness and how it should be treated. That these opinions are often at odds with the views of psychiatric professionals is illustrated by the public debate on the legitimacy of the "insanity defense" and by the frequent neighborhood hostility to the placement of mental health group homes in their "backyards" (Winerip 1994). Despite some probable recent changes in public understandings of mental disorder toward acceptance of the view that it stems from an illness process, the general public still regards this perspective with some suspicion. Moreover, public attitudes are affected by media portrayals that range from the sensitive to the sensational.

While the understanding of mental disorder among lay persons may reflect socialization and media processes, professional psychiatrists and psychologists have their own ways of diagnosing disorder. Psychiatrists have constructed an elaborate diagnostic system to describe and differentiate psychiatric problems—that is, to label mental illness. This system has been devised to resemble the system used to label physical health problems (Kirk and Kutchins 1992). However, it does not seem to do well at differentiating disorders and it can often seem arbitrary and culturally and socially biased. At best it is a primitive system but one that still affects social reactions to those defined as mentally ill. We need to investigate this diagnostic system because it is the basis for treatment by professionals and it affects the reactions of lay persons. Since professionals have the cultural authority to confer labels that can have significant effects on people's lives, we need to understand how these specific labels are constructed.

THE MEDICALIZATION OF DEVIANT BEHAVIOR AS MENTAL ILLNESS

In the earlier part of this chapter, we argued that medical models explaining the causes of mental disorder dominate the way mental illness is generally understood. This is largely because the deviant behavior we associate with mental disorder has been "medicalized." That is, the labels we apply to disorder are *illness* labels. The "medicalization of deviance" represents an extension of the labeling perspective that explains how the medical system has acquired jurisdiction over specific deviant behaviors (Conrad and Schneider 1980).

As certain behaviors become recognized and defined as deviant, the fate of persons in these categories is significantly affected by how we classify the behavior. The medicalization of deviance argument suggests that the categorization of behavior as evidence of illness follows a social process. Even a quick review of the range of mental disorders contained in the standard diagnostic handbooks used by psychiatrists and psychologists suggests that physiological processes are unlikely to account for all types of disorder that are contained in the classification system. Indeed, diagnostic categories are sometimes voted into or out of existence by psychiatrists. This strongly implies that the behavior that leads to many of these diagnostic categories is a matter, in part, of the willingness to claim control over such behaviors. Attention deficit disorder is a good example. Once regarded as a discipline or behavior problem, it has been "claimed" by psychiatrists as mental illness and has become a medical problem as a result. Notice that we approach the treatment of the problem very differently when we think of the problem as an absence of youthful self-control as opposed to when we think of it as a biological-genetic illness.

We will see that medicalization is not always a bad thing. For example, people are not held responsible for physical illness. Illness just happens. To the extent that mental illness can be thought of in the same way, persons so labeled may be perceived and perceive themselves less stigmatically. A child who is "diagnosed" with attention deficit disorder may receive much more appropriate attention than a child labeled as a disruptive student.

MENTAL HOSPITALS AND COMMUNITY-BASED CARE

There is another way in which the labels we confer on individuals affect their social experiences. The societal reaction to persons labeled as mentally disordered includes the construction of specialized institutions that address the source of deviance in various ways. We will use the societal reaction perspective to examine the creation, maintenance, and history of social institutions that deal with persons labeled as mentally ill. Ordinarily labeling theory, as such, is not applied to the examination of this question. The perspective applies because of the common element of societal reaction. The construction of social institutional responses (e.g., the mental health system) represents a societal reaction to "mental illness."

Ideas about the causes of disorder are linked to the construction of social institutions to control that disorder. For example, when disorders were thought to be a function of moral failure, the treatment devised was geared toward restoration of moral orientations. When disorder was seen as a function of the pressures of modernization, urbanization, and industrialization, the treatment was designed to create pastoral, rural environments. The history of responses to mental disorder in society is closely tied to cultural and social assumptions about the way the world works and how people can act within these assumptions. The medicalization of treatment systems is also a function of the general growth of medical authority in contemporary society. Although ideas about the causes of and "cures" for mental disorder follow cultural and social assumptions, they do not move in perfect synchrony. Institutional responses to mental disorder have their own history and many factors govern the exact form of response. Nevertheless, we can make substantial progress in understanding the nature of mental health systems by linking historical transformations in the structure of such systems with social, economic, and scientific changes in the general society. In other words, we can trace the changes in the social meaning (labeling) of mental illness and the mentally ill.

This process culminates for now in a description of the current system of community mental health services. The current system of community-based services represents some of the contradictions that arise because there are various ways of explaining the causes of mental disorder and, therefore, various ways of reacting to (treating) the disorders (Mechanic 1986). We will see that the community-based system is consistent with the socio-medical model that recognizes the difficulties of social and personal adjustment experienced by persons diagnosed as mentally ill. On the one hand, the "worried-well" are thought to suffer largely from problems of living while the "chronically mentally ill" are thought to be suffering from organic-related disorders. Much of the service provided by community mental health systems is geared toward improving social skills and teaching people how to cope with everyday stressors. As such, the system recognizes the importance of social characteristics as keys to successful adjustment.

A Sociology of Mental Illness

The application of a sociological perspective to the general questions of the causes and treatment of mental illness has engaged the attention of large numbers of sociologists for a number of years. However, even among members of a single discipline, the volume of research makes it difficult to obtain an overall picture of what has been discovered. In this book we attempt to consolidate some of this information to provide a sociology of mental health. That is, we plan to utilize a significant portion of the work of these sociologists to create a systematic summary of the sociological perspective as it deals with the phenomenon of mental illness.

Two major theoretical approaches underlie the majority of research and this book is divided into two major parts. Each of these major parts begins with an explication of one of these theories and ensuing chapters explore the research evidence related to each theory. By the end of the book we expect the reader to have attained a familiarity with the sociological perspective on mental illness and an appreciation of its contribution to understanding the phenomenon.

Part I, "Social Causes of Mental Illness," outlines the theoretical argument for the sociological study of the stress process. It reviews research findings that help explain how positions in social structures affect feelings of well-being or distress. Chapters 3, 4, and 5 review findings related to how gender, socio-economic status, race and ethnicity, and age affect people's sense of well-being or distress. We will illustrate how positions in stratification hierarchies directly affect daily experiences and the ability to react to them. In Chapters 6 and 7, we investigate how the central adult roles of spouse, parent, and worker are related to levels of distress. Our daily lives consist largely of experiences and behavior related to the roles we occupy and these can be significant sources of stressors. In Chapter 8, we suggest that social roles are enacted within structural positions and that the intersection of statuses and roles affects our ability to respond to stressors and, therefore, affect our chances of experiencing distress.

Part II, "Social Reactions to Mental Illness," deals with four forms of social reactions: the social process of labeling deviant behavior as mental illness (Chapter 9), the lay public's attitudes toward persons with mental illness and the professional system of labeling (Chapter 10), the social construction of mental disorder as illness (Chapter 11), and the history of institutional forms for organizing the treatment of people labeled as mentally ill (Chapter 12). Chapter 13 provides additional detail on the structure of the current mental health system in the United States for the public provision of services to the mentally ill (the community mental health system).

Finally, in Chapter 14, we revisit the argument made in this introduction that a sociological perspective on the causes and consequences of mental illness provides a fruitful addition to our understanding of this class of behaviors. The result of this "tour" of the sociological research on topics related to mental illness will be the first such summary of this rich area of social research.

A NOTE ON TERMINOLOGY

In the first part of this book, our discussion will focus on the social origins of psychological *distress*. The use of this term, rather than *mental illness*, is deliberate because distress refers to ways of feeling that do not always correspond to categories of illness. Nevertheless we need to link distress to mental illness. In the second part of the book, we begin by talking about the labeling of *deviant behavior* and then argue that some deviant behavior becomes identified as *mental illness*. We need to link deviant behavior to mental illness, as well.

DISTRESS, DEVIANCE, AND MENTAL ILLNESS

We distinguish between *distress, deviance, and mental illness* to clarify the various meanings that are given to psychological problems and the way they are addressed in the research literature. These three constructs are strongly related but also differ from one another.

Distress refers to the feelings of an individual about his or her affective state. An individual who feels unhappy and/or highly anxious feels distress (Mirowsky and Ross 1989). These feelings of distress do not necessarily translate into forms of deviant behavior nor are they always identifiable as mental illness. Most people who can be diagnosed with a mental illness express relatively high levels of distress but such distress is not always a diagnostic criteria nor equivalent to the identified mental illness. Distress is uncomfortable and it represents a psychological condition that does not correspond to our ideal of the happy, satisfied person. Mirowsky and Ross (1989), however, argue that distress is also not the same as the psychological phenomena defined by cognitive forms of mental illness such as schizophrenia. They argue that cognitive problems reflect disorders of the thought processes while distress refers to problematic emotional conditions. The implication is that distress is not mental illness. This is both true and untrue. It is true in that distress is a very diffuse state of general emotional discomfort while illness refers to a very specific set of diagnostically relevant symptoms. Not everyone who feels distress is also mentally ill. It is also true in that some of the phenomena we identify as mental illness, such as schizophrenia and other problems of thought processes, are conceptually distinct from distress. It is untrue because specific ways of feeling distress can correspond to diagnosed mental illnesses (e.g., depression). It is also untrue because feelings of distress accompany virtually all forms of diagnosed mental illness even if such distress is not regarded as a diagnostic symptom.

Deviance as a general category refers to the violation of social norms. In the case of psychological deviance or disorder, it has a more specific meaning as violations of social norms that do not fit other general categories of deviant behavior, such as criminal deviance, and it seems to stem from motives or stimuli that observers find incomprehensible. Members of an individual's family, their friends, neighbors, acquaintances, and strangers may observe and categorize as psychological deviance behavior that violates social norms but that cannot be otherwise understood. While distress refers to a feeling state in an affected individual, deviance refers to the perceptions of others. The deviant behavior observed may initially result from feelings of distress, but this is not necessarily the case. The evaluation of behavior and thoughts as deviance represents one level of the social reaction to psychological problems. It can have profound consequences for individuals whose behavior is so-labeled. Sometimes the label results in the more specific label of mental illness.

Mental illness refers to societal categorizations of observed deviant behavior. We are most familiar with the idea of mental disorder as illness. Illness, however, refers to a socially devised categorization that distinguishes between different forms of behavior with the further intention that such distinctions should facilitate treatment. The notion that mental disorder is a form of illness has been with us since the Greeks but has dominated the way in which most of us think about mental disorder only recently. Describing forms of deviant behavior as mental illness also indicates that the societal reaction to such deviance is defined through the application of public values and their classification as medical problems.

Distress, then, refers to generalized feelings of depression and/or anxiety. These feelings do not necessarily result in the production of deviant behavior that we regard as incomprehensible and, therefore, as mental illness. However, labeling of deviant behavior as psychological in origin can lead to its diagnosis as mental illness. Distress does accompany most states of feeling and thinking that we have come to define as specific mental illnesses.

In Part I, we describe the social origins of feelings of distress. In Part II, we trace the social processes whereby deviant behavior (whether related to distress or not) is recognized as mental illness, and then we discuss how mental illness has been treated in the past and is treated today.

THE STRESS PROCESS
AND MENTAL ILLNESS

How is stress related to that which we may perceive as psychological distress or mental illness? How has the understanding of this relationship changed? How can the stress process be viewed as sociological? These are the main questions addressed in this chapter.

In a class discussion of how the environment can influence behavior, a student used as an example an event she experienced as a child. Apparently a cousin, employed as her baby-sitter, dangled her outside an apartment window ten stories high. She never told her parents how this cousin, in spite of her screams, held her outside the window, upside down by her ankles, for what seemed like an endless amount of time. The student announced during our class discussion that she was terrified of heights and refused to enter elevators or look out a window more than five stories high. In a city like New York, this can be particularly incapacitating. Would you say this student suffers from mental distress? Can we say she is mentally disturbed or mentally ill? How might we view her fears in light of her life experiences? Can we say she suffers from a stress-related disorder? Questions such as these, relating to the study of stress, have been addressed vigorously by scientists over the past several decades. Stress can be viewed as a multifaceted phenomena and studied in a variety of ways. For example, it has been viewed as a biological process, a biosocial occurrence, and as a sociological phenomena.

THE BIOLOGICAL BASIS OF STRESS

The modern biological understanding of stress is based on the work of Dr. Hans Selye (1956). Selye's contributions included demonstrating the links between physiological stressors and physiological consequences or stress reactions. This relationship is depicted in part A of Figure 2-1. One of the main components in Selye's (1956) definition of stress is that a non-specific biological response ensues when there is any demand for change as represented by physiological stimuli. Selye viewed this demand for change as a universal experience for all biological creatures and he interpreted stress as being produced by stimuli he referred to as "stressors." The stress response is then perceived as a general bodily arousal immediately following exposure to some type of stressor. Selye generalized his stress theory to everyday life by suggesting that since homeostasis is constantly being threatened, stress becomes part of life.

According to Selye's view, stress is with us from birth to death. The only way to avoid any negative consequences of stress is to transform "bad" stress (dystress) into "good" stress. Selye considered that the stress response occurs in three phases: (1) the alarm phase, during which defenses are mobilized and the sympathetic and pituitary-adrenocortical

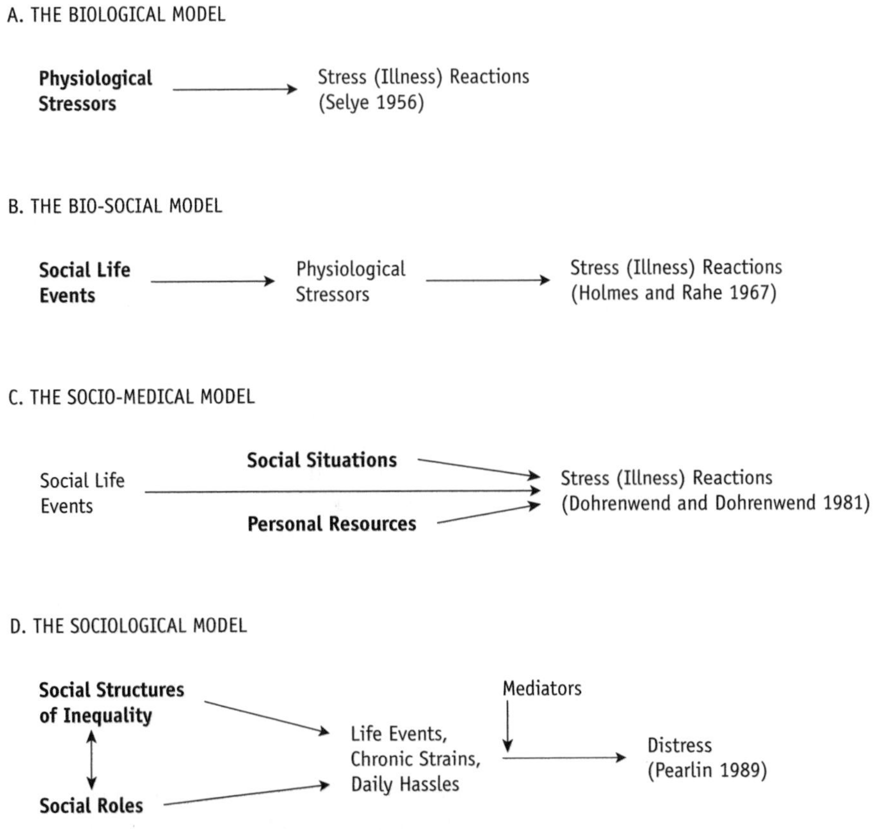

A. THE BIOLOGICAL MODEL

Physiological ⟶ Stress (Illness) Reactions
Stressors   (Selye 1956)

B. THE BIO-SOCIAL MODEL

Social Life ⟶ Physiological ⟶ Stress (Illness) Reactions
Events   Stressors   (Holmes and Rahe 1967)

C. THE SOCIO-MEDICAL MODEL

Social Situations ⟶
Social Life ————————————⟶ Stress (Illness) Reactions
Events   (Dohrenwend and Dohrenwend 1981)
Personal Resources ⟶

D. THE SOCIOLOGICAL MODEL

Social Structures   Mediators
of Inequality ⟶ Life Events, │
        ↑↓   Chronic Strains, ↓ ———⟶ Distress
Social Roles ⟶ Daily Hassles   (Pearlin 1989)

Figure 2-1   The Evolution of Stress (Mental)-Illness Models

systems are triggered into action; (2) the stage of resistance, during which adaptive defenses are maintained; and (3) a stage of exhaustion, in which defenses are overcome. This three-phase response was termed the "general adaptation syndrome." Thus, stress is a physical state of exhaustion brought about by external stimuli and the biological inability to adjust to the stimuli.

From a biological evolutionary viewpoint, stimulation of the sympathetic nervous system is essential to the life-preserving "fight or flight" reactions of primitive man, but the nature of stress for most individuals today is different. It is only occasionally and unexpectedly that one is confronted with overwhelming, life-threatening exposure to extreme biological threat. The situation of the student mentioned above would be an example of a life-threatening stressor. Typical problems today would be the annoying stress and strain of everyday life, such as getting stuck in traffic jams, coping with financial difficulties, or dealing with family, school, or work problems. However, modern-day people have a major difficulty in that the body continues to respond in an archaic fashion, as though the body was still primitive. The body continues to release epinephrine in response to felt stress even though it may not be appropriate. Additional research in the neuro-chemical area has pointed to other hormones or neurotransmitters, such as prolactin, melatonin, and endorphins, as behaving in the same way. It is important to note that some chemical or hormonal responses can actually be harmful to the body. Stressors can result in a compromised immune system that can result in illness.

It has also been suggested that what health professionals consider as contemporary *stress disorders* could actually be labeled as *diseases of civilization* (Anthony 1988b). What is of particular significance about "stress disorders as diseases of civilization" is that the emotional and environmental components of stress take on considerable importance regarding the initiation of the stress response. Stressors occurring repeatedly over a considerable period of time can have severe consequences. This view suggests that the chronicity of stressors, as well as the level of prediction and control over stressors, play important roles. This view is consistent with Selye's explanation. Literature indicates that uncontrollable stressors produce significant depletion of the neurotransmitter noradrenaline in the brain and this absence of control over the production of neurotransmitters can have profound and long-lasting effects.

At this point one might ask, how does the "physiology" or "biology" of stress relate to a sociological viewpoint or the likelihood of developing mental distress or mental illness? It is important to realize that the thrust of this book is to demonstrate how society or social arrangements directly relate to feelings of distress that may ultimately be defined as physical and/or mental illness. This view suggests that the structure of society may indeed act as a precursor to stress (in the biological sense) that can result in some type of psychological distress. In other words, we could argue that the origins of most forms of "mental illness" ultimately lie in the way that the organization of social relations, especially statuses and roles, stimulate physiological responses. Although we are emphasizing the social connections to stress, it is important to have at least a cursory understanding of the physiology of the stress process. It may well be that the sociological causes of distress ultimately operate by affecting biological processes.

THE BIO-SOCIAL BASIS OF STRESS

As mentioned in Chapter 1, Holmes and Rahe (1967) conducted research investigating the impact of social life events on the individual. Their main focus in this research was to demonstrate how different "life events," such as marriage, divorce, change of job, change of residence, death of a family member, etc. might lead to physical illness. Part B of Figure 2-1 depicts this model. Their approach to stress was similar to Selye's in stating that the individual seeks a sense of equilibrium in his or her life and when something occurs that disrupts this equilibrium the person needs to readjust to this change. Selye referred to the body's preferred or desired state as homeostasis and viewed stress as an everyday occurrence in which the body needs to learn to adapt. As you might suspect, Holmes and Rahe's "sociological study" is indeed rather "biological," in that their study, like a lot of other studies, originated from the medical model of illness. The medical model attempts to link some type of toxic agent or substance (e.g., germs or life events) to a specific illness or condition. From this point of view, exposure to some "alien substance" (like life events) leads to illness.

Social stressors have long been suspected of being a precursor of cardiac problems, including death from heart attacks. Studies have demonstrated that unexpected stressors, such as job loss, divorce, or the death of a loved one, are associated with heart attacks and sometimes even with death. Other studies suggest that certain personality characteristics are risk factors for heart disease. In other words, behaviors such as hostility, aggressiveness, and time-urgency (Type A personality) may actually make one susceptible to cardiac problems. It has also been suggested that we need to focus on ways to break the link between experiencing stressors and the development of illness. For example, we can change the environment that causes stressors, alter the way we perceive stressors, or change the response to stressors (Merz 1997).

THE SOCIO-MEDICAL MODEL

The socio-medical perspective incorporates social conditions into a stress-illness model but regards social conditions as simply sources of biological stressors. Divorce, for example, is a stressor not because it represents an unhappy event, but because it arouses a physiologic response that may ultimately cause illness. Part C in Figure 2-1 shows this model. Social situations such as those related to income levels, gender, or education levels can contribute to the stressfulness of events such as a divorce because they affect the ability to cope with the effects of social life events. Personal resources such as feelings of mastery or self-esteem can also mediate, buffer, or increase the effects of life events on stress.

In socio-medical models, income levels, gender, race, and education are simply variables associated with stress reactions. In an epidemiological sense we would see that, in the presence of a particular event or set of events, women (for example) are more likely to exhibit stress reactions. We would want to know what it was about being female that affected stress reactions. From a socio-medical perspective, we would suspect differences in biological reactivity to stressors. The bio-social model simply views social life as a source of physiological stressors that can be indexed as life events. The socio-medical model assumes that, in the presence of life events, physiological or psychological reactions are affected by social characteristics. However, this perspective does not really make clear how these social characteristics might affect the biological process. Perhaps women are biologically different from men and rich people are biologically different from poor people. Even if this is true, it is unlikely to explain all of the difference in stress reactions associated with gender, for example. We know that gender is much more than simple biological difference. Gender has important social consequences related to one's access to valued resources and opportunities. In order to extend the meaning of social distinctions to include variations in access to resources, we need to adopt a perspective that emphasizes the effects of social structures of inequality on distress.

THE SOCIOLOGICAL MODEL

One of the first theorists to make the connection between mental distress and social organization was Emile Durkheim (1897/1951). In his classic book, *Suicide*, he argued:

> Suicides do not form ... a wholly distinct group ... but rather are related ... by a continuous series of intermediate cases.... They are merely the exaggerated form of common practices.... They result from similar states of mind. (pp. 45–46)

As Scheff (1984) points out, Durkheim saw societal norms as so powerful that he gave them a life of their own apart from the people who created them. From this framework, suicide rates are viewed as the result of social influences occurring within the larger social structure. In this particular case, Durkheim felt that suicide was not simply an individualistic response to hopelessness or disappointment. Certain social categories of individuals were more likely to commit suicide because of the relationship of members of those social categories to general norms of society, regardless of their individual bio-psychological constitution. This theoretical framework supports the view that socially induced stressors are directly or indirectly linked to degrees of well-being. But it goes farther. It suggests that the organization of society plays a role in determining who experiences distress and who does not.

Pearlin (1989), Aneshensel et al. (1991), and Turner, Wheaton, and Lloyd (1995) have written extensively about the links between structural arrangements (and the inequalities these structures represent) such as gender, social class, race and ethnicity, and their association with distress. Pearlin (1989) suggests that it is the very structure of society that causes mental distress resulting from stressors. From a sociological point of view, stressors need to be investigated as outcomes of their naturalistic sources in structured inequalities. The sociological model is illustrated in part D of Figure 2-1.

The sociological model used in this book emphasizes that structural inequalities such as those related to gender, socioeconomic status, and race are fundamental causes of psychological distress (Link and Phelan 1995). The structural status of being female, poor, or of a minority racial group directly affects the experience of life events, chronic strain, and daily hassles. In turn, exposure to sources of strain are directly related to the experience of distress.

The essence of social inequality is that not everyone has the same access to valued social resources such as money, power, influence, education, and the things these resources can be used to obtain, such as goods, housing, and jobs. The result is that, when faced with threats to well-being, some people will have more resources with which to deal with these threats. But the argument goes beyond this consequence of inequality. The argument also includes the assumption that stressors arise in an individual's life because of the very conditions defined by structural inequality. For example, single mothers face considerable chronic strain such as economic hardship simply because they are unmarried, female, and single parents. Single mothers are much more likely to face economic hardship because of the inequality of the distribution of socially valued resources based on gender, marital, and parental status. Women, for example, earn an average of seventy-one percent of what men earn.

The inequality of social structure also affects the quality of social roles that lead to events, strains, and hassles. While these sources of distress can be mediated by other social and psychological resources, the primary emphasis of this model is focused on how social statuses and roles directly influence the experience of stressors and the ability to deal with those stressors.

This is not to suggest that other factors are not important; however, societal arrangements (i.e., statuses and roles) are certainly related to feelings of distress that may subsequently be defined by society as mental illness.

LINKING STRESS WITH MENTAL ILLNESS

What exactly is the relationship between stress and mental illness? Which factors are more important? Is it the emotional or psychological concomitants of physical stressors that are the important factors in the initiation of the stress response or the chronicity of the stressor(s)? Regarding these questions, two factors become increasingly important—prediction and control. At the beginning of this chapter it was mentioned that stressors that are not in one's control can produce physiological or chemical changes in the brain. It has been suggested, for example, that decreased levels of neurotransmitters, such as noradrenaline, can have a lasting effect. From a physiological standpoint the role of uncontrollability of stress is an important one. The implication is that events or situations over which we have no control are potentially even more physically damaging than events or situations in which we can anticipate some degree of control.

The same holds true for stressors as precursors of mental illness. From a social structural viewpoint, it is the chronicity of the situation(s) that exacerbates the harmful effects of stressors. It is the continuous lack of control, lack of support, and lack of access to mediating resources that contributes to rates of mental distress. The focus is not on stress-induced brain stem changes but rather on the social conditions that may stimulate these consequences. In turn, physical reactions to biological stress are often defined as "mental illness."

SUMMARY

We can conclude that a number of factors contribute to distress. This chapter has focused on a variety of approaches that address the same theme—how is stress experienced and what makes it become "dis-stress." In industrialized societies, patterns of living have become increasingly complex, demanding, and stressful. It is believed that stress is encountered in all stages of life and is, therefore, "part of the human condition" (Anthony 1988a). However, stress varies in degree of severity and frequency and in terms of who is likely to experience it. It seems that some individuals experience more stress than others. Responses to stress also vary. Some people are quite resilient in response to stress and others are very vulnerable to its effects. Differences in outcomes related to stress are also present.

It has been suggested that more emphasis needs to be placed on the role of societal structure and its ensuing effects as explanations for these differences. The focus of sociological inquiry has been on explaining the development of stress as a product of life circumstances—based on social statuses and roles. The amount and type of stress exposure will vary, as well as the level of mental distress experienced. The next chapter will focus on the effects of gender. The main question addressed in Chapter 3 is: What does it means to be female or male, as defined by society, and how do gender roles differ in what society defines as mental illness? Which statement is true: "To be alive is to be under stress" (Selye 1956), or, to be under stress is to be female?

SOCIAL STATUS: GENDER

The sociological study of the stress process emphasizes the relationship between statuses, social roles, and the likelihood of experiencing some type of psychological distress. The perspective argues that statuses and roles expose people to different types and amounts of stressors and also provide people with different types and amounts of resources for dealing with stressors. Nowhere is this perspective better illustrated than by the consideration of differences in levels of distress based on gender.

In this chapter we will examine how gender affects well-being. Gender affects well-being for two reasons: Gender is a means for stratifying access to resources and a way of defining appropriate role sets. In turn, access to different levels of resources and role set differences affect levels of distress experienced by men and women.

HOW GENDER IS DEFINED

What do we mean by "gender?" How is "gender" distinguished from "sex?" From a sociological perspective, gender refers to cultural expectations and obligations of men and women. It is distinguished from sex, which refers to biological differences and specific innate and physiological attributes and characteristics. Neither sex nor gender differences and similarities are clear-cut. There are various physiological abnormalities, such as hermaphroditism (having both male and female sexual organs) and Turner's Syndrome (the second X chromosome missing in females) that can "muddy the waters" regarding human attributes of sex. Similarly, changing definitions of appropriate sex-roles, such as whether married women should work outside the home, can blur distinctions about socially defined gender differences.

The "nature/nurture" argument regarding male/female characteristics reflects the distinction between sex and gender. The nature side of the debate suggests that differences in psychological well-being, for example, are a simple function of biological differences based on physiological sex. The nurture side of the debate emphasizes the importance of cultural values and social organization as explanations for differences in the experiences of men and women. In this chapter it will not be our goal to decide between the sides of this debate. Rather, we will simply describe differences in distress levels by gender, thereby emphasizing the sociocultural definition of gender over the biological definition of sex.

According to Webster's New World Dictionary, *stress* refers to some type of strain or exertion. Alternately, the letters s-t-r-e-s-s can be used as a suffix referring to a female person associated with something specific, e.g., seamstress or songstress. It may not be a coincidence that *female* can be associated with *stress*. This may be a trivial, but meaningful, reflection of societal perceptions of gender differences and the organization of male and female roles and statuses.

THE RELATIONSHIP BETWEEN GENDER AND MENTAL HEALTH

The literature has consistently reported higher rates of depression and anxiety disorders among women when compared to men (Aneshensel et al. 1981). On the other hand, men have higher rates of substance and alcohol abuse and are more likely to be diagnosed with personality disorders (Aneshensel et al. 1991; Kessler et al. 1994). Aneshensel et al. (1991) have conjectured that these diagnostic differences reflect alternate behavior responses to sources of stress. That is, they argue that men and women are equally likely to experience psychological distress but the behavioral symptoms of that distress differ for men and women. It is possible that differences in the diagnostic frequency of disorders for men and women are due to biological/physiological differences. It is equally likely that these differences reflect socialization and social contextual differences. Most of the research on gender differences in distress have examined depression or depressed mood as indicators of distress. Hence, our discussion of gender differences in mental health will reflect this research bias.

SOCIAL STATUS EXPLANATIONS OF DISTRESS

If gender is a status indicator, it means that access to resources varies by gender. Access to resources is important for two reasons. First, greater social resources are associated with exposure to fewer stressors (Turner,

Wheaton, and Lloyd 1995) and, second, resources are helpful for dealing with stressors when they do occur. Since the principle means of acquiring resources are related to income and work status, we will focus on the relationship between gender, work, and distress to illustrate the relationship between status and distress. On average, women earn about 71 percent of what men earn. Part of this difference is explained by unequal pay for equal work but most of it is explained by differences in occupational segregation and the "value" of "women's work."

Men and women who work often do so under very different structural conditions. Their labor is differentially distributed across economic sectors, organizations, occupations, and specific job characteristics. For example, women are much more likely to be employed as secretaries, school teachers, nurses, and sales clerks than are men. These differences have well-documented effects on job outcomes, ranging from differences in income and authority to distress (Barnett and Marshall 1991).

Compared to men, women constitute a group of workers whose employment is typified by job characteristics that have been found to be stressful. Women's work is concentrated in low-paying occupations, smaller organizations, and peripheral, nonunionized industries (England and McCreary 1987). This occupational segregation is also related to characteristics of the jobs that women typically encounter. Women tend to predominate in occupations that are less flexible and that permit less autonomy than those occupied by men—precisely the characteristics related to high levels of job-related distress (Tomaskovic-Devey 1993; Rosenfield 1989). Even when men and women work in the same occupations it has been shown that women tend to occupy jobs with less power than men (Wolf and Fligstein 1979). In short, social and economic environments play a prominent role in structuring work opportunities and specific job characteristics that, in turn, affect individual well-being. Differences in these environments for men and women may explain differences in gendered reactions to changes in these environments.

The consequences of women's occupational segregation are not limited to restricted labor markets, mobility chances, and stress-causing job characteristic changes. Women may also perceive greater risk of job instability during economic downturns because, as employees of firms that are more likely to be threatened by economic crises (firms in peripheral sectors, for instance), their perceptions of personal threat may increase. Women's job mobility is often limited to lateral changes and even this mobility is limited by widespread unemployment. Further, it is possible that women's jobs will be sacrificed in order to create resources to retain other valued workers (males) during economic downturns. The over-representation of women in economic sectors and industries that favor replacement rather than retention strategies when faced with economic threat, coupled with personnel policies that seek to retain "valued" employees, increase women's perceptions that they are at greater risk of unemployment even if they manage to remain employed. Hence, this becomes another source of distress for women.

Women's job-related distress is, therefore, affected both by the macroeconomic and social conditions that channel women into specific occupations and industries and to the specific job characteristics they encounter. Moreover, the differences in occupation and industry also lead to different consequences for men and women during periods of economic change (Tausig and Fenwick 1992). Gender is a stratification variable that clearly affects distress because of the differences in access to economic resources.

SOCIAL ROLE EXPLANATIONS OF DISTRESS

Women and men also differ in the way they are exposed to stressors because of the status-related consequences of differences in roles typically enacted by men and women. Part of gender-related status differences comes from the assignment of men to external, economic roles and women to domestic roles. While this is changing, of course, for purposes of discussion we will use stereotypes about typical role sets to illustrate our argument. Several approaches have been used to account for differences in distress as they are related to roles.

ROLE OCCUPANCY

The explanations that have gained the strongest support regarding gender differences in distress have been the "social in origin" views that suggest that higher distress rates among women are due to the roles they typically occupy. Researchers such as Gove (1972), Gove and Tudor (1973), Aneshensel (1986), Thoits (1986), and others reported that married women are more likely to become depressed than married men. The "role occupancy" perspective suggests that women have too few roles compared to men, and that this absence of roles leads to boredom and then depression, particularly when women are homemakers (Gove 1972; Gove and Tudor 1973). This perspective is limited in scope, since it mainly focuses on married women who are unemployed, and does not consider other roles. Inherent in this perspective is the assumption that playing the role of "stay at home spouse" becomes one's "master status." In this case the master status of homemaker lacks prestige and societal worth for the homemaker but allows the employed husband to benefit from his wife's role, which is viewed as having limited societal worth.

ROLE FULFILLMENT

Some studies have challenged the "role occupancy" perspective by pointing out that in recent years women have increasingly been working outside the home—however, depression rates are still higher than among male counterparts (Aneshensel et al. 1981). Another "social in origin" view suggests that men and women occupy different roles, therefore, they are not at comparable risk of exposure to specific events (Thoits 1986; Menaghan 1989). The issue here may not be whether married women have too few roles but whether they are fulfilling or unsatisfactory (Aneshensel and Pearlin 1987). When one considers that women tend to occupy low-level, low-paying jobs more so than men, such institutional arrangements may indeed be the precursors of distress leading to depression.

Women are also more exposed to poor working conditions, discrimination, sexual harassment, job instability, lack of mobility, and a highly segregated labor market (Lennon 1987). Within this literature, what has become increasingly important is not how many roles women occupy, but whether a role or roles are satisfying (Barnett and Baruch 1987). Therefore, role fulfillment is an important determinant of well-being for women; however, the subjective evaluation of roles also needs to be considered in addition to their objective properties (Pearlin 1983).

MULTIPLE ROLES

Another key element in the social role explanation of gender differences in distress emphasizes the impact of family roles on employment roles. Some studies suggest that women have better mental health when they are part of the paid labor force, compared to nonemployed women. Other studies indicate that employment has significant costs for women's well-being (Roxburgh 1996). According to Thoits (1986) and Menaghan (1989), many role combinations are very gender specific and cannot be adequately contrasted between men and women. Therefore, disentangling gender differences in distress resulting from particular role combinations becomes problematic. However, Thoits (1986) also claims that employment complicates life for married women but is the basis for men's mental health advantage. Another possibility is that women's greater distress is the result of higher exposure to stress. This differential exposure perspective focuses on the combination of work and home roles that may create *unique* stressors for women (Aneshensel et al. 1981; Barnett, Biener, and Baruch 1987). Other studies support the position that when the multiple roles of both men and women are contrasted by specific role combinations, such as the roles of parent, spouse, and worker, some gender differences in depression disappear, whereas others remain. For example, in one such study that examined specific role combinations by gender, it was found that the role of parent is more stressful for women than for men whether women are employed or not and regardless of marital status (Michello 1989). What is implied is that it may actually be the role of parent that is more stressful for women when compared to men, and not necessarily employment or marital status, since women tend to be the primary caregivers regardless of other role obligations. Within this view is the assumption that stressful conditions reside within the institutional settings of work and family roles (Pearlin 1981) and some roles such as the role of parent, whether viewed by itself or in combination with other roles, is indeed intrinsically more stressful for women.

ROLE STRAIN

Pearlin (1983) has suggested that, in addition to strains associated with specific roles, we need to examine how role conflict and role overload (among other types of role-related strain) affect well-being. This suggestion is particularly relevant to the consideration of gender-related differences in well-being. Women are now as likely to be in the employed labor force as men—even if they are mothers of small children. At the same time, women are not less likely to have principal responsibility for child rearing, and home-related chores such as cleaning and cooking. If women have added the role of worker to their typical role set, they have not reduced other obligations. Thus, role conflict, such as when paid work requires overtime and one's husband demands a hot meal when he comes home, are likely to arise. Women are sometimes described as working two shifts (Hochschild 1989). They may not have enough time to fulfill the separate role obligations of paid and unpaid work and this may result in distress. From the role occupancy perspective, women should benefit from the added role of paid employee but from the multiple role perspective, the combination of roles that includes paid employment, motherhood, and spouse, increases obligations and strains women's capacity to deal with the demands of day-to-day life.

In summary, the social role explanations of gender differences in distress support the view that such gender differences are primarily due to the constraints of social roles. The implication is that, as men and women occupy the same roles, gender differences in distress, like gender differences in coping, are likely to vanish (Rosario et al. 1988). This may prove to be especially true for the role of parent as men and women move into similar social roles. However, for the moment women are still more likely to experience negative consequences from role equality because the expectations of what it takes to be a spouse, parent, or worker differ by gender. When roles are the same for each gender and role expectations for each role are identical, then it is possible that distress differences by gender will decrease.

SUMMARY

The social circumstances affecting distress, particularly by gender, are indeed complex. Although rates of mental disorders, such as depression, have been consistently higher for women than for men, overall, the rates of depression in the United States have been increasing across genders as we approach the twenty-first century. People born after 1940 have a greater chance than people born prior to 1920 of becoming depressed at some time in their lives and they also tend to develop mood disorders, such as depression, at an earlier age. The implication is that twentieth century social changes have been provoking or exacerbating mood disorders and are in need of considerable research attention. The further implication is that, to the extent that gender-related role differences are declining, men and women are equally exposed to and vulnerable to stressors in the social environment.

Overall, this chapter has reviewed the dominant themes in the literature regarding mental health differences by gender. Intrinsic in each theme presented was how mental distress or mental illness is linked to social status and social roles. Other chapters in this book review similar types of disparity by addressing socioeconomic status, race, age, marital status, employment status, and the intersection of statuses and roles as they affect distress. Whether we recognize it or not, our overall well-being is very much connected to the organization and structure of the society in which we live and the roles that we play.

SOCIAL STATUS: SOCIOECONOMIC STATUS AND RACE/ETHNICITY

oney buys happiness. Americans believe that you don't need to be rich to be happy but the research data show that money helps a lot. Differences in education, income, and occupation affect just about every aspect of a person's life. They affect where one lives, how one's life is organized, the types of experiences one has, and one's basic outlook on the world. We speak of people with money, education, and good jobs as "advantaged" and that is exactly how we want to think about them in terms of mental health status. By and large, those with greater income, higher education, and better, more prestigious jobs are happier than other people.

In the United States, African Americans are not as happy as non-Hispanic whites. While some of this difference may be due to the fact that a greater proportion of African Americans have low incomes, lower levels of education, and less prestigious jobs, racial status has its own effect on well-being.

In this chapter we will discuss how and why these status characteristics, socioeconomic status (SES) and race, affect well-being. The general argument is straightforward. Persons in higher status positions live lives that include fewer threatening experiences and they have better access to resources that permit them to deal with the stressors that do arise in their lives. This is not to say, of course, that all poor people are unhappy, that all African Americans are unhappy, or that all well-to-do people and all whites are happy. But, as a generalization, individuals with better access to resources report being happier. Socioeconomic status differences, in particular, have a much greater effect on well-being than do gender differences (Mirowsky and Ross 1989). There is a very real and significant sense in which money buys happiness. As we come to understand why this might be so, we will also develop our understanding of how social structure affects well-being and distress.

SOCIOECONOMIC STATUS (SES) AND WELL-BEING

The relationship between socioeconomic status and mental illness has been recognized for some time. In 1939 Faris and Dunham explained differences in the rates of mental disorder in areas of the city of Chicago as the result of differences in the economic, educational, and ethnic backgrounds of each area (Faris and Dunham 1939). They viewed mental illness as a sign of social disorganization and as a social problem and they correlated these differences with levels of crime, poverty, general and infant mortality, and unemployment in the various areas. While they concluded that social conditions might not be primary causes of disorder, they discovered that stressful circumstances associated with living in certain neighborhoods, such as isolation, dealing with adjustments related to recent immigration, and frustration in a career (i.e., unemployment) were precipitating factors for many mental disorders. Their study was not explicitly concerned with the relationship between social status and disorder but the strong relationship between urban neighborhood, the economic status of neighborhood residents, and mental disorder strongly suggested that economic status played a role in the appearance of mental disorder.

In 1953 Hollingshead and Redlich reported that persons in lower social classes were more likely to be treated for mental illness and that, among treatment populations, those in the lower classes were more likely to be diagnosed with more severe forms of disorder (i.e., psychoses rather than neuroses).

Since these original discoveries of status-based differences in the prevalence of and types of disorders, there have been numerous community surveys that have continued to document class and status-based differences in rates of psychiatric disorder. Some of these surveys have documented differences in rates of diagnosable disorder and some have documented differences in well-being or distress (as opposed to specific disorders). Ortega and Corzine (1990) reviewed sixty studies conducted between 1972 and 1989 about the relationship between social status and disorder and reported that forty-six of these confirmed that persons in lower social status positions had higher rates of psychiatric disorder. The remaining studies were unclear or focused on specific disorders and did not find an association. The review found that most studies report a strong, consistent relationship between low social status and schizophrenia, personality disorders, and "organic" disorders. Studies that assessed minor depression or psychological distress were found to consistently demonstrate a relationship between lower status and higher rates of these psychological outcomes as well. The studies also show that there is a weak or even a positive (as status rank goes up, so does the rate of disorder) relationship between status and certain affective disorders such as manic-depression. Overall, most researchers agree that lower social status, measured in terms of income, education, or employment, is associated with higher rates of disorder and distress.

Mirowsky and Ross (1989) report that persons with incomes below $7,500 annually have average depression scores that are twice those of persons making over $45,000 per year. Kessler et al. (1996) report that those earning less than $20,000 are twice as likely as those earning $70,000 or more to report symptoms that would define them as severely mentally ill.

Mirowsky and Ross (1989) also report that persons with less than an eighth grade education have depression scores that are almost twice those with postcollege levels of education. Kessler et al. (1996) found that persons with 0–11 years of education are more than three times as likely to report symptoms of severe mental illness as those with sixteen-plus years of education. However, even those with less than a college degree are twice as likely to report such symptoms compared to college graduates.

Turner, Wheaton, and Lloyd (1995) report that persons in "major" professions have depression scores that are only about 65 percent as high as those reported by persons in semiskilled or unskilled positions. The likelihood of reporting a major depressive disorder among major professionals in a given one-year period is less than one-quarter of that for semiskilled or unskilled workers.

EXPLAINING THE RELATIONSHIP

Selection / Drift Two different types of explanation have been developed to account for this observed relationship: the *selection / drift* hypothesis and the *social causation* model. The explanations differ in the way they relate social structure and social status to mental illness (and/or distress).

The first of these explanations is called the selection/drift hypothesis. This explanation suggests that mental illness causes social status (not that social status causes mental illness). According to this argument, sicker (physically and mentally) persons are less able to compete for social resources such as education, occupations, and income. Therefore, unhealthy people are "selected out" of higher SES positions in the same way that evolutionary theory explains the natural selection of physical traits among living species. In this Darwinian (or Lamarckian) process, those who cannot compete occupy social statuses that are inferior to those who can compete. Since mental illness represents a handicap in this regard, we find persons with mental illness in lower SES positions because they lack the ability to attain higher social status. The reason we find greater rates of mental illness and distress in lower SES groups is because lower levels of the "right stuff" mean you can only attain lower levels of socioeconomic resources.

We also observe greater levels of mental disorder and distress in lower SES categories because persons with mental disorders "drift" down into lower SES levels as a result of their mental illness. An individual who otherwise could compete for higher SES levels, but who becomes mentally ill, will fall down to inferior SES levels because the illness prevents him from competing. Selection suggests that some people lack the mental health to compete as a fundamental biological handicap and so they never reach higher SES levels. Drift suggests that the occurrence of a mental illness can also cause previously successful persons to lose status as the illness interferes with their ability to compete.

In selection/drift explanations the common conditions such as poverty, neighborhood violence, high levels of divorce, etc. that Faris and Dunham (1939) first observed in association with high levels of disorder are simply correlates of these high rates of disorder or results of high rates of disorder. For example, persons with a disorder might not be able to maintain good interpersonal relationships and may be more likely to become divorced. Finding oneself in these negative social conditions is a consequence of mental disorder, not a cause of it.

The selection/drift explanation is not a truly sociological model. However, the arguments made for this model are almost certainly true. Numerous investigators have shown that persons who receive a diagnosis as schizophrenic often lose jobs and status. What is really at issue is the extent to which such a model accounts for most of the association between social status and mental illness/distress. This turns out to be a very difficult question to answer. Studies that test the selection/drift model mostly require very long-term data, specifically, intergenerational data. That is, the selection/drift hypothesis is best tested when it can be shown that members of the same biological family remain in the same SES locations over generations due to recurring mental illness, and that the onset of mental illness causes long-term status decline. This is difficult data to obtain and difficult to analyze. In addition, it does not appear that the number of persons who drift down in status as a result of their disorder is sufficient to account for all the persons at a given status level who are suffering from a psychiatric disorder. Also, the type of general distress that we have been contrasting to well-being does not often cause changes in socioeconomic status. Hence, we need to consider an alternate explanation.

Social Causation   The social causation model says that SES causes mental illness (not that mental illness causes SES). This is the model that we have actually been using to describe the relationship between income, jobs, education, and well-being, and it seems to be the model that is most significant (compared to selection/drift) as well (Aneshensel 1992). In this model people arrive at their SES level largely through their acquired education and the access to jobs and income that education makes possible. People in lower socioeconomic statuses live in a social environment that exposes them to more stressful situations and they are more vulnerable to the effects of these stressors because they lack the financial, intellectual (educational), and personal resources to deal with stressors. People with poor educations get jobs that pay less, are unpleasant and uninteresting, are more subject to layoffs during economic recessions, and often lack health and other benefits. They face day-to-day circumstances in which making ends meet and dealing with changes can become a significant challenge to their sense of well-being and, the social causation theory argues, they are more likely than people with higher levels of education and income to feel this challenge to their sense of well-being.

Good jobs, high income, and high education cause well-being because they supply people with the resources they need to deal with the events, conditions, and daily hassles in their lives. At the opposite end, bad jobs, low income, and low levels of education expose people to more stressors and leave people without helpful resources and so they are more likely to feel distressed. Hence, the relationship between lower SES and higher rates of distress is explained by suggesting that low SES exposes occupants to higher levels of stressors to which they are also more vulnerable. Social status causes distress.

THE SOCIOECONOMIC DISTRIBUTION OF STRESSORS

Almost 37 million Americans were living in poverty in 1992 (U.S. Bureau of the Census 1993). Such statistics suggest that a large number of people struggle with economic issues on a day-to-day basis. Poverty or low income has negative effects on the quality of housing, the quality of diets, the quality of medical care, and the ability to deal with the economic impact of needs that arise in the course of everyday life. Poverty also increases the likelihood of being a victim of a crime and the chances of being arrested.

Thirty-two percent of all family groups with children were headed by a single parent (mostly mothers) and fifty-four percent of poor families are headed by women (U.S. Bureau of the Census 1997). Since women earn about 71 percent of what men earn, female-headed households with children represent a social situation with a high likelihood of financial stressors related to poverty.

Turner, Wheaton, and Lloyd (1995) measured stressful life events, chronic stressors, and childhood and adult traumatic events for a sample of Canadian adults. They showed that having an occupation that was classified as "major professional" or "lesser professional" was uniformly related to the reporting of fewer stressors of all types. By contrast, those in semiskilled or unskilled occupations reported the highest rates of all types of stressors.

Ross and Van Willigen (1997) report that poorly-educated people are more likely to be employed part-time (versus full-time) than are more educated persons. Poorly educated persons are more likely to experience layoffs, and they are more likely to work in jobs that are routine, do not offer a variety of tasks, and offer little chance for continued learning and development. Of course, persons with lower education also have jobs that pay more poorly. Households in which a main earner has less than a ninth grade education average an income of $15,000 per year while households in which the main breadwinner has a bachelor's degree earn almost $53,000 per year (U.S. Bureau of the Census 1997). Thus, financial hardships are a major category of stressors for persons with low levels of education.

THE SOCIOECONOMIC DISTRIBUTION OF RESOURCES

Differences in access to resources (including financial and social) that can be used to mediate or buffer the effects of stressors are also based, in part, on income, education, and occupation. Differences in access to resources explains vulnerability to the effects of stressors and the likelihood that exposure to stressors will result in feelings of distress. In other words, those with higher SES can deal with stressors better.

You will not be surprised to learn that economic resources are not equally distributed among American households. It is estimated that the richest 2.5 million Americans (about 1 percent of Americans) have as much income as the poorest 100 million (about 40 percent of Americans). Clearly, persons in low-income households have substantially lower access to economic resources that can be used to solve problems than do the wealthy.

Money and wealth represent one type of resource that can be easily understood to help offset the stressful nature of some life experiences. We said that money can buy happiness because money (and the material things it buys) can eliminate many potentially stressful conditions once they arise. Although people with higher incomes may not experience as many potentially stressful situations, part of life for everyone includes dealing with stressors. When your car breaks down, does it make a difference to your mood if you know the repair is affordable or not? The breakdown becomes an annoyance when its repair creates a minor interruption of your day and has no meaningful affect on your bank account. The same breakdown creates a highly stressful condition when it causes you to choose between having it repaired and paying the rent.

Education produces resources related to income, intellectual flexibility, and types of jobs. First, education is strongly linked to income. College graduates, for example, have average incomes that are twice those for high school dropouts. At each higher level of educational attainment, there is a "payoff" in terms of higher income that lasts throughout one's work career.

Education is also related to the development of flexible, creative ways of thinking about problems and this characteristic affects the way people go about solving problems in their lives (Kohn and Schooler 1983). Flexibility may be seen as a resource that can offset the stressfulness of life. In this instance, it does so by making it more likely that you will be able to consider several ways to deal with a given problem in your life. The more ways one can think about a problem, the more likely a better solution can be found. The ability to think in more complex terms and to uncover alternatives is related to the level of one's education and becomes an important resource for dealing with problems.

Education is also strongly related to the type of job one can obtain. This principle may be exactly why you are attending college. Professionals, for example, have high levels of education and income. Day laborers, unskilled laborers, and those in clerical positions generally have much lower levels of income and education. Persons with better education are much more likely to have jobs that are considered desirable because they allow workers more personal control (decision latitude or autonomy) over how the job is done, give the worker control over other workers, and expose the worker to far fewer hazardous environmental stressors. Such workers are also less likely to lose their jobs during downturns in the economy.

Link, Lennon, and Dohrenwend (1993) have shown that higher SES leads to occupations in which employees have greater control over the work of others. In turn this leads to a greater sense of mastery and personal control that lowers depression and distress. There is substantial evidence that the sense of personal control derived from high levels of income and education and having a good job is an important asset for coping with most contingencies in life. Feelings of personal effectiveness and control are a key resource for solving problems and enhancing well-being (Mirowsky and Ross 1989). To the extent that personal control is derived from income, education, and occupation, then this resource is status-related and helps explain the social causes of mental illness and distress.

Social status also provides access to another type of resource—social networks. Social networks describe the relationships we have to other people and they also describe our access to resources controlled by these others. For example, if you are looking for a new job, one way to find it is to reply to want ads listed in the newspaper. But then you are competing against everyone who is also looking for the same type of job. It would help if you knew someone at the firm that was looking for a new employee. That insider could put in a good word, get you an interview, and increase your chances of landing the job. The person you know in the firm is a member of your social network and he or she represents a resource for you. In getting a job, we sometimes say, "its not what you know, but who you know."

Now suppose the job you are looking for is that of a bank teller and that you know someone at the bank. Would it make a difference to your chances of landing the job if that person was another teller or the president of the bank? It turns out that your chances of knowing the bank president or knowing someone who knows the bank president is related to your social status (Lin 1982; Campbell, Marsden, and Hurlbert 1986; Tausig 1990). The bank president would be the better contact and the greater your own social status in occupational or economic stratification systems, the greater the likelihood that you will have access to the president or others of equal or higher status. Hence, to the extent that social networks provide access to opportunity, information, influence, and practical support, networks play a crucial role in dealing with life events, strains, and hassles and their effects on well-being will be related to the quality of help you can obtain.

The idea that social networks provide access to people who may be considered resources for dealing with stressors includes the notion of social support. Social support refers to the assistance that others provide to a person as they deal with the stress and strain of their lives. This assistance can take a number of forms. It can be emotional and expressive when someone relays their affection and esteem to another. Support can also be instrumental when someone provides tangible assistance such as money, information, or influence to someone.

Most studies of social support deal with the effects of emotional exchanges. They show that having a close, confiding relationship with someone is very important for offsetting the effects of stressors and reducing levels of distress. Few of these studies, however, explore the relationship between socioeconomic status and the availability of a close confiding relationship. In fact, confidants are mostly spouses or lovers and they probably share socioeconomic status with their companion. The emotional closeness of persons appears more important than their socioeconomic characteristics for explaining the effects of emotional support on distress.

This is not true for instrumental support. If one is looking for a job, it is far better to seek help from someone with higher status with whom one has a "weak" tie (Granovetter 1974; Lin, Vaughn, and Ensel 1981). In this case, the higher one's own standing in socioeconomic terms, the higher the socioeconomic status of instrumental supporters you can reach and the better the outcome for you (Lin 1982). Contact the bank president (if you can) rather than the teller if you want a job. This same logic extends to the need for information. Persons who are in higher status positions generally have more information (they probably have higher education) and they are more likely to have a better variety of information than people at a lower socioeconomic level.

In truth, very little research has been done that relates socioeconomic status to network support resources. We do know that network structures differ by socioeconomic characteristics (Campbell, Marsden, and Hurlbert 1986) but we do not know exactly how those differences affect the support that is available to persons in different socioeconomic statuses. We should note that while emotional support seems to be clearly related to emotional well-being, instrumental support can also contribute to well-being. Persons who are out of a job will certainly feel better if they get a new job. If getting the job is facilitated by using weak, higher status ties, then the instrumental support received from one's network will also have an effect on the job finder's well-being.

SECTION SUMMARY

The selection/drift and the social causation explanations each have some ability to account for specific ways that disorder and SES are related. For example, there will always be people who start in relatively high socioeconomic positions but who, because they develop symptoms of distress or disorder, will be unable to keep their jobs and income. These persons will drift down into lower levels. Moreover, sometimes the stigma associated with the diagnosis of a mental illness will prevent persons who can function from getting jobs consistent with their levels of education and experience. These people also drift down into lower SES levels. At the same time, such an explanation does not account for the majority of cases in which persons in lower SES positions are observed to have signs of distress or disorder. Most have not come from higher socioeconomic levels nor did they manifest any symptoms of mental illness prior to arriving at their current SES level.

Therefore, we conclude that something about high levels of education, income, and good occupational conditions causes people to be happy. That "something" is reduced exposure to stressful events and conditions, and reduced vulnerability to the negative effects of stressful conditions due to better access to financial, intellectual, psychological (control), and social network resources that come with education, income, and good jobs. In this sense, money can buy happiness.

RACE/ETHNICITY AND DISTRESS

In the United States, race and ethnic status also represent means of ranking persons in hierarchies and so we would expect that membership in a "lower" racial or ethnic category would be related to lower levels of well-being. This assumption, however, would not give us a complete picture of the relationship between race/ethnicity and distress. While it is true, for example, that African Americans have higher average distress scores when compared to non-Hispanic whites, it is not clear whether the difference can be attributed to race or to socioeconomic differences. Since African Americans are more likely than whites to be poor, their higher levels of distress may be a reflection of their relative poverty and not of race-based differences. At the same time, it would not be unreasonable to think that various forms of institutional and informal racial bias would have a separate effect on distress beyond the effects of socioeconomic conditions.

There is not a great deal of research on racial differences in distress but the existing literature does address the issues suggested above. The first of these issues can be called the "social class versus the minority status" explanation for race-based differences in distress scores. The second issue is whether racial minorities are differentially vulnerable to the effects of life events and chronic strains.

Class-based explanations for distress suggest that racial identity has no effect on distress once social class effects have been removed. Thus, if we were to match whites and African Americans so that each group was composed of the same variety of educational levels, jobs, and income, we would find that there would be no differences in distress scores for these groups over and above those due to educational, occupational, and income differences.

By contrast, the minorities argument suggests that persons are differentially exposed to stressors based on their racial identity even when they are matched on the basis of education, occupation, and income. In this argument African Americans would report more distress because they experience more stressful events and strains simply because they are members of a racial minority. Even if education, income, and jobs were equal, experiences based on discrimination and bias represent stressors that would be unique to members of racial minorities.

In fact, these two explanations are not entirely inconsistent with one another. It is quite possible that differences in distress scores are explained in part by socioeconomic differences and in part by the special circumstances of racial minorities.

African Americans do have lower average educational levels, incomes, and occupations. In 1996 African Americans were more likely than whites to have between 9 and 12 years of education and less likely to be college graduates. African Americans earned sixty-two percent of what whites earned on a per capita basis, and sixty-three percent based on household income (U.S. Bureau of the Census 1997).

A number of studies have shown that when differences in income are controlled, racial differences in distress are reduced or eliminated. Kessler and Neighbors (1986), however, argued that these findings do not fairly test class versus minority arguments. They suggested that the effects of class and race differ by class level. They suggested that lower-class African Americans (but not upper-class African Americans) are more likely to show the consequences of minority status. That is, race differences in distress will be particularly large within lower socioeconomic categories. They reasoned that poor African Americans were more likely to be exposed to racial discrimination in addition to economic hardship. Their findings confirmed their expectations but they were unable to explain exactly what was taking place in the lives of lower-class African Americans to cause the observed differences in levels of distress. Takeuchi and Adair (1992) explored the same question although they compared native Hawaiians to Caucasians, Japanese, and Filipinos in Hawaii. They found that when they controlled for life events, differences in distress between the racial/ethnic groups disappeared. In this case, the finding indicates that different minority groups are exposed to different amounts of life events and that these differences explain differences in distress. Ulbrich, Warheit, and Zimmerman (1989) also found that differences in exposure provided an explanation for racial differences in distress. In their study, African Americans were found to be exposed to more undesirable life events and to be exposed to more chronic economic problems. However, it was undesirable life events that explained more of the difference between whites and African Americans in terms of distress.

Exposure to more undesirable life events is not the entire story, however. Vulnerability to stressors must also be considered. Both the Takeuchi and Adair (1992) and Ulbrich et al. (1989) studies considered the additional consequences on distress of differential vulnerability to stressors by race. They both found that racial groups differ in terms of their vulnerability to stressors. Takeuchi and Adair found that Native Hawaiians were more vulnerable to life events than other racial/ethnic groups, and Ulbrich et al. found that African Americans were more vulnerable to life events and less vulnerable to chronic economic problems.

When these studies are considered together, they support both a class and a minority explanation. When class-related indicators such as education, income, and occupation are controlled, many of the differences in distress levels based on race disappear. This means that much of the racial difference is due to differences in socioeconomic status rather than race itself. The fact that African Americans are more likely to have lower

SES standing partly explains why we observe average differences in distress by race. On the other hand, we have also discovered that lower-class African Americans report greater exposure to undesirable life events than do lower-class whites, and they report that these events affect them to a greater degree.

Race affects distress in two ways. First, races are not equally distributed across educational, income, and occupational levels. In particular, African Americans are more often found in low education, low income, and low occupational groups. This distribution (or mal-distribution) is certainly a partial function of historical patterns of racism and discrimination. Poor African Americans share with poor whites a greater exposure to stressors and fewer resources with which to deal with those stressors. Like poor whites, poor African Americans report higher levels of distress, in part because of their relatively poor socioeconomic status compared to others of higher status.

However, educational, income, and occupational differences are not sufficient to account for the observed differences in distress. Rather, we must add that race-based causes of distress include an additional increment of exposure for poorer African Americans and additional vulnerability to these stressors.

Race, as a status characteristic, operates somewhat differently than the socioeconomic differences we have discussed earlier in the chapter. Only part of the difference in race-based distress levels is explained by differences in access to resources. Thomas and Hughes (1986) argue that, despite the ability to document some changes in the relative socioeconomic standing of whites and African Americans over the past forty years, race is still a significant determinant of psychological distress. Researchers suggest that racial patterns of discrimination may still persist, that they may be changing very slowly or that, if attitudes have changed, it may take several generations for equal access to resources to translate into equal educational, income, and occupational profiles, and equal levels of distress.

Willie (1979) has suggested that African Americans are subject to a racial "tax" that is equal to the income differential between African Americans and whites who have the same qualifications for jobs but are paid at different rates. Thomas and Hughes (1986) conclude that, since differences in well-being continue to exist after we account for educational, income, and job characteristics, African Americans are also subject to a racial tax in terms of psychological health. If this is truly the case, then the effects of membership in a racial minority compound the effects of socioeconomic status. The findings of Kessler and Neighbors (1986) suggest that the racial tax is more likely to be paid by lower SES minorities. This leads us to conclude that access to resources is affected by more than education, income, and occupation. The assumed relationship between education, income, job quality, and access to resources is that of a free market in which socioeconomic standing directly and uniformly provides access to resources regardless of race, ethnicity, or gender. The existing literature examining the effects of race/ethnicity on distress suggests that race/ethnicity affects life chances by modifying the connection between education, income, occupations, and distress. It is still the case that resources affect distress or happiness but access to resources is determined by multiple status characteristics.

This is very similar to the way that gender affects access to resources. Race and ethnicity modify the relationship between education, income, occupation, and distress. They do so by influencing the relative "payoff" from education in terms of income and in occupational segregation. Race and ethnicity also affect the number and types of stressors that will be encountered as a result of unequal access to resources.

SOCIAL STATUS: AGE

What are the best years of life? Is it good to be young and carefree? Is it better to be older and wiser? We are concerned by the rising incidence of adolescent suicide but did you know that the elderly are more likely to commit suicide? As we go through life, there are transitions and events that we experience that are linked to our age. Young people gain an education, get married, and have children. Middle-aged people raise families and solidify careers. Older persons retire, deal with physical aging, and the loss of roles and statuses. Age is related to distress because our capacity to deal with transitions and stressors is affected by the resources we are able to mobilize and these resources are affected by age. Age is correlated with our physical health status (but by no means perfectly correlated). Age provides an interpretive context for events. For example, the death of a spouse has different meanings when the spouse is twenty and when the spouse is eighty and the couple has been married for sixty years. Age is also an indicator of biography that reminds us that our past experiences may affect our present.

We can consider the relationship between age and distress from several perspectives. First, we can consider the trajectory of distress over the life course. This approach traces shifts in well-being or distress reported by community samples of respondents who are members of different age groups. Second, we can examine stressors and resources that are characteristic of age groups or life stages and see how they are related to levels of distress. Third, we can think of age as a marker in an individual's life course and consider how events, chronic strains, and resources in an individual's life can accumulate over time.

THE AGE TRAJECTORY OF DISTRESS

So, who are happier—young people or older people? The answer is, nei-ther. Community-based surveys of the population reveal that the rela-tionship between age and well-being is not a simple straight line. Rather, beginning with young adults (because we don't know all that much about adolescents and younger children), levels of distress slowly decrease with age until about fifty-five, when the curve turns upward to reflect increased distress for older persons (Mirowsky and Ross 1989).

This pattern makes sense if we trace some normal characteristics of social status and role obligations across the life course. In general, the research findings about the way that social status (SES) or social roles (spouse, parent, worker) are related to distress does not take into account how age affects the observed relationships. Yet there are clear normative expectations about the ways our life should go at certain ages. Thus, we are expected to marry in our twenties (men should be older than their wives). We should get our education in our late teens and early twenties. Children are grown up and leave the nest by the time parents are in their fifties. Retirement from work occurs in the mid to late sixties (certainly by seventy). Women can expect their husbands to die sooner than they will, so women can expect to live the last years of their lives as widows.

In fact, there is a great deal of truth to this sequence of life stages. There is a great deal of variation, too. Indeed, some of this variation is associated with distress. For example, parents of disabled children may remain in a caregiving parental mode well beyond the expected age at which children leave the nest. The normative expectations we have for the parental role change with age and when these expectation are vio-lated, the situation may represent a stressor.

The trajectory of distress related to age is clearly associated with the trajectory of our acquisition and loss of social resources. Distress goes down, for example, as income goes up and income goes up as people age (until retirement). To put this another way, over time a worker's income tends to go up and so economic security increases and one feels better and more in control of life. Most people begin to work full-time in their late teens or twenties. Their earnings at these ages are probably the low-est they will have. As workers add more skills and acquire job tenure, their incomes go up and this trend continues until retirement. At retire-ment, income generally goes down and distress levels go up. This normal trajectory means that social resources based on income and occupation are at a maximum just before retirement and it strongly links age to social status and status transitions.

We also tend to marry in our late teens and early twenties. Marriage, as we will see in the next chapter, has mostly positive effects on well-being. Stable emotional relationships provide social support and companionship and they tend to increase family income because of the increasing prevalence of dual-income families.

Age can also be used as a general proxy indicator for health status. There is a very strong relationship between physical well-being and psychological well-being. In this case, the health trajectory is a bit different than that associated with distress. Health is best in youth and declines thereafter. But we need to be extremely careful about this generalization. Perceptions of health (rather than diagnoses of illness) do not always follow this trajectory. Rather, people tend to view their health positively until they reach about sixty-five. People are not especially sensitive to objective changes in their health or physical capacity unless health problems interfere with daily activities. However, when they do interfere, physical health problems can be an independent stressor leading to distress. Thus, age is both a social marker of status and an independent factor affecting well-being.

In this regard, there is evidence that we are aging better with each successive generation. Our parents are in better health than their parents; we are in better health than our parents. As we age, therefore, the effects of physical ill-health on our psychological distress will be less important until we experience an illness or disability that limits social activity. There are two ways to plot the trajectory of health: one objective based on physical status and another trajectory based on social resources, expectations, and limitations on social activities. It is probably the latter trajectory, the one associated with social age, that generally affects psychological well-being.

Consideration of age as a status characteristic emphasizes the trajectory of our involvement in the social world and it also emphasizes the transitions that occur in our lifetime access to resources. Therefore, we should find it useful to take a closer look at the transitions associated with age and how they can affect well-being.

AGE, RESOURCES, AND DISTRESS

If we view age as a marker of social status and role occupation, then age ranges become social contexts for defining stressors and for predicting our ability to deal with these stressors. The earliest attempts to relate life events to distress, represented by the social readjustment rating scale of Holmes and Rahe (1967), contained a list of events that was somewhat age-specific. That is, some events listed in the scale are much more likely to occur at specific ages (or narrow ranges) than others. The birth of a first child is much more likely in one's twenties than in one's fifties, for example. The scale also asked about getting a new job, graduating from school, getting married, and taking on a new mortgage. Part of this age-specificity is an artifact of the types of events that the scale included but the main point is simply to note that many events are age-related. Marriage, birth of children, retirement, and the death of a spouse are examples of age-related stressors.

Establishing a family, completing education, buying a house, and starting to work in a chosen profession are events that are characteristic of the age range of twenty to thirty-five. Completing education and starting to work are directly related to the acquisition of social resources, income, and occupation. It follows that individuals will be increasingly able to mobilize resources to cope with life's problems. Of course we are already aware that this increasing access to resources is not uniform. Those who terminate their education after high school or fail to complete college will be at a disadvantage in the acquisition of resources during this age period and throughout their lives (Ross and Wu 1996).

The acquisition of resources during this life stage is related to the decrease in distress that we begin to observe toward the older side of the twenty- to thirty-five-year-old age bracket. Youth, however, is not without negative events that may strain acquired resources. Married people get divorced, employed people lose jobs, and children can represent a drain on economic resources. With the acquisition of resources and demands on resources in mind, let us look a bit more closely at age-related stressors.

CHILDREN AND ADOLESCENTS

We don't actually know a great deal about the psychological distress of children and adolescents. While there are extensive literatures about the emotional growth of children, there is little discussion of the relationship between life stress and strain (Irwin 1987). There are no national epidemiological studies of mental disorders for children and/or adolescents that have been conducted in the United States. However, various regional studies indicate that, at any given time, approximately 20 percent of children and adolescents suffer from a diagnosable mental disorder (Friedman, Katz-Leavy, Manderscheid, and Sondheimer 1996). We also know that poverty is associated with demoralization and distress for children. Every parental generation believes that their children have a harder time growing up. They feel that there is more pressure on children and that they are subject to more danger from drugs, or exposure to violence. How much of this is true? We actually have no good way to measure generational differences in exposure to stressors and strain, but we can describe what we know about the current generation of children.

Parental divorce and separation rates are very high. The average child has only a fifty-fifty chance of growing up in the same household with both biological parents to the age of eighteen. Children who live with their mothers in single-parent households have a high likelihood of living in poverty or in low-income households (Rosenbaum and Starfield 1986). When a divorced parent remarries, it often necessitates the blending of families. This can be a significant source of stress for children. Children are also exposed to abuse or witness to spousal abuse.

A parental divorce becomes a life event for a couple's children. It is not uncommon for children to feel sadness, anger, confusion, and fear following a divorce. Wallerstein and Kelly (1980), however, conclude that the degree of instability in the child's routine, the pre-existing quality of the parent-child relationships, and the ability to continue to meet the child's developmental needs are most predictive of distress related to parental divorce.

Single mothers with small children have extremely high rates of poverty, which means that the children of divorced mothers are also likely to feel the effects of poverty. Moreover, in single parent households, role models for behavior are absent and parental time and attention are spotty.

Gelles and Straus (1979) claim that the family is one of the most violent social groups and that the home is one of the most violent social settings. This claim dramatizes the exposure to abuse that is part of some children's lives. In turn, exposure to violence is related to higher levels of distress. It is difficult to know whether exposure to violence has increased or decreased over time because of the way such violence is (and is not) reported. However, the relationship between violence exposure and distress is not questioned.

In the school system today, children are routinely screened for learning and behavior problems. More children are routinely labeled as learning disabled or diagnosed as having Attention Deficit Disorder (ADD) than at any previous time. Yet it is unlikely that children today are really any different from children of previous generations. Rather, the labeling of childhood behavior as a psychological disorder is part of a more general social process called the medicalization of deviance. The discussion of this process is the subject of a separate chapter. Children who are diagnosed with this and other forms of psychological disorders are part of the growing number of children who are recognized as having symptoms of psychological distress.

Though it is tempting to relate the incidence of childhood distress to higher rates of divorce, single parent households, poverty, and family abuse, it is really very early in the research process to draw many conclusions. There is no doubt that children experience distress. To the extent that divorce, poverty, and violence do affect distress, it is ironic to note that the distress is brought about by adult behavior that has consequences for children. Children, themselves, have few resources that they can directly control and they have poorly developed coping skills. If age is a status variable, then the youngest members of the social system have the lowest status and, therefore, the fewest resources to apply to deal with stressful events and chronic strains.

Although adolescents have access to more resources than children, adolescents more closely resemble children than adults when it comes to characterizing their resources. Adolescents can work as a means of generating their own incomes, but they are still subject to parental control. Adolescent responses to strain may be manifest in different ways than among children. Suicide and accidents are the leading causes of death among adolescents. Schizophrenia (or at least, its symptoms) is most often first evident in adolescence. Moreover, there are high levels of substance abuse that may or may not be a response to stress. Adolescents share with younger children the possible exposure to stressors in the form of divorce, poverty, and violence and they are only marginally better equipped to deal with these stressors.

YOUNG ADULTS

Young adults, say between twenty and thirty-five, report relatively high levels of distress. This stage in the life course includes many changes in roles and status and also includes many events that require substantial adjustment. These transitions are well-known. They include completing education, getting married, having first children, getting a first job, buying a house, and probably moving away from childhood community. If the sheer number of events were a predictor of distress, younger adults would be expected to show high levels of distress, and they do. However, distress declines across this age range as well. Something is going on as age increases. Young adults are acquiring statuses and roles that provide them with resources. In turn, increased access to resources permits better coping and reduces distress.

Objectively, young adults do not represent the age group with the highest set of social resources. Normatively, young people expect their early adulthood to be somewhat anxious and uncertain, but with the promise of more security and comfort to come. This normative expectation probably offsets some of the distress that young adults might feel based on their objective control of resources. Interestingly, Mirowsky and Ross (1989) find that both depression and anxiety decline with age but that anxiety does not increase among the elderly as depression does. This suggests that, until younger adults develop a sense of their ability to survive in the adult world, distress contains a high level of anxiety. However, as they develop a sense of their ability to deal with adult life, levels of anxiety decrease.

The sense of ability to survive is otherwise known as sense of personal control. This sense develops, in part, from the way one deals with transitions and events associated with age. Perhaps the most crucial of these transitions is the one associated with education. The importance of education lies, not only in its role in determining the type of work and the income one can expect, but in the development of a sense of personal control. In turn, high levels of personal control are associated with lower levels of distress.

The higher levels of distress reported by young adults compared to older adults is not solely a function of their improving, but initially lower, socioeconomic status. Some age-related events and transitions are negative and raise levels of distress. Perhaps the most prominent of these is divorce. We are all aware of the high rates of divorce in the United States, and most divorces occur within the first five to seven years of marriage. For younger adults the consequences of divorce can be very serious. Divorce is a financially damaging event, especially for women. The average income of households headed by women who are divorced is drastically less than the income in a married household and it is further reduced by the lower average wages of women compared to men. Since women are also most likely to obtain custody of their children, the finances of female-headed households are further strained by the need to support those children.

In summary, the ages from twenty to thirty-five represent an age range in which distress is initially high but declines as young adults acquire resources and develop a sense of personal control. The major life transitions that occur among people in this age group mostly contribute to this growth in resources. However, some of these age-related events and transitions have the potential to cause distress. Divorce is an undesirable event at any age but it is more likely to occur in young adulthood when couples have relatively fewer resources and may have substantial demands on those resources (e.g., young children).

MIDDLE-AGED ADULTS

Adults between the ages of thirty-five and fifty-five have, on average, the highest levels of well-being and the lowest levels of diagnosable psychiatric disorder (Kessler et al. 1994). They reach their maximum level of income, highest levels of personal control, and are generally in excellent physical health. Middle-aged adults have developed their occupational identities, their children are reaching the age at which they leave to attend college or establish their own households, and the frequency of life transitions is very low. This combination of social status, resource access, and low events leads to a relatively high sense of well-being.

Persons with high education and high income show the highest levels of well-being within this age group and persons with the lowest levels of education and income show the lowest levels of well-being. In this way, the outcomes of earlier life transitions continue to be felt as one ages. It is important to note that, even though distress is lowest within this age group, status and role differences are reflected in variations in distress within the age group. The particular salience of observing well-being levels in this age group is to reemphasize the importance of resource control for well-being.

OLDER ADULTS

It is a myth that old age is uniformly associated with decline, loneliness, and isolation. Nevertheless, the average measure of distress for adults over fifty-five increases throughout this age group. It would not be accurate to associate this decline solely with declines in physical health status because aging is not a perfect predictor of illness and long-term health problems. While long-term health problems do increase as people age, many people are in good health until very shortly before their deaths. It would also not be accurate to assume that all older adults become unhappy. Old age can be a time of great satisfaction and peace. Many older adults are able to take advantage of their accumulated resources to enjoy their later years.

What does decline at a fairly steady rate is resource access and control. People begin to retire, which affects their income and their sense of identity. Transitions in statuses and roles present challenges to older adults. This is especially so because most of these transitions involve the loss of resources.

Retirement often has two important stress-related consequences. Of course, loss of income is the largest, most evident consequence. Older adults are often concerned about their ability to support themselves following retirement. People today don't believe that Social Security benefits will be available when they retire and most people have not saved enough to afford to live without such retirement benefits. Loss of income following retirement is a substantial concern for many elders. Work is also one of the principal sources of adult identity and its loss through retirement can also be stressful. The first thing we usually do to identify ourselves to a new acquaintance is tell them what we do to earn a living. When that identity can no longer be claimed, it can affect our well-being. Work gives purpose to our lives and it involves us in a set of social relations with coworkers that help to integrate us into society and to provide us with social support. For some people, retirement is a major status and role transition and it leads to increases in levels of distress because it results in loss of income and identity.

There are other losses to deal with. Perhaps the principal event associated with the elderly is widowhood. Women's life expectancy is about seven years longer than men's and so it is fairly likely that women will experience the loss of their husbands. Virtually life-long intimate relationships are severed by widowhood and this certainly decreases well-being.

Friends and other family members also die, which results in the loss of social support and often reminds one of one's own mortality. This loss of social relations is also a loss of social resources that would be helpful for dealing with stressors.

Physical health status does play a role in our sense of well-being. Elders who experience health problems that restrict activities are often depressed by these limitations. Moreover, spouses (particularly women) often become caregivers to physically ill husbands. Caregiving, itself, can be a source of strain and distress. Ironically, we are only now beginning to appreciate the wide-spread levels of distress among the elderly. Depression, for example, includes the symptoms of withdrawal from social activities, disinterest in friendships, and loss of energy. These same symptoms are often stereotypically associated with old age and are presumed to be physical correlates of old age. We are now learning that this is not the case. What we previously believed to be signs of physical decline in the elderly may actually be signs of distress that have gone unrecognized. It is estimated that 25 percent of all suicides in the United States are committed by older persons, far higher than their proportion in the population. Men, whose identities are most strongly tied to their employment but are often retired, have the highest rate of all.

This review of stressors by age groups serves to indicate the importance of life course for understanding distress. Here we have treated age as a status variable that is associated with both variations in exposure to particular stressors and with the acquisition and control of resources that can be used to deal with stressors. In the next section, we will consider another life course perspective that emphasizes the consequences of earlier life experiences on later ones. Thus far we have been dealing with age-related issues as though a given individual's biography meant nothing. In fact, we know that a large part of the explanation for current distress is related to prior levels of distress.

THE CUMULATIVE NATURE OF WELL-BEING

To this point we have been summarizing the social context of age, which helps to explain the trajectory of psychological distress over the life course. Age is an independent factor whose importance comes from the normative association of age with characteristic life events and transitions. Age is also an independent indicator of status that represents access to resources. Exposure and vulnerability to events and transitions varies by age and helps to explain aggregate levels of distress within age groups.

Age is also a way of representing individual experience. People's biographies explain many things about their current character and it makes sense to think that prior levels of distress influence current levels of distress. As a biographical characteristic, age summarizes an individual's unique life history. This is essential knowledge for psychiatrists and psychologists who are attempting to treat an individual's distress. In order to understand where one has arrived, it is essential to understand where one began and where the journey has taken them. We understand that an individual's current psychological state can be a function of their previous states.

Sociologists are beginning to apply this reasoning to the study of the relationship between age and distress. In this case, their interest is in the ways in which status and access to resources at earlier ages affects status and access to resources at later stages of life. This perspective is described as "cumulative advantage" (Ross and Wu 1996). In addition, sociologists have also begun to look at the role that childhood traumas and stressors play for predicting adult levels of distress. This perspective is called "cumulative adversity" (Turner and Lloyd 1995).

CUMULATIVE ADVANTAGE

The essence of this perspective on cumulation (the adding up of advantage over time) is the argument that social positions in earlier life affect the physical and psychological health of individuals in later life. If most people complete their education by their twenties, but some complete high school while others complete graduate school, we would expect that these differences in educational attainment would explain health differences all through life. Age does not equalize access to resources. Even if resource access rises for all until age fifty-five, some people start with better access to resources and the differences in access should have effects on health.

Let us use the example of education as an illustration. We have already seen how education is strongly related to occupation and income and to levels of psychological distress. Higher educational attainment is strongly related to higher income, which is related to lower levels of distress. This generalization, however, is not made with reference to age. Do differences in education have consistent effects over the life course? Would the probability of experiencing distress be different at age thirty and at age fifty for someone of a given educational level or would the likelihood of distress grow (or narrow) as time goes by? In the context of age-related transitions and events, do different resolutions of these transitions and events affect well-being at older ages?

The answer appears to be yes. Persons who start at different status levels are consistently likely to differ in their probability of reporting levels of distress across the life course and the differences by status may actually increase over time (Ross and Wu 1996). If we all go through similar status transitions, those who go through these with better resources, will have better psychological outcomes and, over time, the difference in outcomes will increase (cumulative advantage). Alternately, those with lower resources are more likely to have poorer psychological outcomes and, having had poorer outcomes, they will have even worse outcomes from dealing with subsequent stressors (cumulative disadvantage).

From the cumulative advantage perspective, initial status-related differences in access to resources and opportunities operate over the life course to preserve or even widen status-related differences in well-being. Age is not a "great equalizer." In this perspective age simply represents the passage of time that permits the consequences of other social inequalities to play out.

CUMULATIVE ADVERSITY

The other way in which age affects well-being reflects the fact that life events and traumas that occur early in life may have effects on adult psychological status. A number of authors have noted such a relationship with regard to childhood experience of abuse, parental divorce and death, and parental mental illness and parental alcohol and substance abuse. Kessler and Magee (1994) suggest that childhood adversity is associated with difficulties in making successful transitions to adult roles and that such difficulties affect adult well-being. In other words, experiences such as childhood abuse or parental divorce might affect educational attainment, job hunting, interpersonal skills, or likelihood of marriage. Since these transitions lead to increased access to resources, if adversity prevents or delays these transitions, it will lower well-being.

Turner and Lloyd (1995) asked adult respondents to report childhood traumatic events, including serious childhood illness, failure at school, history of abuse, parental divorce or death, and parental substance abuse. They found that the more of these events an adult reported from their childhood, the greater the likelihood that adults would report current distress and psychiatric disorders, including depressive disorders and substance use disorders. Moreover, they noted that the average age of onset of psychiatric disorder was twenty-one years old, which means that such individuals are likely to miss making certain adult status and role transitions. Kessler and Magee (1994) found that persons with a previous history of depression were significantly less likely to be married and more likely to be divorced or separated but did not have lower educational attainment or income.

The cumulative adversity perspective reminds us that the consequences of exposure to stressors (perhaps traumatic stressors, especially) may persist for a considerable time, perhaps for life. It sensitizes us to the role that age plays as an indicator of personal biography.

SUMMARY

Age is a social status variable that is associated with normal life events and role transitions. Age affects exposure to stressors. Age is also a status variable that reflects variations in access to social resources. Age affects vulnerability to the effects of stressors. Thus, age is related to levels of psychological distress that arise from exposure and vulnerability to stressors. Finally, we have learned that age also provides a biographical context in which differences in initial levels of well-being based on other social structural characteristics are preserved or expanded and in which childhood exposure to traumatic stressors can affect adult well-being.

Regardless of where one is positioned in social structures defined by education, income, occupation, gender, or age, one also enacts roles such as parent, spouse, and worker. Roles create demands on our time and resources. The sociological perspective on the stress process requires that we also examine how roles and role combinations affect well-being. This is the subject of the next two chapters.

6

SOCIAL ROLES: SPOUSE, PARENT

In this chapter, we are going to examine the social roles of spouse and parent as sources of strain and distress. Social roles are embedded in social structures and consist of sets of duties, expectations, and obligations that govern behavior. Roles thus make demands on individuals to fulfill role expectations. Most individuals typically perform many roles, such as those of spouse, parent, and worker. Problems in meeting the expectations and demands of multiple roles because of role overload or role conflict are almost inevitable. In turn, such problems may lead to feelings of distress.

The roles of spouse and parent are played out within the context of the family. The family is thus an important setting for the study of the stress/strain process. Family members have high emotional investments in family matters and, consequently, the performance of roles and the content of relations among family members can lead to stress when they do not go well. Family structures have undergone rapid change in the past several decades, so marital and parental roles have also undergone change. There are more single parent families and more dual-earner families today, for example. A working single mother of a small child may be under considerable strain when childcare needs conflict with work demands. The family is also an arena in which problems generated elsewhere (i.e., at work) may spill-over into family life and affect relationships. Finally, even "normal" life events and transitions that the family experiences throughout its life cycle can provide fertile grounds for feelings of distress. As Pearlin (1983, 7) puts it, "The family is truly many things to its members. It is commonly an active and rich source of pain, it is sensitively reflective of problems whose roots are outside its boundaries, and it is commonly where people turn to find relief from pain. In the stress process, it has a uniquely pivotal position."

We will describe the roles of spouse and parent within families, and the effects playing these roles have on distress. The chapter will begin with an examination of marriage and marital roles as they are related to emotional well-being. Is being married better for you than not being married? We will then briefly describe recent aggregate changes in family structures such as the high rates of divorce, the increasing number of working mothers, and the growth of single parent households, and consider the way that these changes may affect the emotional lives of family members. Next, we will analyze some marital transitions, especially divorce and widowhood, as they affect distress. We will examine the impact of parenthood on well-being. Are children a blessing or a curse for adult sense of well-being? The chapter ends with some general conclusions about gender differences in marital and parental role strain.

Marriage, Marital Roles, and Emotional Well-Being

Are married people happier than unmarried people? Before the results of general community surveys in the 1960s were known, most social researchers believed that married men led stressful lives due to economic and job demands associated with supporting a family. Single men led less stressful lives than married men, who had to bear the daily stress of workplace travel and tension due to burdensome family economic responsibilities. Married women who did not work were thought to lead relatively content and stress-free lives, staying at home and taking care of household and childcare tasks and needs. General community surveys revealed some different patterns that have now been confirmed many times. Among these patterns are the following: (1) Married persons are less distressed than singles; and (2) housewives are more distressed than their husbands.

This research suggests two things. First, there is something about marriage that acts as a buffer against stress and distress, and, second, staying at home and fulfilling family and marital role obligations is not as stress-free and satisfying as thought earlier. In fact, further research has indicated that there are significant gender differences in the effects of marriage on well-being. In general, fewer married women than married men experience emotional well-being as a result of being married. In comparison to married men, married women are more likely to be depressed, to be unhappy with their marriages, and to have a negative image of themselves (Gove 1972; Pearlin 1975b; Radloff 1975).

The question thus arises: What is it about marriage that helps emotional well-being, and what are the reasons for the gender differences in emotional well-being of married persons?

Many explanations have been offered. At first researchers believed that the presence of an adult partner helped to reduce isolation and loneliness. Marriage was also thought to create a sense of security and belonging. Hughes and Gove (1981), however, studied three groups of unmarried persons—never married, separated or divorced, and widowed—and found that living alone per se does not cause distress in unmarried persons. A significant difference in levels of distress appears to exist between married persons and others, and not between persons who live alone and others.

Gove, Hughes, and Style (1983) surveyed married persons about the relationship between happiness with marriage and levels of emotional distress. They found that those who reported that they were very happy with their marriage were less distressed than the unmarried, those who reported that they were somewhat happy with their marriage had similar levels of distress to unmarried persons, while those who reported that they were not happy with their marriage were more distressed than unmarried persons.

The emotional well-being of married couples is thus determined by the type of marriage. A good marriage helps emotional well-being by providing something important—a friend and confidant and a sense of being loved, respected, and valued as a person. Pearlin (1975b) found that a close, confiding marital relationship actually protected couples against certain stressful life events. On the other hand, where there is no confiding, equity, or reciprocity in marriage, couples, especially wives, feel unhappy and frustrated. It is, therefore, not enough to be married. It is better to remain unmarried than to be in a marriage characterized by a lack of caring, consideration, and equity. Similarly, it can be speculated that if married persons have higher levels of emotional well-being compared to unmarried persons due to the presence of a close, confiding, and sharing partner, then unmarried persons with similar partners and high levels of social support should have comparable mental health levels to happily married couples.

Ross, Mirowsky, and Huber (1983) conducted a survey of married couples in 1978 in which they analyzed the psychological well-being of husbands and wives within four types of marriage patterns.

The first type of marriage pattern they studied was the traditional marriage in which only the husband works outside the home. Due to his economic advantage, the husband is the head of the household, has more power than the wife, and is the major decision-maker. The wife, by agreement, stays at home and is dependent on and subordinate to her husband. She is responsible for all the housework and childcare. This type of marriage is internally consistent because both the husband and wife share similar values—a husband's priority is his job while a wife's place is at home. According to the researchers, because preferences match behavior, this type of marriage is psychologically beneficial. There is a slight difference, however, in that the wife tends to have a somewhat higher level of depression than her husband.

In the second type of marital structural pattern, both the husband and wife work, although neither of them believe that a wife should have paid employment. In this type of marriage the wife works not because she wants to, but out of necessity. Further, even though she has a job, the wife is still responsible for all or most of the housework and childcare. The researchers found that this type of marriage is most detrimental psychologically for both partners. The distress level of partners in this type of marriage is greater than in any other type of marriage. The researchers feel that this may be due to the fact that the wife thinks that it is not right that she has to work, that she is not a "good" mother, that her husband was a poor choice, and so on. On his part the husband's psychological distress may stem from feeling that his wife's employment reflects unfavorably on him and his capacity as a provider. This may lead to feelings of guilt, shame, worry about loss of authority, self-doubt, and poor self-esteem. Interestingly, the husband is more distressed than the wife in this type of marriage.

In the third type of marriage, both husband and wife are employed and the husband accepts his wife's employment status. The wife is still responsible for the home and childcare. The husband is better off psychologically in this type of marriage than in any other type of marriage—his standard of living is higher, and the flow of family income is more secure. Things are not, however, as positive for his wife. She is better off than in the second type of marriage but still has to carry a double burden of paid work and housework. She feels that the division of household labor is not fair. Her level of distress in this type of marriage is about the same as in the first type, while the gap between her level of distress and that of her husband is greater than in any other marital structural type.

In the final marriage pattern, both husband and wife are employed, have no problems with the wife's employment, and share housework and childcare equally. This type of marital structure was found to be most positive for the mental health of both partners. The researchers conclude that couples who share economic and household responsibilities maintain higher levels of psychological well-being than other couples.

AGGREGATE CHANGES IN FAMILY STRUCTURE AS A SOURCE OF DISTRESS

Over the past century, the American family has been radically altered and reconfigured. These changes have been both liberating and stressful. According to Elkind (1994, 1), the nuclear family (as the one portrayed traditionally) is disappearing, and in its place is a new structure—"the postmodern permeable family that mirrors the openness, complexity, and diversity of our contemporary life styles."

The nuclear family provided clear-cut, often rigid rules of behavior and expectations, as well as boundaries between public and private lives. These firm boundaries and well-defined rules were beneficial to children, married couples, and parents. These boundaries were, at the same time, confining and demeaning for many. Today, in the permeable family, the distinctions and boundaries have become blurred. The new postmodern family is more flexible, but more vulnerable to pressures from outside. Thus, although the loosening of old constraints provided some relief from the stresses of family life, the crumbling of these boundaries, along with the ambiguity and flux of new norms and lifestyles, have become new sources of stress (Elkind 1994).

There are three historical trends in particular that mark the transition from "old" family forms to "new" family forms. First, there has been an increase in rates of divorce. A first marriage has a one in two chance of ending in divorce. Moreover, one in three adults will marry, divorce, and remarry so that "blending" families is often a necessity. Second, the majority of married women, even those with young children, now work outside the home. Third, there has been a large increase in the number of families headed by a single adult, mostly women.

Each of these aggregate changes in marital structures and patterns has the potential to increase distress. High rates of divorce, for example, expose more people to the traumatic life event of divorce. Higher rates of divorce also suggest that more families will need to deal with remarriage and the blending of families that is often associated with remarriage. Moreover, divorce has important financial consequences for the divorced partners, particularly for women. High rates of divorce mean more women will need to cope with financial hardship. Working women need to manage both work and household demands (even if their husbands support their work status). Access to quality daycare becomes a concern only because women work. Single parents need to deal with financial problems, child rearing issues, and a lack of companionship.

MARITAL STATUS TRANSITIONS

The changes described above are statistical alterations in family structure and characteristics. They reflect the probability that persons will experience marital status transitions and life events associated with the marital role that contain the potential to affect well-being. In the larger social context of these historical changes, transitions in marital status or role obligations within the family are still experienced as personal and individual events that have direct effects on how people feel.

Death, separation, and divorce are role transitions or passages
that involve the loss of roles and the acquisition of new roles. These
role transitions (losses and additions) are capable of evoking considerable distress. The death of a spouse, separation, or divorce are non-
scheduled transitions that people can never be adequately trained to
anticipate.

Structural changes in families that lead to new statuses and
roles—widow, widower, single parent, divorcee—are also changes that
profoundly restructure the lives of the people involved. Dohrenwend
(1973) calls such life changes "status loss" events. These are events that
mark transitions of individuals to lower status, for example, from
employed to unemployed, from married to divorced, from wife to widow,
husband to widower.

The death of a spouse involves considerable restructuring of family circumstances and roles and can cause significant levels of distress.
Often the effect of a spouse's death can be extremely detrimental, for
example, if it involves the premature or unanticipated sudden death of
a spouse. A number of factors, however, influence mental health outcomes: (1) the nature of the death experience of the spouse; (2) the presence or absence of a social support system; (3) individual personality
characteristics; and (4) concurrent stressors in addition to this life event
(Vachon and Stylianos 1988).

With old age comes an increased risk of widowhood. Widowhood in
the elderly has been found to be associated with feelings of isolation and
despair, and these feelings often lead to the occurrence of depression.
Depression in old age is twice as common in women as in men and usually follows the loss of a spouse (Cox 1988). Apart from the event itself,
the death of a spouse leaves people without the support levels they had
previously. According to Mirowsky and Ross (1989), relatively few people under age fifty-five are widowed, but once they reach their eighties,
almost 70 percent of such persons experience the death of a spouse. At
this time, the person may experience increased distress due to the loss
of friends and other family members as well.

Divorce often leads to a new type of family structure—the single-
parent family. A few decades ago this type of family was always referred
to as a "broken family." Studies maintained that this type of family was
characterized by functional disruption that led to a wide variety of problems involving its members, such as crime, delinquency, and mental illness (Chen and Cobb 1960; Beiser 1969).

Today, research typically recognizes the fact that single parent
families face certain special adverse circumstances that cause a variety
of stressful conditions. Decision making, disciplining the children, han-
dling family emotional and instrumental needs, especially finances, and
managing individual and family health needs are special hardships that

single parents have to deal with. Thus, there can be an overload of tasks and responsibilities.

Economic hardship is the single most significant problem in most single-parent families. Today, over 85 percent of single-parent families are headed by divorced mothers, who, with their children, are being recognized as the new poor in the United States and who represent the "feminization" of poverty (i.e., the increasing proportion of poor people who are single women). Many single mothers are unemployed or cannot work due to the presence of small children and the lack of adequate day care opportunities. Even when working, most single mothers work in jobs that pay poorly. The lack of socioeconomic and social supportive resources are recognized as causes of distress in single-parent families. A two-parent family, by definition, has the potential advantage of dividing responsibilities between two income-earning and parenting individuals. In contrast, the single-parent family is more often economically vulnerable and is less flexible regarding parenting responsibilities. The role overload of the single parent causes high levels of stress and this, combined with the lack of adequate economic and supportive resources, often leads to anxiety and depression and causes behavioral and psychological problems in the children as well.

IMPACT OF PARENTAL ROLES ON EMOTIONAL WELL-BEING

The relationship between parents and children has been of interest for several decades. Mirowsky and Ross (1989) suggest that in this culture a strong value is placed on children since they are believed to bring joy and happiness. Women in particular are believed to feel empty and unfulfilled without them. Having children is thus considered good and valuable, and those who decide not to have children are viewed as selfish or immature.

Research findings, however, suggest that children do not improve the emotional well-being of parents (Gove and Geerken 1977; Pearlin 1975a; Cleary and Mechanic 1983; Ross, Mirowsky, and Huber 1983). The presence of children in no way enhances the emotional well-being of parents compared to nonparents. This is because parenting brings with it plenty of everyday conflicts and frustrations as well as numerous daily demands.

Children are most detrimental to the mental health of divorced and single mothers (Pearlin 1975a; Aneshensel, Frerichs, and Clark 1981; Kandel, Davis, and Raveis 1985). Although it is not surprising that children increase anxiety and depression in divorced and single mothers, children have also been found to lower emotional well-being among married mothers. On the other hand, children do not seem to increase distress among fathers as much (Mirowsky and Ross 1989).

Scott and Alwin (1989) argue that this sex difference in parental role strain occurs because the role experiences and expectations of men and women are very different. Women are expected to spend more time than men looking after children. Some of this inequity may stem from differences in employment, but as mentioned earlier, even when women work outside the home, they are still held responsible for the majority of housework and childcare functions. This may be coupled with role conflict and feelings of guilt and anxiety for not being a full-time parent, especially when the children are young. Empirical studies have confirmed that working mothers are more likely to experience emotional distress than working fathers (Radloff 1975), and that mothers of young children have elevated rates of depression (Brown, Bhrolchain, and Harris 1975; Weissman and Klerman 1977).

Why would children increase distress and lower emotional well-being? Ross and Huber (1985) suggest that children increase economic strains on the family. At the same time, the presence of small children often means the mother cannot work outside the home. If she continues to work, funds are needed for day care. Economic hardship is associated with increased depression for both men and women.

Children may also affect the quality of and satisfaction with marriage (Rollins and Feldman 1970). With the birth of the first child, satisfaction with marriage decreases and does not return to the original level until all the children have left home. As the number of young children increases, marital satisfaction decreases (Campbell, Converse, and Rodgers 1976; Veroff, Douvan, and Kulka 1981). Due to the presence of children, husbands and wives spend less time together. Brown and Harris (1978) report that husbands are less likely to be confidants or to be there to talk when needed after the birth of the first child.

Young children put constant demands on mothers who are full-time housewives, leaving them little privacy or time for themselves. Research shows that mothers who are not employed are much more likely than employed mothers and fathers to feel that others are making demands on them (Gove and Geerken 1977). On the other hand, children are also bad for the emotional well-being of employed mothers due to role conflict and role overload.

It should be noted here that the strains of parenthood do not end when children reach a particular age—"parental strains have a persistency that can extend across the entire life cycle" (Pearlin 1983, 12). The newborn imposes stressors on parents very different from those created by adolescents or young adults. Thus, events such as childbirth, entrance to school and schooling, becoming teenagers, and eventual departure from home are family transitions that can be particularly stressful as they often necessitate changes in parental activities or interfere with previous patterns of interaction between spouses (Menaghan 1982).

Since the advent of community mental health and community mental retardation services, many parents have been thrust into a new role, that of a caregiver to a chronically or often severely mentally ill, retarded, or developmentally disabled son or daughter. Often these children are adults who live at home and require help for day-to-day management and functioning. In addition, most of these adult children are also unemployed. This caregiving role thus puts great demands and often economic strains on parents. Women are particularly affected by this role, as research indicates that women are much more likely than men to become primary caregivers.

Parents and, again, women in particular, have also become caregivers to their own (and their spouse's) aging parents. In this instance, the role of parent can be extended to include obligations to care for one's parents even though this is far from the conventional definition of parent. Caregiving obligations can be very time consuming. They can sometimes force a caregiver to give up employment (and, thus, an emotionally beneficial role). Caregiving, itself, can be financially, emotionally, and physically draining and it can disrupt other family relationships. Working mothers not only perform a "second shift" of house work, but can also become members of the "sandwich" generation with parental-type responsibilities for both an older and younger generation.

GENDER DIFFERENCES

In the 1960s, community surveys identified and confirmed relationships between certain basic social patterns, distress, and mental illness. One of these patterns showed that women report more distress than men and are more likely to suffer from depression and anxiety disorders than men, and a second pattern showed that married persons are less distressed than all other marital status categories. Married women especially are less distressed and less likely to suffer from depression than unmarried and other women.

Gove and his colleagues were among the earliest sociologists to examine why women are more distressed than men (Gove 1972; Gove and Tudor 1973; Gove and Geerken 1977). They reasoned that some of the apparent differences in levels of distress stem from differences in the lives of men and women. They also utilized analysis of the different occupational and familial roles of men and women to explain sex differences in mental disorders, and depression in particular. Some of the same explanations can be applied to understand why more married women than married men seem to be unhappy and depressed.

As discussed earlier, a couple of decades ago the majority of adult women were exclusively housewives and men were the bread winners and job holders. Due to their limited access to the job market, most women lacked economic independence and power, and this often led to power differentials between husbands and wives (Blood and Wolfe 1960). Although housework and childcare represented a full-time job, this work was not accorded the status of 'real' work in a cash-oriented economy. Feeling less appreciated and with little access to opportunities for self-enhancement and fulfillment, many housewives felt caught in unsatis-factory marital and family roles and obligations. This caused distress and often led to mental health problems, in particular depression.

Research has consistently indicated that women who are employed are less distressed than women who are housewives (Gove and Tudor 1973; Gove and Geerken 1977; Kessler and McRae 1982). This may be because employment provides women with opportunities and contacts outside the home, some economic and decision-making power, and often support and help from husbands. Kessler and McRae (1982) found that employed wives whose husbands help with housework and childcare have lower levels of distress and emotional problems than employed wives whose husbands do not help at all.

Since the 1970s, compared to men, women's roles in the family and workplace have altered rapidly and radically. As large numbers of women, including wives and mothers, joined the labor force and began to gain economic independence, their roles within marriages, families, and society have changed. Today, the majority of wives and mothers work out-side the home. For women, the changes outside the home should have been accompanied by changes at home. Research, however, reveals that this has not necessarily occurred. Most women have become worker by day and housewife by night. Instead of other family members, including husbands, changing their responsibilities and sharing housework and childcare duties, these tasks have been left largely to wives and mothers (Vanfossen 1981, 1986; Yogev 1981; Hobfoll 1986).

Therefore, for women both the role of housewife and the role of employee can be stressful. When women are not employed, the lack of equity and support by husbands and other family members and perceived discrepancy between tasks performed and rewards received are factors associated with distress and disillusionment with marriage and marital roles, negative self-image, and depression. Similarly, many working wives are caught in a world of role overload and role conflict, trying to juggle career and home responsibilities. This accounts for the lower lev-els of emotional well-being of married women compared to married men. Pearlin and Lieberman (1979) also report that women are more vulnera-ble than men to persistent problems within their marriages. These per-sistent strains often lead to symptoms of anxiety and depression.

According to Mirowsky and Ross (1989), for wives the central cause for distress is associated with whether or not the husband shares in household and other familial responsibilities. They conclude that couples who share economic and household responsibilities also share similar levels of emotional well-being, and are less distressed than other couples. In contrast, for men, stress and distress are largely related to work roles and relationships. For husbands, family or marital role stress stems from adapting to the wife's employment and overcoming any embarrassment or guilt.

In conclusion, as Aneshensel (1986, 100) puts it, marriage "appears to benefit the psychological health of women, but marital stress appears to result in psychological distress"

Summary

In this chapter we have discussed how the central adult roles of spouse and parent can affect psychological well-being. Marriage, on average, is a good thing for people's mental health although it tends to be a bit better for men than for women. Parenthood is not so good.

The structures of families and, hence, the meaning of roles within the family have changed extensively during the twentieth century. These changes have both expanded possibilities and created new burdens. Wives, for example, are not necessarily stuck in the role of housewife. They can become workers as well, and the addition of that role has generally beneficial effects. At the same time, wives who work, particularly mothers, sometimes face the difficulty of reconciling their work status and their expectations about good role performance as a spouse and parent.

Families have changed in other ways. The probability of divorce has increased and this has increased the number of single women who need to support children on their own. In light of the typically lower wages they receive, single working mothers are likely to be under considerable stress. Divorce and other transitions in family structure and function often require the renegotiation of role definitions and obligations.

Parenting creates many burdens for families that do not appear to be offset by the benefits of parenting. Particularly when children are young, they place time, financial, and other obligations on their parents. These burdens generally appear to create emotional distress among parents. In addition, parenting increasingly includes the obligation to care for chronically ill and disabled family members even when those family members are older than a family caregiver.

It must be pointed out here that not all individuals and family units experience high levels of stress and distress. Most individuals and families seem to have the ability to manage life's changes and demands through successful coping strategies—personal and social.

In this chapter we have tried to describe the effects of spousal and parental roles on well-being. This has not been entirely easy or satisfactory. We discussed the additional role of worker and we considered gender differences in how the roles of spouse and parent are perceived and carried out. In the next chapter we will describe the effects of the work role on personal well-being, and then we will consider how the combination of statuses and roles that can be used to characterize a person can also be used to understand the likelihood that a given person will experience feelings of distress.

SOCIAL ROLES: WORKER

L ove it or hate it, work consumes a major portion of most adults' waking hours and it is logical that the way one feels about work, what one does and how one does it, will have an impact on feelings of well-being. "Until recently I'd cry in the morning. I didn't want to get up. I'd dread Fridays because Monday was always looming over me. Another five days ahead of me. There never seemed to be any end to it" (Terkel 1972). "Stressful working conditions have driven postal workers to kill, claim union officials attending the American Postal Worker's biennial convention..." (Trent 1994). Between 1983 and 1993 there were thirty-four deaths resulting from shootings among employees of the postal service (New York Times 1995).

Work can be a major source of stress, as the quotations above suggest. In fact, the relationship between work and mental health has been a subject of discussion for a long time. In the mid-1800s, Karl Marx (1964) raised the concern that work performed in factories for the primary benefit of capitalists was, by definition, alienating for the worker. This type of paid labor does not belong to the person who performs it, but to the owners of factories. Since the individual does not own his own effort, Marx argued that the worker is unable to get any satisfaction out of his labor. This estrangement (alienation) from work prevents the worker from developing a true sense of self. This alienation also leads to distress (Mirowsky and Ross 1989).

This argument by Marx has been debated and studied using a number of different terms: alienation, job satisfaction, worker control, and job stress. Surveys of workers routinely show that about 20 percent of employees are dissatisfied with their work and their employer (Tausky 1984). In addition, recent large-scale layoffs by companies otherwise known for the stability of their work force, international economic competition, computerization, boring simple jobs, and other factors suggest that workers may be increasingly anxious about keeping jobs or about having enough money to get by, about supporting their family, and planning for the future. It is also possible that the mental well-being of such workers will be lower than among workers who do not face these conditions.

In this chapter we will take a systematic look at some of the work-related factors that researchers have found to be related to distress. To be consistent with our arguments about the social sources of distress, we will examine evidence that relates conditions in the general economy, particularly labor market conditions and changes, and conditions on the job, to psychological well-being. We will also observe how the status variables of gender, socioeconomic status, and race/ethnicity affect the relationship between work and well-being.

THE ECONOMY, LABOR MARKETS, AND DISTRESS

Open the morning newspaper. Listen to the news on television. You will almost certainly read or see a news report concerning the general state of the economy, unemployment rates, the downsizing of a corporation, the merger of two companies, a plant closing or its relocation to another country. For many people the importance of these changes in the general economy are related to their possible impact on jobs. Economic conditions define the labor market in which individuals seek jobs, hope to hold jobs, and compare their jobs to other opportunities.

We will define the labor market very broadly to mean all characteristics of economic activity related to the acquisition, retention, and loss of jobs, whether an individual works for others or is self-employed. Labor market structures affect the ability of workers to land "good" jobs and the likelihood that they will keep those jobs. It refers to historical trends in the types of jobs that are available and to other factors that affect whether and where an individual works.

It should be clear that an individual will have very little or no control over labor market structures. Nevertheless, these structures can have profound effects on individual well-being (Brenner 1976; Catalano and Dooley 1977). During the Great Depression of the 1930s, the general collapse of the economy virtually destroyed the labor market, putting vast numbers of persons out of work and making them unable to support dependents. An enduring, if somewhat exaggerated, image from that time is the man jumping from a building ledge to commit suicide because he is depressed by his financial losses. Unemployed men did sometimes leave their homes each day as though they were still working so as not to reveal to their neighbors that they had been laid off and in order to retain some sense of identity for themselves.

THE EFFECTS OF UNEMPLOYMENT

The work role is a central source of identity, an organizer of time, a primary source of social interaction, and the major source of income for most adults. Unemployment, then, could be expected to have many negative effects on workers' well-being. Given that we often define ourselves by our jobs, "I'm a professor," "I'm a bricklayer," the loss of a job means that an important source of our identity, based on our employment, is threatened. Unemployment, of course, also has significant financial effects. Most of the research on the effects of unemployment on worker's well-being focuses on these two matters, threats to identity and financial strain. The typical study of the health effects of unemployment shows that unemployment is related to increases in drinking, more physical illness, higher rates of depression, anxiety, "bad days," suicidal ideation, and the increased use of tranquilizers (Kessler et al. 1987).

If the health effects of unemployment are not much debated, then the question turns to the causes of unemployment. It is here that we can see some of the ways in which social and economic structures affect worker well-being by affecting the opportunities for work.

Why do people lose their jobs? They move elsewhere, they don't like their jobs or their employers, they decide to go back to school, or they want to raise children. These reasons for job loss are defined as "voluntary" reasons for unemployment. And people voluntarily leave jobs all the time. Sometimes people leave one job to take another and suffer few consequences from the loss of a particular job, but sometimes, even though job loss is voluntary, the loss causes strain and distress.

The vast majority of job losses, however, are not voluntary. Involuntary unemployment has greater consequences for personal well-being than voluntary unemployment. One nonvoluntary reason for job loss is that the worker cannot perform the job adequately. People get fired all the time because they appear to lack a physical or intellectual skill that is crucial to the successful completion of their jobs. Workers also get fired for excessive absenteeism, insubordination, and using drugs. In these circumstances we would expect unemployment to have negative effects on health. Yet these reasons are peculiar to individual workers and individual employers. They are also not the main reason for unemployment.

The loss of employment for reasons unrelated to personal characteristics or specific job performance is a permanent, built-in, structural feature of the United States and other capitalist economies. Loss of employment (for whatever reason) has significant negative effects on individual well-being. Economic cycles, as well as shifts in the distribution of jobs across industries and occupations that occur for historical and technological reasons, have the same effect on individuals—they create stressful situations that can lead to psychological distress. In our day-to-day lives we are generally unaware of the effects of these cycles and trends on the probability of holding, losing, or finding a job, but these structural effects account for more of the change in labor markets than do personal reasons for unemployment or employment.

ECONOMIC CYCLES AND UNEMPLOYMENT

The main reason for unemployment is structural. That is, the economy goes through cycles of growth and decline and, during decline, jobs are lost simply because employers cannot afford the labor force costs they incurred when times were better. The number of unemployed persons swells during recessions and that is when the prospects for quick reemployment are lowest. By definition, involuntary unemployment means that workers do not have control over the basic condition of their access to financial and identity security. Several authors (Brenner 1976; Catalano and Dooley 1977) have shown that rates of both physical and mental illness rise and fall in parallel with changes in unemployment rates. There is also evidence that even among workers who do not lose their jobs during recessions, elevated levels of insecurity brought on by concern over the economy increase symptoms of depression and other forms of psychological distress (Catalano and Dooley 1983; Kuhnert and Vance 1992; Heaney, Israel, and House 1994).

DOWNSIZING

Jobs can also be lost in other ways related to economic and social changes other than economic cycles. The so-called downsizing of American corporations is characterized by the planned reduction of a firm's labor force for purposes related to the reduction of labor costs and/or the reorganization of the firm. In either case the net effect is that significant numbers of people have lost long-term employment and are subject to the uncertainty of the labor market. The economic, political, and social issues surrounding downsizing are often complex and controversial. What is clear is that jobs are being lost on a large scale and that many workers are being exposed to the stressors associated with unemployment because of this systematic process. Some downsizing occurs in the context of plant closings. Rather than a mere trimming of a work force, downsizing is often accomplished by simply shutting down entire plants or divisions of larger firms.

SHIFTS IN THE ECONOMIC DISTRIBUTION OF JOBS

When recessions or downsizing or plant closings cause workers to lose their jobs, the evidence suggests that reemployment will largely erase any short-term consequences on worker physical or mental health (Kessler et al. 1989). However, there are other factors that affect the likelihood that persons will become reemployed. During a recession the labor market will be both competitive and small. This indicates that fewer workers who lose jobs will become reemployed within a relatively short period. When plants close down, there may simply be no jobs in that community that provide alternate employment opportunities. Jobs in one type of industry may also disappear as the economy shifts from manufacturing jobs to service jobs. There is no assurance that if a job, say as a steel worker, is lost, that another job in the steel industry will eventually be found. In fact, one of the historical trends in employment opportunities is the shift from manufacturing to service industries as the primary source of employment. This means that employees who lose their jobs in manufacturing industries such as steelworking may not be able to find new jobs as steelworkers. To the extent that our identities are tied to the work we do, the loss of a job and the decreasing likelihood that one's next job will be similar, undermines one's sense of identity. In addition, the types of jobs that are more widely available in the current economy may pay lower wages. Thus, persons who become unemployed while the economy is shifting the kinds of jobs that are available may not be able to offset financial strains or threats to work identity because they will be reemployed in a different industry that pays more poorly and involves work that is not the same as their previous job (Turner 1995). We would expect that such displacement leads to distress.

Today the labor market has produced the "displaced" worker, someone who has lost a job because a business closed or moved, or a worker whose position was eliminated via downsizing. Between 1991 and 1993, 13 million U.S. workers fit this definition (New York Times 1996). To make matters worse, 36 percent of those displaced workers were still unemployed two to four years later (in 1995), 18 percent were reemployed at less than 50 percent of the income of their old jobs, and only 27 percent were reemployed at the same or higher incomes.

When a steelworker is unable to find a new job in the steel industry because of the shift from an economy in which manufacturing jobs dominate the labor market to one in which service jobs dominate, this shift has several additional consequences with potential psychological impact. Manufacturing jobs are often found within large firms that are capital intensive, highly stable, offer internal career ladders and good pay, and that are often unionized. These characteristics are associated with job security, job satisfaction, and well-being. By contrast, service jobs tend to be found in smaller, less stable firms in which there is no internal labor market and where the pay is not so good. These firms are seldom unionized so that workers do not have a sense of protection regarding their jobs and their income. Thus, workers who are forced to trade stable, high paying jobs in manufacturing industries for unstable, lower paying jobs are likely to find this situation disturbing. Workers who enter service jobs without having worked in manufacturing jobs will also find the instability and low pay to be problematic.

DESKILLING OF JOBS

The other long-term trend in the American economy that can be related to increased distress among workers is the so-called "deskilling" of work content (Braverman 1974). Hall (1994, 24) defines deskilling as, "... the systematic reconstruction of jobs so that they require fewer skills and so management can have more control over workers." To the extent that such deskilling occurs (and there is some debate about whether it actually does), one would expect jobs that require low levels of skill to be repetitive and demoralizing. Those who argue for the existence of deskilling see it as an outgrowth of capitalism itself. Jobs that require lower skill levels justify lower levels of pay and make workers' experience and skills less relevant to hiring decisions. Anyone can do these jobs and so no one can feel secure about keeping such jobs. Workers are highly replaceable. At this point, research on the actual psychological consequences of changes in the labor market distribution of jobs (manufacturing versus service) or the needed skill content of jobs is only suggestive and partial. However, the conditions represented by both trends are consistent with known work-related stressors that have been shown to be related to distress.

TEMPORARY AND CONTINGENT JOBS

The last major macroeconomic trend that has implications for worker well-being is the growing practice by employers of hiring workers on a "temporary" or contingent basis, rather than on a regular, permanent basis. Firms argue that in today's competitive economy, they must maintain a "flexible" workforce—one that grows or shrinks quickly in reaction to demand for the output of the firm. Of course, this strategy also permits firms to offer fewer employee benefits, such as health care plans and retirement benefits. Temporary or contingent workers represent the fastest growing segment of the job market, and by the year 2000 it is expected that one of every two jobs will be contingent or nonpermanent in nature. If work is essential to the development of an identity and sense of security, then the contingent worker role has the potential to undermine both. That is, contingent workers are likely to feel distress based simply on the general understanding that their work cannot be expected to provide them with stable identity validation and support.

JOB CONDITIONS AND DISTRESS

The previous discussion suggests that there is a direct relationship between changes in the economy and how people feel psychologically. This occurs principally through the effects of unemployment on distress and through anxiety about the likelihood of continued employment, uncertainties associated with worker displacement, deskilling, and employment stability. However, this is not the only relationship between work and psychological well-being, and this relationship may not be very strong in comparison to how our specific job affects us. What we actually do on our job and how we are able to do it have strong effects on the relationship between work and well-being.

In our day-to-day lives we go to work and we like it or we don't, and it gives us a sense of well-being or it does not. Some researchers argue that how we feel about our work is a function of the match between our skills, interests, and personalities, and the characteristics of the work we do. Others argue that the conditions of our jobs, particularly the scope of job demands and the freedom to meet these demands, determine how we feel about our work and/or ourselves. In this section of the chapter we will examine the evidence that shows how job conditions create distress for many workers. Again, these conditions are generally not the making of individual workers but of their employers. They cannot be attributed to personal characteristics. The way in which work is organized represents a social structure, and so any characteristics of the organization of work that affect health are structural rather than individual.

The bulk of research concerning the relationship between work and mental health has been conducted at the level of specific work conditions rather than at the level of the general economy. More specifically, it has been demonstrated that the relationship between the demands of work and the freedom to meet these demands is of crucial importance (Karasek and Theorell 1990). Think about this for a moment. How would you feel if the boss was piling on job duties but was not giving you the time or tools to meet these demands? What if you risked being fired for failure to meet those demands? Moreover, it appears that the ability to control the balance between job demands and capacity to meet demands is central to the development of identity, intellectual flexibility, and the well-being of workers (Kohn and Schooler 1983).

From the perspective of Karl Marx, all work in a capitalist economy is alienating. However, research suggests that some people are well-pleased with the work they do and the way they do it. One argument that has been advanced to explain differences in worker reaction to their jobs is called the "Person-Environment Fit" explanation (French, Caplan, and Harrison 1982). This approach suggests that when individual biological and psychological characteristics do not match job requirements, workers will report higher job dissatisfaction, alienation, and illness. Distress related to work, then, is a function of how well or how poorly the individual has matched job and personal characteristics. Research, however, suggests that this explanation for work stress cannot account for most of the distress (though it can account for some of the distress) observed among workers (Baker 1985).

The model that accounts for more of the variations in feelings of distress is the classic stress-illness model we have been using all along. In this model, specific characteristics of jobs have been shown to increase levels of felt distress among workers, regardless of their biological or psychological makeup. In short, it is the way the job is defined, organized, and operationalized by an employer that affects the worker's psychological reaction to work.

JOB DEMANDS AND DECISION LATITUDE

The research literature suggests that several characteristics of the job have important effects on well-being. The most important of these seems to be the degree of autonomy or control one has over the way that work is done. In addition, the amount of work demanded by the job, the intrinsic interest and complexity of the work, co-worker and supervisor support, control over the work of others, and the perception of security about one's job have all been shown to be important features of work that affect mental health.

Robert Karasek and his colleagues (Karasek and Theorell 1990) have outlined a "demand/control" model for explaining worker well-being that has received widespread empirical support. In this schema, the way that a worker can balance work demands with decision latitude (autonomy) in the way one does the work is strongly related to worker mental health. The worker who experiences a high level of demands on the job and who has little flexibility in the way he or she can meet these demands is at high risk of developing signs of psychological distress. In this model, stress comes from the inability of the worker to find and use the tools available to do a good job. Note that some jobs have high levels of demand but do not produce distress because the job also permits the worker to control how the job will be done. People do not become distressed by the presence of challenge in their work, but by the inability to meet the challenge.

Job demands are usually indexed by asking workers if they must work very fast on their job, if they have too much work, or if they have enough time to get everything done. Job demands can also be used to indicate if the work is paced by machine and whether it is boring and repetitive. The effects of machine pacing have been of concern for some time. In the stereotypical image of assembly line manufacturing, a worker's rate of activity is determined by the speed of the assembly line and the image of the worker falling behind the pace of the machine is a symbol of the stress of manufacturing jobs. Machine pacing has been associated with higher levels of boredom, anxiety, and depression (Caplan et al. 1975; Hurrell 1985).

Decision latitude is typically measured by questions about a worker's belief that he or she has the freedom to decide what to do on the job, has a lot of say about what happens on the job, feels that he or she has responsibility to decide how the job gets done, and that the job requires some creativity. Decision latitude also contains the notion of "closeness of supervision." The findings suggest that persons who are closely and constantly monitored by their supervisors, who perceive that they are unable to make decisions about their work on their own, and who have no opportunity to disagree with their supervisors will display increased levels of anxiety, low self-confidence and low job satisfaction (Kohn and Schooler 1983).

Decision latitude appears to be the most crucial variable related to work satisfaction and the onset of psychological distress. It is central to the notion of personal control and autonomy. This aspect of work structure is the most direct way to operationalize the meaning of autonomy and personal control as used in the current research literature. It is intended to reflect how the characteristics of the job, as defined by the employer, affects the employee. In its simplest version, decision latitude assesses whether the worker has the ability to complete assigned tasks in a way that permits individual preferences to be respected. That is, to what extent can an individual participate in the design of his or her work? Consider the assembly line worker. She has no decision latitude. A piece of work comes down the line and the worker's job is to add to the value of this piece in a precise, predefined way. The process must be completed in exactly the same way for each piece. There is no room for creativity, variation, or independent input from the worker.

Karasek's model suggests that the combination of high demands and low decision latitude is particularly stressful. However, there is ample evidence that decision latitude alone is strongly related to feeling of distress (Fenwick and Tausig 1994). Since we are taught that individualism is among the highest virtues, the opportunity to make decisions about one's work as an individual is central to self-identity. Link, Lennon, and Dohrenwend (1993) argue that direction, control, and planning of occupational activities affects one's sense of mastery and personal control. They argue, further, that both control over one's own work and the ability to control other's work are essential to perceptions of mastery and personal control. In turn, such perceptions are linked to psychological well-being.

JOB COMPLEXITY, CO-WORKER SUPPORT, AND JOB SECURITY

In discussing changes in the general nature of work earlier, we mentioned the idea that jobs were being "deskilled." That is, that the actual jobs we are hired to do seem increasingly simple and require less mental effort to accomplish. The "substantive complexity" of jobs is another feature of work that affects psychological well-being. Jobs that require more thinking to complete or that are more complicated to complete are associated with lower rates of anxiety, higher self-esteem, and higher life satisfaction (Kornhauser 1965; Caplan et al. 1975; LaRocco, House, and French 1980; Kohn and Schooler 1983). This explains the concern with deskilling. If more and more jobs in the economy are less complicated and complex, what effects will this have on worker self-esteem and well-being? How does an employer balance the lower labor cost related to hiring a person who does not possess high education or experience to do deskilled work with the psychological costs to individual workers of doing work with low substantive complexity?

Work is also a social setting. Generally we talk with our co-workers and our supervisors during the day. Often people develop important friendships among co-workers that are carried on after working hours. The opportunity to interact with one's co-workers fills a general need for socializing that we all seem to have. Interactions with co-workers and supervisors offer the possibility of receiving support in times of strain or distress. Jobs that permit workers to interact and to form relationships (i.e., those in which one does not work alone, where the surrounding noise is not too great) also permit workers to obtain support and advice regarding work-related (and maybe family-related) problems. Having someone who is trusted to talk to about problems is essential to well-being. Thus, opportunities to make friends and to obtain social support from co-workers and supervisors on the job can have a positive effect on well-being (Etzion 1984; LaRocco, House, and French 1980; Winhurst, Marcelissen, and Kleber 1982; Billings and Moos 1982; Karasek, Triandis, and Chandhry 1982).

Finally, jobs vary in the extent to which they offer a sense of security to their occupants. Job insecurity is defined as, "... perceived powerlessness to maintain desired continuity in a threatened job situation." (Greenhalgh and Rosenblatt 1984). A worker's belief that her job will still exist in a year and that she can expect to keep the job if she chooses are important to a sense of well-being. Even when economic times are generally good, employees worry about the stability of their employment. When times are bad, fear of unemployment can have severe psychological effects on individuals (Joelson and Wahlquist 1987; Heaney, Israel, and House 1994). The absence of job security is associated with increases in anxiety and decreases in job and life satisfaction and self-esteem. It is important to remember just how central work is as a source of financial security and identity. As such, threats to the stability of either financial or identity resources would be expected to provoke anxiety and distress. Given the increase in the number of workers who are hired as "temporaries," the importance of employment security is becoming magnified as a source of well-being.

In this section of the chapter we have outlined dimensions of work itself that are directly related to worker well-being or distress. Work in which demands and capacity are in balance, that is inherently interesting and complex, in which employees can maintain social networks, and that seems secure from unemployment offers workers the healthiest work environment. Work in which there is too much to do and no way to do it all, where workers cannot control their work activities, where the work is simplistic and boring, in which the worker is isolated from other workers, and where the employee is uncertain about continued job tenure undermine individual sense of well-being, mastery, and identity. In turn, jobs with any or all of these characteristics are associated with higher rates of psychological distress and physical illness. Once again, it is clear that these are characteristics of the economy and the job and not of the individual.

THE EFFECTS OF THE GENERAL ECONOMY ON JOB CONDITIONS

Thus far we have shown that the characteristics of the larger economy and of one's job can each affect well-being. In fact, changes in the larger economy can also produce changes in the job conditions of employees. For example, during recessions companies often reduce their labor force as a way of dealing with reduced economic activity. In turn, they often pressure their remaining workers to do more work (increased job demands) and they often increase the level of supervision to assure that work is done more cost effectively (reduced decision latitude) (Fenwick and Tausig 1994). Thus, job conditions can become more stressful for workers even when they are not actually laid off during recessions.

The major effect on work structures attributed to changes in the economy, however, is unrelated to regular economic cycles of good times and bad times. Job security (and insecurity) has become a central issue related to the psychological well-being of workers. In the last decade or so, more and more jobs have been designed to be temporary or contingent. Fewer and fewer employees can feel secure in their jobs, even in industries where such security was once a defining characteristic. Job insecurity is, as a result, becoming a greater and greater source of psychological distress.

GENDER, SES, RACE, AND JOB CONDITIONS

Jobs that are vulnerable to the effects of economic change and jobs with stressful characteristics are not randomly distributed within the economy. Rather, such jobs are differentially likely to be held by women, those with lower socioeconomic status, and racial or ethnic minorities. We need to look at how these status variables affect the mental health of workers.

In the previous sections we have suggested that work is a central activity of social life and that the conditions under which we work can be a major source of psychological distress. Because work and jobs are social creations and because individual workers have little control over how jobs are constructed, it should be clear that the relationship between conditions of the job and well-being are also, in large part, a result of social organization and social processes.

When we think about this idea in the "real" world, it is easy to spot exceptions, however. Many people like their jobs, feel fulfilled by their work, and trust that they will be able to work as long as they wish. Who are these people? As you might expect, they are most likely to be people with high levels of education, in high status professions, males and whites. That is, the quality of jobs and their stress-producing characteristics are distributed like other social resources. Hence we would expect that being a member of a group with lower education, and/or being female and/or being nonwhite would be associated with jobs of lower quality and more stress.

In previous chapters we have already seen that the status characteristics of gender, SES, and race/ethnicity strongly affect rates of psychological disorder. In general this is ascribed to variations in the life chances of persons that are determined by their positions in these social structures. Additionally, social statuses are associated with characteristic levels of social resources that can be mobilized by individuals in an attempt to deal with the day-to-day demands of life.

Another way to characterize such status differences is by describing differences in the characteristics of the jobs that people do that are associated with these status levels. For example, if women often work in jobs that are typically high in work demands but low in decision latitude, then we would expect to observe more work-related distress among women.

GENDER EFFECTS

Women have entered the paid labor force in large numbers in the twentieth century. In fact, almost 70 percent of all women between the ages of eighteen and sixty-four work in the paid labor force and close to one-half of all workers in the United States are women (Baca-Zinn and Eitzen 1993).

Men and women react fairly similarly to the specific characteristics of their jobs. Both men and women are affected by time pressures, job demands, control over work load, support from co-workers and supervisors, and the absence of conflict between workers and supervisors (Miller 1980; Karasek, Gardell, and Lindell 1987; Lowe and Northcott 1988; Lennon and Rosenfield 1992). Women react a bit more to low work complexity and less to close supervision (Miller 1980; Lennon 1987).

However, women are also concentrated (segregated) in occupations that tend to have stressful job conditions. One-third of all women work in just ten occupations including: secretary, elementary school teacher, cashier, nurse, bookkeeper, and waitress. Moreover, only 11 percent of women work in occupations that are at least 75 percent male. Women get paid less, too. In 1995, women earned from five to fifteen percent less than men when they worked in similar jobs but, because of the gender segregation of jobs, women are most often employed in traditionally low paying occupations. Thus, the average pay for women is just 71 percent of what men earn (U.S. Bureau of the Census 1997). While there are also instances in which women get paid more than men in similar jobs, these situations continue to be relatively rare.

The employment statistics just mentioned suggest that women may find themselves in more financially stressful situations compared to men, especially if they are unmarried. A single woman who may also be raising children will find these financial stressors to be quite significant. The observed job segregation by sex affects exposure to stress-related job conditions too. Tomaskovic-Devey (1993) has shown that, on average, women have less complex jobs than men, women have less access to internal labor markets (promotions within organizations), less managerial authority, and less supervisory responsibility. Fox and Hesse-Biber (1984) reported that the typical woman's job tends to be relatively unstable (insecure), among the lowest paid, and with little opportunity for advancement. Hall (1991) found that women have less control over the content and process of work than do men and that this is even true within female-segregated occupations.

These and other studies confirm that the jobs that women perform contain many of the characteristics that have been found to be stressful, in general. The jobs that women hold are in low paying occupations, in companies without internal labor markets, and in nonunionized industries. Women's jobs are less flexible and permit less autonomy than those occupied by men. These are precisely the conditions that we have suggested lead to work-related distress.

While men and women react to similar conditions in their jobs in similar ways, women are more likely to be exposed to stressful work conditions. Thus, the effects of gender on worker well-being are largely felt through the consequences of gender segregation in the labor force and labor market and the specific conditions of jobs in "women's" work. Even when women and men hold similar job titles, however, women are generally paid less, and have less authority over their own and others' work (Wolf and Fligstein 1979).

Many questions have been raised about how family-related factors affect women and their well-being as employees. How does motherhood affect a women's ability to manage the demands of work and family? How does a woman manage a household and a job? What effect do interruptions in labor force participation in order to bear and raise children have on the types of jobs women employees can get? In fact, there is evidence about the role that marriage and family-related responsibilities play in explaining the well-being of women workers. We will defer a detailed discussion to the next chapter in which the intersection of statuses (e.g., female) and roles (e.g., spouse, mother) will be explored. Marital status and parental status do have effects on well-being both separately and jointly, with work-related sources of distress. In addition to the likelihood that women's jobs are more stressful than men's, the division of household labor, child-rearing duties, and marital status appear to have different effects on men and women.

SOCIOECONOMIC STATUS EFFECTS

Socioeconomic status has separate but similar effects on the well-being of workers. We have already discussed the general association between socioeconomic status and mental health. Here, however, we focus on the types of work that blue- and white-collar employees typically perform, the characteristics of those jobs, and the relative well-being of employees in blue- and white-collar occupations. Socioeconomic status is defined, in part, by occupation. Therefore, the relationship between socioeconomic status and distress owes much to the relationship between occupational (job) characteristics and distress. Just as we suggested that the typical jobs that women perform have features that make them more stressful, a similar argument can be made about the characteristics of jobs held by persons of lower socioeconomic status (Link, Lennon, and Dohrenwend 1993). Socioeconomic status can also be defined in class-related terms that distinguish between those who own the means of production and those who work for owners. Research confirms a relationship between status defined in class-related terms, job conditions, and distress (Kohn et al. 1990; Tausig and Fenwick 1992). Link, Lennon, and Dohrenwend (1993) suggest that the crucial characteristic of work that links socioeconomic status to distress is the extent to which occupations permit workers to control the work of others, a characteristic of work that is consistent with class-based distinctions between ownership and nonownership of the means of production.

Studies of the relationship between socioeconomic status defined in terms of education, income and occupation, and distress are complicated by the fact that occupation is part of the way status is measured. For example, Karasek (1991) has cross-tabulated job demands and decision latitude scores for different occupations in the United States. High stress occupations (high demand, low latitude) include those of gas station attendant, waiter, telephone operator, and keypuncher (data entry clerk). While we might see these as "low" class occupations, other such occupations including sales clerk, construction laborer, machinist, or janitor are not classified as high stress occupations. Thus, we cannot use simple distinctions such as blue- versus white-collar, skilled versus unskilled or manual versus nonmanual labor to define occupations in terms of status and potential to cause distress (Wallace, Levens, and Singer 1988).

When we measure a worker's socioeconomic status in terms of father's SES and the worker's education (as is typically done), there is a strong relationship with the type of job and job conditions that the worker holds. High SES is associated with "good" jobs and low SES with "bad" jobs. In this way, SES has effects on well-being that are similar to the way gender affects well-being. Just as gender affects occupational choice by segregating men and women, SES affects occupational choice by the way that one's family and one's educational background qualify one for different types of work. In turn, differences in the job characteristics of one's work affect felt distress.

RACE/ETHNICITY EFFECTS

Finally, we need to consider the effects of race and ethnicity on the relationship between work conditions and distress. Once again, we will see that membership in nonwhite racial categories has substantial effects on the likelihood that an individual will be employed in a job that will contain stressful characteristics.

African Americans earn less than whites on average and within identical occupations (Cain 1984). African-American men earn about 73 percent of the amounts earned by white men. African-American women earn almost as much as white women but both earn substantially less than men. When alternate explanations for these income differentials are evaluated, the racial differences observed are mostly attributable to discrimination and occupational segregation. Such studies show that African Americans are systematically excluded from good, well-paying jobs that also tend to be high in decision latitude. Tomaskovic-Devey (1993) found that African-American employees are more closely supervised, have less complex tasks, less managerial authority, and less supervisory responsibility than whites.

These differences remain even when differences in training and skills are taken into account. With the long history of racial segregation, discrimination, and bias that characterizes the African-American experience in the United States, part of the explanation for the relatively poor jobs that nonwhites hold must be based on institutionalized racist policies that prevent people of color from acquiring a good education and/or job-training. However, as indicated, even when training is held constant, African Americans are at a significant disadvantage in terms of occupying jobs with positive characteristics. Therefore, race affects the likelihood of obtaining the prerequisites needed to acquire good jobs as well as the likelihood of acquiring the job itself.

Gender, SES, and race each affect the types of jobs that an individual is likely to acquire independent of other criteria such as education. In turn, working in jobs with stressful characteristics increases the risk that women, lower SES individuals, and nonwhites will report work-related distress. To make matters even worse, the effects of gender, SES, and race interact so that, generally speaking, a nonwhite female with low SES stands the greatest chance of experiencing work-related stressors.

What is common about the ways in which gender, SES, and race affect work-related distress? These characteristics of the individual represent status positions in the social structure and persons with lower positions are at a relative disadvantage compared to those at higher levels. The consequences of lower status position are reflected in labor market opportunities, vulnerabilities to economic change, and in the characteristics of the jobs that can be obtained. Women, those of lower SES, and nonwhites feel the effects of bias and discrimination in terms of the types of jobs for which they may compete. Gender segregation in the workplace, for example, indicates that women are less likely to be successful candidates for "nontraditional" male jobs. Although there will always be exceptions, gender-based segregation of occupations means that, on average, women will work in less complex, high demand, and low decision latitude jobs. In the larger economy these types of jobs are also those in which there is a greater risk of unemployment. Although male and female rates of unemployment do not appear to differ, women are more likely to be laid off and then rehired in the same type of work. Thus, levels of job security are lower for women (and for those of low SES and nonwhites). If the last-hired employees are the first to be laid off, then a pattern of job change (layoff and rehire) means that women are more likely to be last hires. In sum, persons of lower social status are less secure in their employment and systematically "steered" into more stressful jobs.

SUMMARY

In this chapter we have explored the relationship between the nature of a person's job and their well-being. Work is a central aspect of most adults' sense of identity and the primary source of financial well-being. Therefore, it is logical that the quality of one's work should have psychological consequences. Numerous theoretical and empirical studies of work have shown that the more control one has over the conditions of one's labor, the higher one's sense of psychological well-being.

With this simple proposition in mind, we outlined some of the ways in which the general economy, the organization of the labor market, and the characteristics of individual jobs have been shown to affect psychological health. Individuals seek and maintain jobs in a global economic context that determines what kinds of jobs are available. Unemployment is "built-in" to capitalist economies and unemployment has significant effects on well-being. The American economy continues to shift away from manufacturing jobs to service jobs that have more stressful characteristics, and downsizing, deskilling, and plant closures create a context in which employees cannot feel completely secure about their employment status, nor about their ability to find work in their chosen fields.

Even when adults manage to find work, the specific characteristics of their work have profound effects. Jobs that combine high levels of demand with low decision latitude (autonomy) are particularly stressful. A sense of control over one's own work and the ability to control the work of others are strongly linked to psychological well-being. To the extent that jobs do not contain these characteristics, they represent social structures that increase the likelihood of distress independent of personal, physical, or personality characteristics.

As it turns out, the likelihood of holding a relatively stressful job is partly determined by social status characteristics as well. Women, those with lower SES, and those of nonwhite racial origin face social and firm-specific biases that steer these persons into jobs with stressful characteristics. They are also differentially likely to experience insecurity in the labor market.

In Chapter 8, the final chapter in Part I of this book, we will show how the separate effects of status-related and role-related stress intersect in people's lives. In the day-to-day experience of life, individuals are the sum total of their statuses and roles (at least as sociologists see them). Aspects of all of these ways of describing who we are affect our well-being and ultimately explain the sociological perspective on the causes and consequences of mental illness.

THE INTERSECTION
OF STATUSES AND ROLES

In the preceding chapters we have described how a person's major statuses and roles are related to the probabilities of experiencing psychological distress. Describing oneself by sets of statuses and roles is one way to answer the question, "Who am I?" You are a male or a female. You have a certain age, marital status, racial and ethnic background, an occupation (including that of student). You are someone's child and you probably have siblings. You have a religion (including no religion). In short, you are apt to describe your "self" in terms of a collection of social statuses and roles. However you describe yourself, the point we wish to make here is that your description will reflect an intersecting set of characteristics that come together to make "you."

The social causation hypothesis suggests that who you are also describes some things about your likely psychological well-being. If you list all of your statuses and roles, you will notice that some of these are associated with higher levels of distress and some with lower levels of distress. In essence, to predict your level of psychological distress based on statuses and roles, we would have to somehow add and subtract the effects of each status and role to arrive at some estimate of how you might feel. Of course this combined figure would only be a guess anyway. It does not take into account biological and personality characteristics, your personal history, or the effects of multiple roles and role combinations that also contribute to your mental state.

The intersection of statuses and roles is meant to indicate the fact that, in real life, every person possesses a variety of social status and social role characteristics that come together to define that individual. As we have repeatedly indicated, a central tenet of the sociological study of psychological stress is that an individual's exposure and vulnerability to stressful events or on-going stressful conditions is determined, in part, by that person's statuses and roles. A person, just living out his or her life, encounters risks for psychological distress that flow from status and role characteristics. Ordinary people, living ordinary lives, are subject to various levels of risk of disorder simply because of their social characteristics (Turner, Wheaton, and Lloyd 1995). Intersections of statuses and roles do not automatically imply role conflict, role overload, or elevated distress, however. This is simply a way of talking about a whole person by focusing on some important selected parts. At the same time, we recognize some combinations as strong predictors of distress, for example; "supermoms" who both work full-time and raise families, or "women in the middle" who care both for their own family and for their aging parents.

In this chapter we will examine evidence concerning the consequences of some specific intersections of statuses and roles. In particular we will discuss the intersections of gender, work, marital status, and parental status (including the special case of single mothers) as well as the intersections of age, gender, and the caregiving role. These particular combinations illustrate the notion that distress arises in the context of everyday life, and understanding how distress arises in these instances helps us to address important areas of concern within public policy debates. Finally, we will use these examples of the intersection of statuses and roles to draw some general conclusions about the way in which the social context affects psychological distress.

In order to understand a specific person's risk of experiencing distress, we need to take into consideration all of his or her relevant statuses and roles simultaneously (i.e., the way in which statuses and roles intersect) because the answer to the question "Who am I?" is "all of the above statuses and roles." In fact, one very simple idea about the relationship between roles and distress is that the more roles a person has, the better their psychological health. This is called the "multiple role" hypothesis and it is based on the idea that a greater number of roles indicates better access to social resources and a greater sense of integration into social life (Thoits 1983). In this formulation, one simply counts the number of roles a person enacts and the greater the number (regardless of what these roles are), the less distress the person will feel. On the other hand, there is ample evidence that the specific roles enacted and the context in which they are enacted make a difference. This perspective is called the "role occupancy" explanation. The exact roles occupied affect levels of distress (Menaghan 1989). Work stress can spill over to home and family life and vice versa. Parental roles affect whether work conditions are stressful. Finally, in addition to role-related explanations, we also add that status characteristics of individuals enacting roles affect the experience of psychological well-being or distress. Gender affects work, parental and household conditions, and educational levels affect work conditions and parental and marital roles.

While this situation may make it appear that predicting distress levels for particular individuals from their social characteristics is nearly impossible, it turns out that this is not truly so. Certain statuses and roles tend to go together more often than other combinations and this allows us to sort people into a few groups for comparison. For example, we can compare married employed fathers with married employed mothers. These are fairly large categories (there are many people who fit these descriptions) so that, if we find differences in the rates of psychological distress in these groups, we can estimate a particular individual's risk of feeling distress by placing them in one of these groups.

Thoits (1986) and Menaghan (1989) have argued that specific combinations of statuses and roles are associated with a greater likelihood of feeling distress. Men and women tend to occupy different combinations of statuses and roles and this tells us that men and women live in different social worlds with unique experiences of stressors and means for coping with stressors. For example, three role "repertoires" are mostly female; unmarried child rearers without employment, employed unmarried child rearers, and married child rearers without employment. Males are mostly married, employed child rearers, married and employed and not child rearers, or employed, not married and not child rearers (Menaghan 1989, 702–703). Menaghan found that the risk of distress was highest, not for any particular combination of statuses and roles, but when a combination was considered unusual. For example, a man who stays home to raise children and lets his wife work will experience more stress than a man in any of the most common male role configurations. She suggests that "non-normal" role repertoires are inconsistent with the expectations of other societal institutions so that "Mr. Moms" will find few supportive systems and will be more distressed as a result. She suggests that normal problems in normal role configurations are less stressful by contrast. The distress felt by women who work and raise children can be attributed to this non-normal role arrangement. Simon (1995) explains the same observation by arguing that roles mean different things to men and women. For example, employment is often regarded as interference with motherly duties by married women whereas employment is part of being a good father for men.

THE INTERSECTION OF GENDER, WORK, AND FAMILY

Men and women who work do so under very different conditions. Moreover, the relationship between work and family life is substantially different for men and women. We have already documented much of this in earlier chapters, so our task in this chapter will be to bring together what we know about these differences and their effects on mental well-being.

Each of the several characteristics (statuses and roles) that we might use to identify a particular person affect one another. For example, being female affects the types of work one is likely to find, and that will affect household income and the arrangements that can be made for child care. In earlier chapters we have tried to show how each characteristic, by itself, is related to the likelihood of experiencing distress. It may not be so difficult to see that combinations of statuses and roles can have complicated effects on how people feel about themselves. But this is clearly what we must try to understand because it reflects the actual conditions in which people live.

Let's do a quick review of some basic relationships between individual characteristics and well-being and then think about how they might go together. Women are more likely than men to show symptoms of distress (especially symptoms of depression: Mirowsky and Ross 1995). Women are about equally likely to be in the employed labor force (this decreases distress) as are men, but they are most likely to be concentrated occupationally in low-paying, low-control jobs (this increases distress). Working in the paid labor force gives women more leverage in the marital decision-making process (this decreases distress). If not in the labor force, however, they can legitimately take on a maternal parenting role as a substitute (this decreases distress associated with unemployment). Married women are far more likely to do the majority of daily household labor (washing, cooking, shopping, cleaning, child care) than are husbands. This tends to increase distress.

The role of parent plays an important part in explaining distress, especially when children are relatively young. Parenting is stressful for both parents but can be especially so for women. Distress levels related to parental roles are highest when mothers work, regardless of màrital status. The attitudes of husbands about their wives' work and its relationship to parenting has significant effects on the well-being of wives and husbands. If husbands and wives agree about the wife's work status in the paid labor force and about child rearing, then distress is reduced (Mirowsky and Ross 1989).

Marital status has effects on well-being. Both men and women are happier when married than when unmarried. However, parental status and employment status qualify this statement. Working, married women must balance work and home life, usually with little help from their husbands. Women who are employed, especially in professional occupations, gain leverage in family decision making because of their incomes and this makes them less distressed. Dual-earner couples average much higher family incomes than when only one adult in the family works and this reduces distress.

Job structures have been shown to have important effects on distress. Jobs that make high demands and provide little decision latitude produce distress. Such jobs are more often held by women. Almost everyone is concerned about the stability of their jobs so when job security is shaky, levels of anxiety increase. On the other hand, jobs in the paid labor force provide incomes that provide access to supportive resources. Jobs usually provide access to co-workers and personal relationships. They improve the sense of integration into the institutions comprising the social system. Housewives work also (unpaid labor) and the conditions of their work affect their well-being (Lennon 1994). Housewives have less responsibility for things outside their control (which reduces distress) but they also have very routine jobs, which increases their distress.

Now let's consider the way in which statuses and roles can intersect by examining how the performance of housework affects levels of distress. For married women who work, the household division of labor between husband and wife usually needs to be altered from a situation in which the husband is in the paid labor force and the wife is not. Generally when the wife does not work, it is considered reasonable (normal) for her to assume responsibility for most of the daily household tasks such as cooking, cleaning, laundry, and child care. However, when a married woman enters the paid labor force, this division of labor, if maintained, can become a source of strain since the woman would add job duties to household duties, risking overload and role conflict.

Research suggests that employed women do less housework. However, this does not mean that husbands (or children) do a greater share. Less total time may be devoted to household work—thereby allowing for a reduction of amount of housework without a reallocation of the division of labor. On the other hand, in some marriages, the division of household labor between husband and wife does change. Women can use their contribution to the household income to "negotiate" a more equitable division of labor. In one instance, when the negotiation fails and the wife continues to do all or most of the household labor, her levels of distress may rise. When the division of labor does change, it may have negative effects on husbands. In addition, both the husband's and wife's general attitudes about appropriate sex-role behavior will affect the interpretation of the shift in household division of labor. If both the husband and the wife see the new division as consistent with a "nontraditional" idea of sex-roles and they both approve of this orientation, then distress can be minimized. When, however, either the husband or the wife (or both) hold traditional views of spousal sex-roles (Husband works, wife stays home), then the reorganization of household labor, which occurs because the wife has a nontraditional role set, will increase her feelings of conflict and marital dissatisfaction (Greenstein 1996).

This perspective is consistent with the argument made by Menaghan

(1989) about the relationship between distress and non-normative role combinations. Until particular combinations become more normative (say, female, married, employed, child rearer), neither men nor women have ready-made models to refer to in order to give them guidance on how to behave (i.e., how to comfortably divide household tasks). In the absence of such social guidelines and expectations, distress is more likely to arise. For the most part, explanations of well-being that rely on simple role counts (multiple roles) do not appear to be as effective as explanations that take into consideration role combinations (role occupancy). Yet role occupancy is also an insufficient explanation.

The sources of distress that we just described arise only because of the intersection of statuses and roles. Issues of household division of labor do not occur when the husband works and the wife does not. Moreover, the effects of adding work roles on the household division of labor and levels of distress are perhaps most relevant to wives' well-being whereas the effects of losing work roles (unemployment) are probably greater for married men.

There is also a growing literature on the way in which stressors that arise in one sphere of social activity cross over or contaminate activities in another. That is, multiple roles may affect one another (as when work stress causes marital stress). Crossover (when stress in one role causes stress in another role) and contamination (when a husband's distress affects his wife's level of distress) work differently for men and women because the sources of stress in each role and the meaning of experiences in roles seem to differ for men and women (Simon 1995). Nevertheless, such crossover and contamination occurs only because statuses and roles intersect.

Matthews, Conger, and Wickrama (1996) showed that both the husband's and wife's experiences of conflict between work and family can affect the other spouse's feelings of distress, and subsequently, the quality of marital interaction. Rosenfield (1992) also showed that the advantages that women receive from working outside the home can negatively affect the perceived well-being of their husbands. Gender effects related to occupational segregation, low pay, and sex-role stereotypes represent status effects that modify the relationship between work (or parental) role occupation and distress. Similarly, income, education, race, and age also affect the psychological consequences of role occupancy.

SOME NON-NORMATIVE CASES

If Thoits (1986) and Menaghan (1989) are right about the stressfulness of non-normative status and role combinations in comparison with normal combinations, then we ought to observe elevated levels of distress in two particular widespread (but still non-normative) combinations, single, working, child-rearing women, and women who care for either their elderly parent(s) or for chronically disabled children.

SINGLE MOTHERS

The single parent household has become a frequent family form in the last thirty years (Feltey 1995). In 1990 in the United States, about 16 million children under the age of eighteen lived in single-parent households, mostly headed by women (90 percent). This figure represents about one-fourth of all U.S. families. Most of these single-parent households are formed because of divorce, separation, and births to never-married women. Thus, to some extent, the distress we may observe among female household heads could be created by the stressful circumstances of role loss (i.e., married to unmarried). In a typical divorce or dissolution women are awarded custody of the children and fathers are obligated to provide financial support for their children. When such payments are forthcoming—and they often are not—(less than one-half of the mothers who are awarded child support receive the full amount awarded), they rarely cover all household expenses. Women who are single as a result of divorce experience decreases in household income of about 30 percent (Peterson 1996). Hence, women who head such households need to be in the paid labor force. (Obtaining welfare benefits, such as Aid to Families with Dependent Children, is another alternative.)

As frequent as this particular family form is becoming, it still represents a non-normative set of roles. Mothers struggle with how to be "both Mom and Dad" to their children. They may not have access to intimate supporters. Children are sometimes designated as "substitute grownups." Household divisions of labor may become problematic. Baca-Zinn and Eitzen (1993) describe three types of "overload" that can develop from this non-normative role set: responsibility overload, task overload, and emotional overload. The inability to deal with these overloads makes distress more likely among single working mothers. Indeed, studies do show that unmarried working parents experience greater distress than married working parents (Kandel, Davies, and Raveis 1985). Goldberg et al. (1992) report that, for employed single mothers, the intersections of work life and family life are particularly important for the mothers' sense of well-being. Maternal concerns about childcare (only needed because the mother works) and concerns about the consequences of employment for the growth and development of her children arise because single employed mothers are in non-normative role sets.

However, the clearest and most consistent findings regarding the mental health effects of single, employed motherhood are related to the effects of income on well-being. That is, single, employed mothers tend to be poor (Goldberg 1990) and poverty is strongly related to distress. Mirowsky and Ross (1989) and Cohen et al. (1990) have both shown that economic hardship is a dominant factor in the explanation of elevated distress levels among single, employed mothers. Downey and Moen (1987) suggest that low income reduces one's sense of efficacy which, in turn, leads to feelings of distress. But, having found that it is the underlying poverty among single, working mothers that leads to elevated distress, we have not found that the role set itself is irrelevant for explaining where distress comes from. The fact that so many of these women are poor (the feminization of poverty) must be seen in the context of the intersection of statuses and roles. More specifically, being female (a status characteristic) makes it most likely that an employed woman will work in a low-paying job (hence the risk of poverty) and a job with characteristics that are also predictive of distress (Reskin and Coverman 1985; Glass and Camarigg 1992). Thus, the status of being female intersects the role set of single parent and worker in such a way that women find it harder to fulfill role demands because of the negative consequences of being in the lower status position of female.

From a "multiple role" perspective, women should report the highest levels of well-being when they occupy the greatest number of roles. As typically assessed, women who are married, work, and are mothers should have the lowest distress scores because a greater number of roles fulfills multiple human needs and provides opportunities for meaningful social life. In fact, most studies support this expectation (Kandel et al. 1985, for example). A further implication of this notion is that the loss of a role will increase distress. Working mothers who are also the heads of households (i.e., single) occupy one less role than married working mothers. Thus, unmarried, working mothers should report higher levels of distress than women who are married. The data suggest that this is true as well.

Counting roles is not sufficient for explaining distress levels even though it is consistent with this data. Role counts do not reflect the intersection of statuses and roles. More specifically and concretely, the consistent findings indicating that income (i.e., SES) plays a very important role in explaining the emotional consequences of being a single, employed mother, even though it does not affect role counts or combinations, means that distress is not solely a function of role counts or role loss.

The explanation for distress among single, employed mothers, then, does not arise simply from non-normative role combinations (Thoits 1987; Menaghan 1989), but is further and more fully explained by recognizing how gender and income stratification affect role performance. It is the inability to meet role demands and manage role conflicts that stem, in part, from a lack of status-based resources that influences the amount of distress felt by single, working mothers. Both the effects of status on access to resources and the effects of non-normative role sets on well-being are well-known as separate lines of research. Our emphasis on the intersection of status and roles helps to provide a more complete picture.

CAREGIVERS

Another non-normative role combination is one in which adult women (whether employed or unemployed, married or unmarried) are primary caregivers to a dependent family member (elder or offspring). This role set involves the addition of a role (caregiver) and, by the logic of multiple role explanations, should increase the well-being of persons providing care (Hong and Seltzer 1995). As a non-normative role set, it should decrease well-being. To be honest, we don't know exactly which explanation is correct, if either is correct. There are quite a few studies of caregivers that do show elevated distress for caregivers that is attributed to caregiving activities but these studies rarely provide the data needed to directly assess our questions about the effects of role sets and status. It is typical of such studies to examine only caregivers and not a comparable group of persons without the caregiving role. Moreover, studies of caregivers usually are not done with random samples of caregivers so it is frequently unclear whether the findings from any given study can be generalized to the entire population. Subjects in caregiving studies may represent an already "stressed" group of caregivers.

A number of status-related issues cross-cut the explanation for possible caregiver distress. First, age represents both a physical and social status concern. Second, income and education also affect psychological reactions to the caregiving role. Age may count because it represents a proxy for physical health status. A caregiver may be unable to physically handle all caregiving tasks or may be concerned about a disabled family member's future as the caregiver ages. Age may matter as a social status consideration because the role of caregiver may be out of "sync" with expectations about role obligations at a certain age. This is particularly relevant for parents caring for disabled adult children. Adult children should be able to manage their own lives. Age is also associated with a loss of economic resources through retirement, and social resources in the form of friendships and family size.

It is well known that our national population is aging. The percentage of the U.S. population over sixty-five years old has increased from about 4 percent in 1900 to about 13 percent today and will increase to over 20 percent by 2030 (Brody 1990). Although there is some evidence that people are entering older ages in better health, the fact is that, as individuals age, they are increasingly likely to become dependent on others for some amount of assistance in managing their lives. As the numbers of elderly increase, so will the number of people who help elders deal with those aspects of their lives that they cannot handle on their own. Persons who provide this assistance are called "caregivers" and for most purposes this activity defines the caregiver role. Caregiving often arises as an evolution of normal social relationships (Pearlin et al. 1990). That is, a daughter helps her mother or father do grocery shopping as a perfectly normal consequence of the role of daughter, but this assistance can also be defined as caregiving in most uses of this concept. What distinguishes the caregiver role is the change in the relationship between mother and daughter (for example) from a mutual give-and-take to one in which help flows predominantly in one direction.

In addition to the number of persons who take on a caregiving role related to an elder family member, an increasing number of families are also providing care to dependent adult children who are either chronically mentally ill, mentally retarded, or developmentally disabled. These disabled persons were once sent away to large institutions to receive life-time or extended care. Today, however, almost all such persons are cared for in the community and often within their families. In this case, the role of parent generally does not change as a child grows to adulthood. Rather, the parent role is prolonged indefinitely in the form of parent-caregiver. Parenting becomes a non-normative role when children reach a certain age.

Studies of caregivers indicate that, in some caregiving situations, distress does arise. Caregiving has been associated with depression, anger, anxiety, demoralization, feelings of helplessness, emotional exhaustion as well as physical exhaustion, and ulcers (Brody 1990). Caregiving often has an impact on time management, social lives, and financial well-being as well. It has been estimated that as many as one-half of caregivers report one or more of these consequences (Brody 1990).

Hong and Seltzer (1995) point out that the caregiving role is not a desirable role. That is, although it represents an addition to a role set and should improve well-being as a consequence, it often is also an unwanted and demanding role, which partially explains the negative effects of this role addition.

If the role of caregiver has the potential to cause distress simply because it is a difficult one to maintain, the social structural context in which the caregiver functions also has its effects. Women are, by far, the most likely persons to become caregivers (Stone, Cafferata, and Sangl 1987). This is true both for care of elders and care of disabled children and it is explained in several ways. Women are said to be socialized to be nurturant and to be generally oriented to involvement in situations that require the provision of care. Women are also said to be more likely to become caregivers because they are less likely to work—they have fewer other, competing roles. Breslau, Salkever, and Staruch (1982) reported that mothers of young children with disabilities are less likely to occupy employee roles. The birth of a disabled child often "locks" them into a caregiving role. Hong and Seltzer (1995) report, for example, that many of the female caregivers to children in their study had provided care for forty years or more. Stone et al. (1987) reported that, among female caregivers to older husbands, approximately 13.5 percent quit work to become caregivers and 11.6 percent of caregiving daughters gave up the employment role. About 10 percent of caregiving wives to older husbands are employed and almost 44 percent of caregiving daughters to elderly family members work.

Caregivers to disabled children are also less likely to be married. Rates of divorce following the birth of a disabled child are very high. At the same time, almost 30 percent of daughter caregivers to elderly parents are also unmarried. Although situations requiring care of elders or children develop independently of caregiver income or education (status variables), there is a tendency for higher income and better educated caregivers to make use of more purchased caregiving services and to retain their employment status, though it is not clear how this affects caregiver distress levels. Brody (1981) found that the greatest distress from caregiving arises when working women must balance the competing demands of work and caregiving.

Even when male and female caregivers provide the same levels of care, women experience more distress in the caregiving role. Moen, Robison, and Dempster-McClain (1995) studied 293 women who had been interviewed in both 1956 and 1989. In 1989 some of these women had provided or were currently providing care to an aging parent. They found that college educated caregivers had higher self-esteem scores than caregivers with only a high school education. They also found that, for married caregivers, the more caregiving provided, the lower the self-esteem. In a study of factors leading to decisions to institutionalize elders who were recipients of family caregiving, Aneshensel, Pearlin, and Schuler (1993) reported that family income (higher) and lower caregiver education were linked to the decision to institutionalize a family elder. They noted that, "The impact of exposure to care-related stressors may depend upon access to various resources—such as social support, self-concept, or being healthy..." (63). In turn, we suggest that access to these resources may be a function of social status variables such as gender, age, education, and income. As such, the intersections of these status variables with the caregiving role need to be explored further. The evidence suggests that caregiving itself (even when the demands for caregiving assistance are held constant) does not affect people equally.

Women are more likely to become caregivers but even when men become caregivers, they do different types of caregiving service. It is unclear whether this occurs as a result of differences in socialization between men and women or to the generally better financial situation of men, because the difference in caregiving assistance provided by men and women is mostly related to men's greater use of paid services as compared to women's use of paid services.

Caregiving to either an aging parent (or parent-in-law) or to a dependent child often entails considerable work and readjustment of daily routines and other role relationships. As a long-term source of stress (a chronic stressor), its effects on caregivers can be expected to be negative, based on the stressor-illness model. Moreover, it is not uncommon for role sets to change in response to caregiving duties. The complexity of these possibilities makes definite statements difficult but it is certain that individual reactions to caregiving roles are partly a function of the social status and role contexts of the caregiver.

COMBINING STATUSES AND ROLES TO PREDICT DISTRESS

Now that we have examined how some specific combinations of statuses and roles affect well-being, it would be helpful to develop a more general understanding of how sociologists explain the ways in which the intersection of statuses and roles affect distress. This general level of explanation will permit us to apply the analysis to any specific combination of statuses and roles. We will make use of the material presented in this and the preceding chapters to construct our explanation.

Figure 8-1 presents a visual description of the way the research data we have described can be organized to provide an explanation for the relationship between social context and well-being or distress. In the stress-distress model we explained that humans beings are constantly exposed to situations in which they must readjust their activities (life events) and that they are also constantly required to deal with the ongoing problems of daily living (daily hassles and chronic stressors). Experiencing events and on-going problems can lead to psychological distress. However, it is often true that people do not feel distress under these same conditions. Moreover, not every person has the same risk of being exposed to any or to many of these stressors. In the preceding chapters, for example, we showed that differences in social status and role occupation are related to different rates of reported distress. Therefore, status and role differences must be related to either differences in exposure to stressors or to the ability to deal with stressors (resources) or both.

We suggest that exposure to stressors arises from at least two

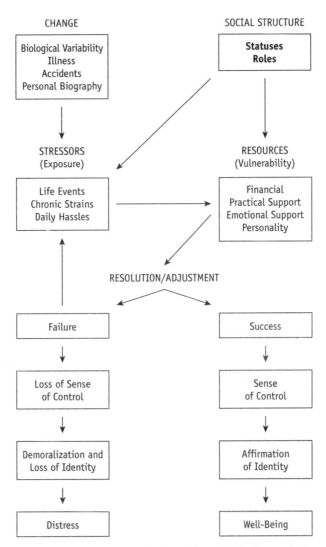

Figure 8-1   How Statuses and Roles Affect Well-Being and Distress

sources: chance (which includes biological variability, illness and accidents, personal biography, and the general unpredictability of life) and social structure (statuses and roles). Since our emphasis is on the social causes of distress, we make a provision for nonsocial causes of stressors but do not develop this part of the explanation.

We also suggest that people differ in their ability to deal with stressors (their vulnerability to the effects of stressors), in part because of differences in access to social and personal resources (practical and emotional support and personality attributes) that are also related to social status and roles. The ability to resolve problems related to various stressors (the application of resources to deal with problems) affects one's sense of control over life. Finally, we suggest that distress arises not from the inability to mobilize the appropriate social resources to deal with a given stressor but from the loss of identity and the demoralization that occurs because of a loss of sense of personal control coming from the inability to mobilize the appropriate resources. This formulation (as it will be elaborated) seems to account for a majority of the findings reported in prior chapters and also for the varieties of explanations offered for those findings.

Stressors arise in a number of ways and their presence in a person's life is referred to as "exposure" to stressors. The most frequently studied source of stressors is life events. Things happen. However, as we have already seen, many of these events are not random, freak occurrences. Rather, they arise from existing social relationships (Turner, Wheaton, and Lloyd 1995) or are secondary consequences of other types of stressors (Pearlin et al. 1990). Even such random-seeming events as death can be related to social structural positions to some extent. There is a strong relationship between physical health status and socioeconomic status, for example. Life expectancy is also linked to SES. Still, things do happen without rhyme or reason and events are a potent source of exposure to stressful circumstances. Sometimes events happen to other people but involve us (Thoits 1987; Kessler and McLeod 1984) because roles often define interpersonal relationships.

Eventful stressors, however, are by definition relatively rare. Enduring or chronic stressors are much more common. Concerns about financial conditions, personal relationships, children, work, physical health, the balance between work and family, etc. are often ongoing sources of stress and strain. Research clearly shows that exposure to these types of chronic stressors is related to social status (Turner, Wheaton, and Lloyd 1995).

If the importance of stressors lies in the necessity for persons to find ways to adjust to the new conditions created by these stressors, then the way that adjustment occurs is through the mobilization of resources to deal with the stressors. People attempt to resolve the problems created by stressors (notwithstanding long-term experiences that discourage attempts at resolution) by using personal and social resources to make adjustments in their lives and reduce the stressfulness of change or chronic problems. Change and adjustment to life is both frequent and necessary. However, we also know that people differ in their capacity to resolve problems or to make changes and adjustments as a function of their social statuses (Turner and Marino 1994). People differ in their access to financial and social resources based on education, income, marital status, and age, for example. Kohn and Schooler (1983) have also shown that socioeconomic status is related to psychological dispositions that affect the ability to resolve problems.

At one level, then, we can argue that social statuses and social roles give rise to stressful circumstances so that persons in different statuses and roles have different exposure to stressors. Moreover, social statuses and roles also affect the resources one can use to make adjustments to one's life (style) and thus affect vulnerability to the negative effects of stressors. Exposure and vulnerability are in turn indirectly related to feelings of distress. Higher stressor exposure and/or greater vulnerability to the effects of stressors (i.e., fewer resources) ultimately increase the chances of experiencing distress.

The above formulation does not entirely explain, however, how the failure to resolve or readjust to problems ultimately leads to distress. Part of the answer is simply that the stressful conditions persist when attempts to resolve stressors are less than completely successful—hence the return arrow in Figure 8-1 from Resolution/Adjustment back to Stressors. Chronic stressors may become chronic simply because eventful stressors cannot be resolved. We think, however, that there is more to the story.

People are not simply passive victims of events and chronic conditions. They try to resolve problems by using material and emotional resources and, to the extent that people are activists in their own behalf, they seem to suffer fewer negative emotional consequences (Thoits 1994). Successful resolution of problems increases the sense of personal control, reaffirms identities, and leads to well-being. Unsuccessful resolution leads to a decreased sense of personal control; it increases demoralization and loss of identity and, finally, it leads to distress. Sense of control appears to be the key link between the resolution of stressful life circumstances, identity affirmation, and feelings of well-being (Mirowsky and Ross 1989; Turner and Roszell 1994).

SECTION SUMMARY

So, let's review. People's identities are provided by their positions in the social structure and the roles they play (the frequent answer to the question, "Who am I?"). These positions and roles are both sources of stressors and resources for dealing with those stressors. The effective resolution of stressors affirms personal control and sense of self, leading to feelings of well-being. Alternatively, failure to resolve the issues created by stressors leads to loss of confidence, demoralization, identity loss, and feelings of distress.

The importance of social positions and roles lies not only in their relationship to stress exposure, but also to stress vulnerability. The same characteristics of statuses and roles that generate stressors also affect the level of resources that an individual can mobilize to offset stressors. The consequence is that persons in lower social positions and/or with conflicting or demanding roles are also less likely to control the resources that could offset these stressors. In turn, they are the most likely to display signs of distress, as we have documented in this part of the book (Part I).

Mirowsky and Ross (1989) estimate that social conditions explain at least half of all symptoms of depression and almost three-quarters of symptoms among persons in the lowest categories of social position and personal control. Turner, Wheaton, and Lloyd (1995) estimate that between 23 and 50 percent of observed differences in mental health status are explained by differences in exposure to stressors as a function of gender, marital status, and occupation. Thus, as we stated in the Introduction, understanding the social causes of psychological distress is crucial to a more complete explanation of mental health.

A NOTE ON THE LIMITATIONS OF THIS DISCUSSION

We need to address one other implication of the argument for a social explanation of the causes of psychological distress that you may have wondered about—is everybody (or nearly everybody) crazy? After all, only a small subgroup of people, white, middle class, educated, married men seem not to be at elevated risk of distress. Therefore, everyone else *is* at elevated risk, by comparison. The further implication is that the social system itself creates this large-scale distress so that illness is normal and health is the exception (Gerhardt 1989). Sociologists who believe that social systems are based on models of conflicting interests and patterns of dominance and subordination (for example, Marxists) make exactly this claim. Social systems can be bad for your health. Psychologists and psychiatrists make similar claims for the presence of widespread disorder although they base their claims on genetic and biological characteristics. Later in this book we will see that community surveys of the incidence and prevalence of psychiatric disorders find that almost 50 percent of the population will experience a psychiatric disorder in their lifetime.

The presumption that large numbers of persons will suffer from disorder leads to several processes that we will describe in the second part of this book. This includes the idea that much of social life is becoming "medicalized." That is, more and more of our behavior is evaluated through the "gaze" of medical personnel and evaluated in terms of potential health effects. Further, the presence of illness requires the imposition of treatment (some would say, social control).

Although we are not used to thinking about societies in which illness is normal and health is unusual, doing so raises serious political and social concerns in addition to human concerns about relieving discomfort. For example, should we regard single mothers as ill? Since we know that poverty is related to distress, should we define poor people as ill because they are poor (Mirowsky and Ross 1989b)? On the one hand, it seems silly. On the other, there is evidence that it is happening and the question that we need to think about is how desirable it is to deal with social and personal problems as forms of mental illness?

Part II of this book describes the societal and institutional reactions to behaviors and thought processes that we define as signs of mental illness. In dealing with a sociological explanation for the ways in which we think of mental disorder and arrange for its treatment or control, we will gain perspective on these broader social and political issues. Exploring the societal reactions to mental illness will then permit us to assess the contribution of sociology as a discipline for understanding mental illness.

LABELING DEVIANT BEHAVIOR AS MENTAL ILLNESS

Anyone who has ever watched one of the many talk shows on television knows that there are a lot of "crazy" people "out there." Yet it is doubtful that most of these people are actually mentally ill. There is an enormous amount of variation in people's behavior and ways of thinking but only a small portion of this variation is regarded as a sign of craziness and still less is formally diagnosed as mental illness. In daily life we often witness odd or unusual behavior but we generally ignore it or explain it as due to some temporary stressor or just to "losing it."

This chapter discusses a sociological explanation of how and why some of this vast range of behavior is recognized as mental illness. The principle idea is that mental illness is in the eye of the beholder. We observe deviant behavior that we are unable to readily understand and then we label it so that we can try to control it. We will focus less on the characteristics of individuals who are labeled as mentally ill and more on the characteristics of those who witness behavioral deviance and then label it as mental illness. The recognition of mental illness by others is described as a *labeling process* and more generally as *societal reaction*. We will first address the relationships between deviant behavior, mental illness, and the social control of deviant behavior; then we will discuss the general arguments of this labeling perspective, including some criticisms and modifications of the basic theory. We will then examine the process of recognition as it occurs among family and friends. In a final section we will consider the way in which social status affects the process of labeling deviant behavior as mental illness.

DEVIANT BEHAVIOR AS MENTAL ILLNESS

To begin our discussion of social labeling, we will briefly discuss exactly what we mean by mental illness. Of course one meaning of mental illness is simply the diagnostic categories utilized by psychiatric professionals to identify varieties of mental disorder. More generally, however, we may define mental illness as descriptive of certain kinds of deviant behavior. Some deviant behavior is defined as criminal or bad manners or religious heresy but the deviant behavior we associate with mental illness often does not fit these categories and is distinguished by its incomprehensibility: "[O]bservers perceive that behaviors lack purpose, intent, or reason..." (Horwitz 1982, 14).

Although there can be disagreement between observers, and although different cultures and different historical time periods may have different standards for determining purpose, intent, and reason, the characteristic of incomprehensibility appears to underlie all conceptions of the meaning of madness. In our daily lives we rely on the unspoken expectation that our view of the world closely resembles that of others. These shared expectations allow us to interact with others in meaningful ways, they validate our view of ourselves, and they permit us to act in goal-directed ways. When we encounter someone who does not appear to share these expectations, whose behavior does not appear to be motivated by normal ideas about how the world works, we are apt to view that behavior as "crazy" and the person as "not all there," "out to lunch," or as mentally ill. Our inability to understand the reasoning behind the behaviors we see leads us to regard this type of behavior as deviant and as an example of mental disorder. We understand the motivations of thieves and murderers even if we do not approve of them. Even when crimes are committed in the heat of passion, we still understand such a motivation. It is comprehensible. By contrast, when aliens direct a person to save used candy wrappers, we do not have a framework for explaining this deviant behavior. We are inclined to think of the behavior as an example of mental illness. It is otherwise incomprehensible.

SOCIETAL REACTIONS TO DEVIANT BEHAVIOR: SOCIAL CONTROL

But why should we care if some people don't see the world the same way we do and act in ways we don't understand? The key lies in our classification of such behavior as deviance. The behavior associated with mental illness violates social norms. Moreover, although we find the motivation for this behavior incomprehensible, we hold the individual violator personally responsible for this behavior. Violations of social norms, particularly violations for which we attribute personal responsibility, are generally subject to social control. According to Scheff (1984), deviant behavior offends strongly held beliefs about acceptable behavior and leads to attempts to suppress and control such behavior. Part of what makes normal behavior comprehensible is our ability to relate such behavior to standard models of behavior that we use to regulate our own behavior. If the world is an uncertain place, rules seem to give it a more predictable context. By contrast, the type of deviance that we associate with mental illness can be seen to undermine this sense of certainty because it is incomprehensible. We have an interest, therefore, in preventing or controlling its appearance. From the perspective of functionalist theory, violations of social norms have the potential to disrupt the smooth operation of the social system. From this view all societies create social control mechanisms to safeguard the social system. In either case, deviant behavior is not ignored.

Social control can be established through either informal or formal mechanisms. Informally, we chide persons who violate relatively trivial norms, avoid them, or invoke other forms of control that are designed to restrain or prevent deviant behaviors. An easy way to see how informal social control works is to think of the ways in which children learn acceptable behavior through various forms of parental reward and punishment.

There are also formal mechanisms for the control of deviance, such as the criminal justice system, schools, and the medical/mental health system. These social institutions are intended in whole or in part to identify and control deviant behavior. They represent impersonal social means for enforcing community-wide standards for acceptable behavior.

In order for us to invoke these types of social control we need a mechanism for recognizing when social norms have been violated and a means for determining how to deal with these violations. This is accomplished through the labeling of deviant behavior. The way in which the behavior is labeled (as crime or mental illness, for example) affects the way in which we respond—the societal reaction to deviant behavior. In the following section, therefore, we will explain how the labeling of deviant behavior occurs and how this perspective is applied to the labeling of mental illness.

THE LABELING OF DEVIANT BEHAVIOR AND DEVIANTS

Thomas Scheff (1966, 1984) is largely responsible for providing us with a systematic articulation of the labeling process in which observers come to regard individual behavior as examples of mental illness and the individual as mentally ill. To be labeled as mentally ill is to receive a stigmatic label that implies exclusion and sanctions or social control. The label can have profound negative effects on the lives of persons so labeled.

In brief, Scheff argues that sometimes deviant behavior gets labeled as mental illness, that this label leads to social isolation and rejection and then to self-identification as mentally ill. Mental illness is not initially a property of the individual but an outcome of labeling by others, which then becomes an attribute of the individual. This is clearly not the way we are used to thinking about mental illness. Both medical models and psychodynamic models locate mental illness in the individual and explain its origin in terms of biogenetic or developmental anomalies. By contrast, Scheff argues that the cause of mental illness lies in the evaluations of behavior made by others and *not* in the individual so labeled. As we might expect, then, this perspective is not without its critics and we will discuss their objections after presenting Scheff's argument more completely.

To Scheff, the process starts with the production of deviant behavior by an individual. This deviant behavior has the further property that it is not classifiable (and is possibly incomprehensible) using any other standard way of categorizing deviant behavior such as judging the behavior to be criminal or just a social *faux pas*. Rather, this behavior is "residual," not elsewhere classified. So we have the problem of trying to explain behavior that we regard as deviant but for which we have no ready category. Scheff says that we assign this residual deviance to the category "mental illness," and, further, that once a person's *behavior* is labeled as an example of mental illness, the person becomes labeled as mentally ill. Scheff argues that persons who are labeled as mentally ill develop an identity as mentally ill and then act in ways that confirm the original diagnosis. Since the label is also stigmatic, it leads to isolation, exclusion, and various forms of reward and punishment that are ultimately based on the social function of the mental health system—control.

Scheff has stated his argument in the form of nine propositions that collectively describe the process of labeling and how it "causes" mental illness (Scheff 1984, 189).

(1) "Residual rule-breaking arises from fundamentally diverse sources." Deviant behaviors that are otherwise not classified or are incomprehensible can be caused by organic, psychological, stress, or even volitional sources. What he is saying is that there are a lot of different things that may cause residual rule-breaking but what is important is the way others interpret the behavior, regardless of what caused it. This proposition allows that deviant behavior may originate in biological or psychodynamic processes but it suggests that what is important is the interpretation of this deviant behavior by observers.

(2) "Relative to the rate of treated mental illness, the rate of unrecorded residual rule-breaking is extremely high." This proposition emphasizes the fact that there is an enormous amount of residual rule-

breaking in normal life. We are all guilty of violating behavioral norms of some kind and we do it frequently. This proposition also emphasizes that mental illness is in the eye of the beholder. With residual rule-breaking so frequent, some factor must determine when this rule-breaking is labeled and when it is not. Unless the residual rule-breaking is noted by others, it means nothing. Most community surveys find a high rate of psychiatric symptoms among the population but most of those symptoms go unidentified as signs of mental illness. Not only do these surveys find that most symptomatic behaviors are unlabeled as mental illness, but they also find very low rates of official diagnosis by the medical/mental health system (the rate of treated mental illness). Even for very severe forms of mental illness it is estimated that one of two persons are not getting mental health treatment. So the talk shows are right, there are a lot of crazy people out there but most of the behavior goes unlabeled and persons are untreated.

(3) "Most residual rule-breaking is normalized and is of transitory significance." Usually, when we witness deviant behavior we try to explain it in terms of temporary problems or moods, rather than in terms of more stable mental illness. We "normalize" the behavior as something without long-term meaning. Given how frequent residual rule-breaking is, it wouldn't make sense to label every bit of residual rule-breaking as an example of mental illness. So even if deviant behavior is observed by others, it does not automatically lead to a label.

(4) "Stereotyped imagery of mental disorder is learned at an early age," and (5) "The stereotypes of insanity are continually reaffirmed, inadvertently, in ordinary social interaction." These propositions explain why we seem to know so much about how to identify mental illness. These propositions are also used to explain why, when psychiatrists examine patients, they frequently see symptomatic behavior or behavior that is consistent with a stereotype of madness. That is, they regularly see behavior that is consistent with specific diagnoses because people know how to act crazy. The media, as well as parents and teachers, provide models of persons defined as mentally ill in the form of movies, songs, newspaper articles, and off-hand labeling of behavior. We know how to "go crazy" because we have seen it done. We all have models of mental illness that we can apply to the evaluation of other's behavior or that we can apply to our own behavior.

(6) "Labeled deviants may be rewarded for playing the stereotyped deviant role," and (7) "Labeled deviants are punished when they attempt the return to conventional roles." Here we see one of the hallmarks of the social control perspective in regard to stigmatic labeled behavior. Once an individual has received a stigmatic label, he or she has a "spoiled identity." One is regarded as deviant and therefore is

excluded from normal social life and normal social roles. Moreover, this deviant status implies that the person should continue to be excluded from normal social life. Protests that the label is incorrect or attempts to evade the isolation and exclusion that comes with the label are punished. Don't we want to know if someone with a mental illness is teaching our children or is entrusted (accidentally) with some important job? Sure we do, and so we make rules to prevent such people from assuming these normal roles. In doing so we continue to exclude them. On the other hand, we reward people for playing the stereotyped deviant role by praising their "insight" into their disorder when they acknowledge the accuracy of the label that they have received. The special irony is that playing the stereotyped role is rewarded by allowing access to treatment and therapy but simultaneously justifies current segregation and stigmatization.

(8) "In the crisis occurring when a residual rule-breaker is publicly labeled, the deviant is highly suggestible and may accept the proffered role of the insane as the only alternative." According to Scheff, when the deviant is publicly labeled, the rule-breaker is likely to be confused, anxious, and ashamed. Under these conditions, the rule-breaker may accept the role because they can see no other way out of their dilemma. Since the rule-breaker will be rewarded for accepting the label and punished for attempting to escape it, the easier choice may simply be to accept the accuracy of the label. Moreover, this occurs just at the point where the labeled person is perhaps most vulnerable, when the condition becomes a matter of public knowledge. This is a very controversial aspect of Scheff's theory and one that we don't necessarily need to accept. Scheff thinks that we make use of the stereotypes about how to act crazy to accommodate social control agents (psychiatrists/psychologists) by acting in ways that they will find consistent and as confirmation of their diagnosis of an underlying mental illness.

(9) "Among residual rule-breakers, labeling is the single most important cause of careers of residual deviance." This proposition confirms that the effects of labeling are profound, widespread, and long-lasting. It also affirms the idea that people evolve into the role of being mentally ill over time principally because of their isolation, stigmatization, and the system of rewards and punishments that keep them in this status.

In sum, Scheff says that there is a lot of residual rule-breaking that occurs in daily life but when that behavior is publicly associated with the label of mental illness, responses by others (based on stereotypes of mental illness) to the labeled person keep him or her within the role of the mentally ill person. As a result, the person develops an identity as a mentally ill individual and then continues to act in ways that are consistent with the role of the mentally ill person. Mentally ill persons are "made" by the reactions of others to them and prevented from leaving this role for similar reasons.

CRITIQUE AND MODIFICATIONS

The idea that mental illness is largely caused by the reactions of others to deviant behavior (labeling) is not an easily accepted explanation for the cause of mental illness. First, it is not consistent with the dominant explanations for the origins of mental illness. Second, it assumes that there is a uniformly strong and negative reaction to the label, and third, it assumes that people who are labeled are almost inevitably locked into a deviant status with no prospect of regaining "normality."

Perhaps the most obvious objection to Scheff's notion that mental illness is caused by the reactions of others is that the individual bears no responsibility for the problem in this logic. That is, the label is conferred on the individual without regard to the actual mental state or behavior of the individual. The dominant theories that explain the origins of mental illness focus on the individual as the source of deviant behavior. Both the medical model and psychodynamic models regard the individual as the focus of attention. Either genetic/biochemical conditions in the individual or specific individual issues related to psychological growth (or both) are generally accepted as explanations for mental illness. In the labeling perspective it is not the individual but those who observe and classify behavior who cause the illness.

Critics argue that this is not entirely sensible. They agree that labeling occurs but they argue that the label is applied because it accurately describes behavior and not because others are offended or otherwise in a position to label the behavior for their own purposes. People get labeled as mentally ill because they are mentally ill (Gove 1982).

Sorting out the support for Scheff's perspective versus contradictory evidence about this issue turns out to be very difficult, for a number of reasons. First, the phenomenon that Scheff describes is symbolic and thus difficult to observe directly. When an act of labeling occurs it is usually very difficult to separate the reactions of others from the behavior of the individual. Moreover, changes in the rate at which deviant behavior is observed, once the label has been conferred, cannot be unambiguously attributed to the effects of the label as compared to the trajectory of the psychiatric condition itself.

We do know, however, that there are many people in the general community who manifest diagnosable symptoms of mental illness but who are not, in fact, diagnosed or under treatment (Kessler et al. 1994; Srole et al. 1978). Moreover, we know that some people undergoing treatment do not show the standard symptoms of their disorder. These observations suggest that behavior itself is not a perfect predictor of labels. That is, if all people with schizophrenic symptoms are not diagnosed (and only about 50 percent of them are), then behavior alone cannot explain why some people are labeled schizophrenic and others are not labeled. The fact that some people are labeled even in the absence of "symptoms" also suggests that there is not a perfect correspondence between behavior and labels. These observations support a labeling interpretation.

Some researchers have attempted to discover if people's expectations and reactions change toward a person when they find that the person has been labeled as mentally ill. If expectations and behavior do change, it supports the labeling theory. Labeling theory assumes that there is a uniformly strong and negative reaction to the label and to the person labeled. Think about how you might react to information that a person you met and liked was revealed to have a mental illness.

Labeling theory specifically implicates general public opinion as a source of the meaning of the mental illness label. Propositions 4 and 5 in Scheff's argument refer to stereotypes (standardized conceptions) and to constant generalized reinforcement of stereotypes as factors determining how we label behavior. Research shows that public conceptions of "crazy" behavior and "crazy persons" vary. Attitudes about the dangerousness of persons with mental illness and the feelings of social distance from the mentally ill have actually become more negative over the past thirty-five years (Phelan and Steuve 1997).

This finding is surprising because most researchers thought that attitudes would become more positive because of changes in the manner of providing treatment for the mentally ill in the last thirty-five years. Until the late 1950s, persons with almost any form of disorder who could not afford private community care were sent to large state hospitals that were isolated from the general population. This separation was both representative of the stigma of mental illness and prevented more informed ideas about the mentally ill. A shift from isolated institutional care to community care since then has exposed the general population to the mentally ill more directly and has probably affected the way some members of the general public think of mental illness. Studies do show that familiarity with mentally ill persons reduces the negative ratings of them. Thus, critics argue that stereotypes may not really exist and that the mental illness label isn't all that stigmatic anyway. If these criticisms are true, then a major tenet of the labeling perspective is not supported. However, recent findings that perceptions of dangerousness and unpredictability are associated with the mentally ill more often today than they were in earlier surveys (Phelan and Steuve 1997) suggest support for the labeling perspective.

Another argument made suggests that the general public is not as important to labeling theory as the medical authorities who confer the label. Recall that labeling reflects an attempt to control deviant behavior. Deviant according to whose standards? The answer is, the standards of well-educated, white, heterosexual, middle-class males who dominate the psychiatric profession. For example, studies show that the likelihood that a set of symptoms will be perceived to be consistent with a diagnosable disorder depends on the sex and race of the psychiatrist and the sex and race of the symptomatic individual. There is also some evidence that poor people are more likely to be diagnosed with more severe illnesses and to be treated in more impersonal and traumatic ways. These observations suggest that mental illness diagnoses may be made independently of "symptoms" just as labeling theory would predict.

The other aspect of labeling theory that has been subject to debate is the degree to which labels *cause* individuals to redefine themselves as mentally ill and the degree to which "secondary" deviance (deviance that is consistent with being mentally ill) arises in persons who are labeled. This, of course, is the ultimate cause of mental illness in the labeling perspective and so it is also the most crucial component of Scheff's theory.

In the late 1950s and early 1960s a number of studies of mental hospitals suggested that inmates developed an "institutional" personality (Goffman 1961). They became dependent on the hospital and lost their identities based on preinstitutional roles. Critics of labeling theory argue that this observed phenomenon is the basis for labeling theory's prediction that labeled individuals act like their labels. That is, only persons hospitalized in mental hospitals for long periods of time are prone to take on the identity of the mentally ill. Further, they argue that since confinement for long periods of time in mental hospitals no longer occurs except in very rare circumstances, labeled individuals do not lose their former identities, nor are they likely to produce stereotypically crazy behavior. In short, the label of mental illness does not lead to more behavior that is consistent with the label and, therefore, the theory is incorrect.

Link et al. (1989) have found, however, that there is a basis for expecting that even if labeling does not lead directly to mental illness, it has negative consequences for the individual's self-esteem, earning power, and social support networks, and it makes labeled persons more vulnerable to new disorder or existing disorder. The "modified" labeling theory approach that they propose (and back with research findings) shows that labels make substantial differences in people's lives and that labeled individuals act in ways that not-labeled persons do not. Link and Cullen (1990) conclude, therefore, that the combination of actual symptoms and the nature of the response to those symptoms both strongly influence labeling of people as mentally ill. Estroff (1981) has shown that severely mentally ill persons living in the community know how to "make it crazy" when either the general public becomes intolerant of them or professionals become critical of their lack of therapeutic progress. They can act crazy when they need to.

Time has shown that Scheff's idea that labels are powerful modifiers of interpersonal relationships is probably true. Research also shows that stigmatic labels are particularly "sticky" and particularly damaging to people. And as we shall see, the labeling perspective has some very challenging implications for the diagnostic process in psychiatry.

Despite its critics, then, labeling theory seems to tell us something about the causes of mental illness. The reactions of others to deviant behavior are of great importance in understanding what happens to people who behave in deviant ways. What the theory does not do well is tell us how the person gets labeled in the first place, aside from acting in deviant ways. Who are these mysterious "others" who behold examples of deviant behavior? It turns out that there are two types of others: informal labelers and formal labelers. Informal labelers include family, friends, and neighbors while formal labelers include health and mental health professionals. Since we will deal with the formal institutional responses to mental disorder in detail in other chapters, we now turn to the process of informal labeling. Family, friends, and neighbors are likely to be the first ones to witness deviant, incomprehensible behavior and so it is not unreasonable to think that the labeling process starts among these people.

FAMILY REACTIONS TO DEVIANT BEHAVIOR

The labeling argument outlined by Scheff is clearly a process. That is, the observation, recognition, and labeling of deviant behavior as mental illness occurs over time. Given that the deviance we are talking about is "residual" and that there is a tendency to normalize this deviance, it is likely that reaching the conclusion that deviance represents mental illness takes time. Research shows that there are a number of important variables that need to be taken into account in order to explain how, when, and why deviant behavior gets labeled as mental illness.

Much of this process occurs within the family setting. Although it is important to consider the role that friends, neighbors, and acquaintances play in conferring informal labels and in making referrals to formal treatment, here we focus on the family. The family represents the most intimate day-to-day social context for most people. It is within the family that we spend the majority of our time and family members have the greatest opportunity to observe personal behavior.

Nevertheless, families are not the quickest to label deviance.

Family members share a common cultural, social, and psychological context. They are also tied to one another by strong emotional bonds that tend to increase their tolerance for deviant behavior. Moreover, because family members generally interact with one another so often, they are less likely to detect changes in family members' behaviors that occur over a relatively long time.

We mentioned earlier in this chapter that there is a high rate of residual deviance and that most of this is normalized. These observations suggest that initial signs of mental illness are not perceived as such by observers. There is no fixed pattern of behaviors that reliably leads to mental illness and so we do not normally link distinctive and temporally separated behaviors into patterns until much later in the recognition process.

All of this means that family members are not likely to reach the conclusion that deviant behavior within the family constitutes a mental health problem for quite some time after "initial symptoms" are observed.

Examples of residual rule-breaking are frequent and most of it is unrecorded and normalized (Scheff 1984). Most of this residual rule-breaking doesn't even have to do with mental disorder. Being late for a meeting is an example of a residual rule violation, for example. Even examples of behavior that are considered to be symptomatic of mental disorder are frequently observed but rarely equated with mental illness. Losing one's appetite for a few weeks, losing or gaining weight, changes in sleeping habits, feeling lonely or sad, not being interested in activities, or feeling that one has less energy than usual are all symptoms of depression, and while these must be prolonged and simultaneous to satisfy diagnostic criteria, it is also clear that most of us have experienced each of these "symptoms" at one time or another. Recognition of these symptoms as indicative of a mental illness is not intuitive or obvious. Normal people normally behave in these ways at one time or another. In a study of female ex-mental patients, Angrist et al. (1968) compared the symptoms of hospitalized women with normal women with no hospitalization history. They found very high rates of symptoms among normal women, such as moving about restlessly, acting tense or nervous, getting grouchy, and always seeming worn out or tired, and there were no significant differences between hospitalized and comparison subjects for eleven of thirty-two symptoms. Therefore, much of what we mean by the normalizing of deviant behavior may be nothing more than the lack of recognition of behaviors as consistent with psychiatric diagnostic criteria. Angrist et al. suggest that the real distinction between hospitalized and normal women concerns symptoms that impede adequate functioning and that are defined as disruptive; including abusive language, idleness, restlessness, insomnia, and health worries.

In addition, the observation of symptoms may be spread out over a long period of time. This isolates the individual examples of residual rule-breaking and makes it more likely that each individual behavior will be explained in terms of current (or very recent) situations and not in terms of an on-going progression of symptoms. Moreover, families generally do not have expertise in diagnostic techniques or criteria and are not skilled at "organizing" symptoms into syndromes that might be indicative of disorder.

Community surveys support this view. They consistently find that substantial numbers of people who are not thought to have a mental illness would, in fact, be diagnosed if their behavior was reviewed by someone with psychiatric knowledge. In other words, these surveys suggest that the deviance associated with residual rule-breaking is not necessarily labeled as mental illness (it is normalized) even when it is severe and prolonged.

So, what factors affect the recognition of mental disorder by family members or other lay persons? Mechanic (1989, 108) suggests that the following factors (among others) will affect recognition:

1. The visibility, recognizability, or perceptual salience of deviant signs and symptoms
2. The extent to which symptoms disrupt family, work, and other social activities
3. The frequency of the appearance of deviant signs and symptoms, or their persistence, or their frequency of recurrence
4. The tolerance threshold of those who are exposed to and evaluate the deviant signs and symptoms
5. The degree to which autistic psychological processes (perceptual processes that distort reality) are present

In short, as symptoms become frequent, bizarre (noncomprehensible), and disruptive there is an increased tendency to interpret the deviant behavior in psychiatric terms.

The first appearances of deviant behavior will be explained in terms of the immediate context ("he has been under a lot of stress lately"). However, as deviant behaviors recur and if they cannot be easily related to common explanations, observers of the behavior will increasingly look for more general explanations for the behavior. When the behavior cannot be explained away and when the observer loses tolerance or cannot adjust expectations to accommodate the behavior, then psychiatric interpretations for the behavior are more likely to be applied. Because families vary in the amount of tolerance they have and because they also vary in the amount of knowledge they have about mental illness, there will be variations in the labeling of mental illness by families and others.

NON-FAMILY REACTIONS TO DEVIANT BEHAVIOR

Although family members are the most likely persons to witness behavioral deviance, they are certainly not the only ones who do so. In fact, persons at greater social distance are much more likely to label odd behavior as psychiatric. They are also more likely to make referrals to mental health treatment facilities. Referrals to mental health professionals, of course, begin the formal labeling process that will be discussed in detail in a later chapter.

Friends, acquaintances, neighbors, and strangers are far less familiar with the exact nature of "normal" behavior in a specific family. As a result they are apt to apply general community standards to the behavior they observe. They also have less emotional attachment to the deviant actor and hence, less need of or interest in normalizing the behavior they observe. It is sometimes said that those outside the family can be more "objective" about what is going on inside the family.

Deviant behavior that is observed by non-nuclear family members or others is more "public" and therefore more apt to be labeled as part of "the public crisis" (Scheff 1984) that leads to self-labeling. Because they lack the reasons to deny the presence of mental illness that nuclear family members may have, and because they are less likely to try to explain away the behavior (normalize), nonfamily observers find the deviant behavior less comprehensible and are more likely to define it as mental illness. At the same time, it does not appear that complete strangers have much to do with the labeling process. Complete strangers who observe deviant behavior may informally evaluate the behavior as indicative of mental illness, but they can simply avoid the deviant person and take no further action leading to the imposition of a more lasting label. Horwitz (1982, 36, 47) provides two general propositions related to these arguments: (1) "The tendency to label an individual mentally ill varies directly with relational distance between the observer and the actor" (as long as they have some relationship); and (2) "The tendency to label an individual mentally ill varies directly with the cultural distance between the observer and the actor." By definition, members of a family share a host of relational, cultural, and social traits that make them less likely to label members as mentally ill. With increasing relationship, cultural, and social distance, however, the tendency to label behavior increases.

As one would imagine, these differences in the tendency to label others also affect the likelihood that observation and informal labeling will lead to referrals to mental health professionals and formal labeling. Because families are slower to acknowledge that deviant behaviors might be signs of mental illness, they are also less likely to seek formal help from the mental health system. Often when families become concerned about the behavior of one of their members, they will seek advice from friends and other personal acquaintances. In turn, these informal consultants are apt to suggest that the behavior be interpreted in psychiatric terms and to suggest contact with the mental health system.

Crosscutting the relative tendencies of different observers to label deviant behavior as mental illness are the characteristics of the person to whom the label might be applied. The social characteristics of the deviant actor also affect the likelihood that a label will be applied.

SOCIAL STATUS AND LABELING

In the previous sections we have seen that there is no automatic process linking every instance of residual deviance to a label. Family, friends, neighbors, and strangers have different reactions to such deviance and these differences affect the likelihood that any individual's behavior will be labeled as mental illness. In this section we will discuss how status characteristics of the deviant actor and differences in the social statuses of the observer and the observed affect labeling. Recall that the labeling theory is, at base, a theory of social control that explains how we deal with deviant behavior. As such, we should expect that individuals will have different abilities to resist the imposition of a label that justifies direct control of that person.

Clearly, labeling of mental illness depends on its recognition as such. That is, the deviance observed needs to be thought of in psychiatric terms by the observer. It turns out that individuals have different propensities to label their own behavior in these terms based on their social status. Those with better education (and especially those with a liberal arts/humanities concentration) are more likely to think that their unusual behavior has a psychiatric origin. Women are more likely to label their behavior in these terms, as well. In previous chapters we saw that persons with lower social status attributes (class, gender, race, etc.) are more likely to display symptoms of distress and mental illness. However, persons of higher social class are more likely to label behavior as psychiatric because persons with better education have more general knowledge about mental illness and they have more trust in psychiatric treatment. Their education makes them more familiar with psychiatric concepts and more likely to interpret their behavior in such terms. They are also more likely to make a self-referral to psychiatric authorities because they will be comfortable with the terms of the discussion and because they will be less fearful of their encounter with psychiatrists or psychologists.

Psychiatric interpretations of behavioral deviance seem to require both a familiarity with psychiatric categories and a cultural background in which psychiatric ideas are accepted and legitimated. Psychiatrists, for example, are the most likely occupational group to have actually undergone psychiatric treatment. Similarly, the largest group of practitioners by ethnicity are Jewish and Jews are the most likely ethnicity to make self-referrals. Self-recognition of behavior as representing psychiatric disorder varies by class, education, gender, and ethnicity. When individuals ask themselves, "What's wrong with me?" the answer they get reflects the categories they use to think about the question. For persons with education in the humanities, for example, there is a higher likelihood that psychiatric categories will be familiar to the individual and there is a greater likelihood that the behavior will be "labeled" using such categories.

Although social status characteristics of the individual do affect the likelihood of self-labeling, we are most interested in how these characteristics affect the likelihood that others (particularly psychiatric authorities) will label behavior. As a theory of social control, the essence of labeling theory is that labels are used to control deviant behavior. But, according to whose standards do we determine what constitutes deviant behavior? Since psychiatrists are predominantly males, well-educated, middle to upper class, and white, and since psychiatrists have the authority to formally confer labels, the answer is: according to the standards of psychiatrists with these general social characteristics.

To evaluate this argument we need to find out if women, less educated, lower-class, or minority persons are more likely to be labeled than persons without some or all of these characteristics. The assumption we make is that, because such persons differ from psychiatrists in terms of social characteristics, their behavior is more likely to be interpreted by psychiatrists as deviant. Further, we assume that psychiatrists use the labels they are empowered to confer as a means of controlling deviant behavior.

In practice, the type of information we would need to test this argument is hard to come by. However, a number of studies suggest that such biases exist in diagnostic settings. First, community surveys clearly show different rates of diagnosed and diagnosable disorder by gender, race, and social class. The variations in these rates correspond to the predictions we just made above: Higher rates are observed for women, non-whites, and lower social class individuals. While this data is consistent with the predictions of a labeling theory, they do not directly confirm it. However, in a number of experiments in which psychiatrists were presented with descriptions of individuals with symptoms but with variation in the characteristics of the individual (e.g., the individual is white or black, male or female), there was a clear tendency by white male psychiatrists to diagnosis blacks and women differently than white males (Loring and Powell 1988). The same studies show that nonwhite and female psychiatrists also differed in the way they reached diagnostic conclusions, despite the claim that all the psychiatrists used objective criteria to make their decisions. Rosenfield (1982) found evidence that persons who exhibit psychiatric symptoms that are inconsistent with sex-role stereotypes (such as females with antisocial personality disorders) are more likely to be recommended for hospitalization and are considered to be more disturbed. These findings are also consistent with the labeling argument that the objective of formal labeling is the control of deviant behavior. Existing evidence suggests that persons with social characteristics that differ from those of labelers (psychiatrists) are more apt to have deviant behavior labeled as psychiatric disorder.

While consistent, existing studies do not directly confirm the notion that psychiatric labels are used to control deviant behavior. We must make an assumption that observed differences in the way psychiatric authorities make diagnoses when their own social characteristics differ from those they are evaluating reflect personal judgments about the necessity for controlling deviant behavior. More direct evidence could be obtained by examining some of the specific symptoms that are listed as indicators of disorder and by estimating the likelihood that these behaviors will be produced by men and women (for example) equally. In the chapter on the medicalization of deviance, we will explicitly consider the evidence for gender and other types of status-related bias that might determine the likelihood that behavior stereotyped as "a girl thing," for example, will lead to diagnosis of that behavior as evidence of mental illness.

SUMMARY

The basic premise of the labeling theory of mental illness is that such illness is in the eye of the beholder more so than in the behavior of the individual who is labeled. We began the chapter by considering the meaning of mental illness and found that deviant behavior that is not otherwise understandable in terms of motivation or logic (incomprehensible) can define mental illness. Whether such behavior originates in biological/genetic, psychodynamic, or social causes, the act of labeling the behavior as mental illness has significant consequences for the labeled person. Our review of Scheff's theoretical propositions suggests how the social act of labeling others' behavior isolates the individual and ultimately leads to the production of typical patterns of secondary deviance that we agree constitute mental illness.

The idea that mental illness is not a characteristic of the individual but a result of a social process of labeling, isolation, and role restriction and expectation is not without its critics, who argue that people receive labels because their behavior justifies it. We reviewed these critiques and suggested some ways in which the labeling theory might take these critiques into account.

We also explored the reactions of family members and friends and neighbors to the type of deviant behaviors that characterize mental disorder. The review showed that observers do, in fact, have a role in establishing whether and when a label as mentally ill is applied.

In this book the labeling theory of mental illness is not meant to be restricted to the specific theory of Thomas Scheff, though we have spent much time describing and evaluating his specific ideas. Rather, labeling is to be used as a global way to explain societal reactions to behavioral deviance. This particular way of using the idea of labeling will now be extended to consider the origin of popular and professional labeling of mental illness, the relationship between deviance and mental illness in general, and the historical and social institutional responses to persons labeled as psychologically disordered.

10

The Relationship between Public Attitudes and Professional Labels

In the previous chapter we argued that the labeling of behavior as evidence of mental illness is based on perceptions of certain forms of deviant behavior, popular stereotypes of what mental illness is like, and the context in which deviant behavior is observed. In the current chapter we explore the nature of public stereotypes regarding mental illness and the mentally ill. We will also discuss how professional labels are related to public stereotypes of disorder. Finally, we will take a closer look at the professional system for diagnosing (labeling) mental illness and examine how it reflects general societal (public) notions of deviant and normal behavior.

Consider a stereotypical portrait of insanity. "Wild-eyed, disheveled, talking to the air, laughing at unseen amusements, insensible to others, prone to sudden and possibly violent behavior, a danger to little children."

Although this portrait of mental illness is intentionally overdrawn, it sensitizes us to the fact that stereotypes of mental illness do exist and, we can assume, affect both public and professional reactions to persons who are labeled as mentally ill. We have already explained that to be labeled mentally ill means one can be excluded from normal social relations and stigmatized (marked) as different. Stigma and exclusion based on stigma make it difficult for the general public to relate to the mentally ill in objective ways. When a mental health agency seeks to place a group home for mentally ill clients in a residential neighborhood, for example, appeals to the "rational" side of neighbors' evaluations are difficult because of the strength of negative stereotypes. No amount of assurance by the agency about the regulation of behavior, monitoring of clients, and the unlikelihood of certain "really bad" types of behavior will convince some neighborhood residents that the group home does not represent a danger to their neighborhood. Mental health professionals will also take neighborhood objections into account in guiding their selection of group home residents. In this way professional behavior reflects public attitudes.

We will start our discussion by reviewing public attitudes about mental illness and the mentally ill. We will explain how public attitudes affect professional attitudes and we will examine the professional methods for identifying mental illness (i.e., diagnosis) for evidence that such methods may also reflect the attitudes of the general public and society in general.

PUBLIC ATTITUDES

Do members of the public really believe that all persons who are diagnosed as mentally ill fit the stereotype used at the start of this chapter? Of course not. However, it is important to know what public attitudes are like and how they may affect people who have been diagnosed with a mental illness.

In the late 1950s and early 1960s the treatment of mental illness in the United States underwent a substantial change. Whereas most persons had been sent to large custodial mental hospitals prior to this time, the site of preferred treatment became the community. This meant that persons who had been "sent away" and those who now developed psychological disorders would reside in the community and inevitably interact with the general public. A number of researchers were worried about how the public might react to this new situation. They worried that the general public held unrealistic ideas about the characteristics of mentally ill people and that misinformation and bias might have negative effects on community-based patients and the community-based system of care. They hoped that if they understood the beliefs and attitudes of the general public, then they could design public education and information programs to enlighten the public (Nunnally 1961).

These researchers found that the public had a pretty good idea about the basic facts related to mental illness. That is, the public's general knowledge agreed with professional understandings about such things as the roles of the environment and biology in the causation of mental illness, and about the effectiveness of various ways of treating mental illness. They also found a negative assessment of the qualities of persons with mental illness and evidence for the existence of negative, stigmatic stereotypes of the mentally ill among the general public. Compared to their ideas about the characteristics of "average" men or women, public attitudes toward "insane" men or women reflected the belief that the insane are foolish, ignorant, sad, passive, insincere, unpredictable, weak, slow, delicate, cold, dirty, dangerous, tense, worthless, sick, and bad. This is quite a line-up of negative characteristics and a perfect illustration of stigma. Even though members of the general public had pretty accurate information about the causes and care of the mentally ill, they still reacted in highly negative ways to the label of mental illness. The label is a mark (stigma) that leads to negative stereotyping. In fact, when people were given descriptions of others that were prefaced as descriptions of insane others, the evaluations of these others were immediately much more negative than the same descriptions where no mention of insanity was made. Just knowing that a person was labeled mentally ill biased the reactions of people participating in this study (Nunnally 1961).

These findings were of considerable concern to mental health professionals who knew that the general public would have increased contact with persons diagnosed as mentally ill because of the shift to community-based treatment. They hoped to use the media to enlighten the public.

So, can we resort to the media as a source of information and a method for modifying these unreasoned biases? The answer is a resounding, "Yes and no." On the one hand, when the media attempt to impart factual information about the mentally ill, they can be quite successful while, on the other hand, the entertainment portion of the media utilizes the precise stereotypes held by the public to describe mentally ill characters in dramatic presentations. These portrayals emphasize stereotypically bizarre symptoms of mental illness such as unpredictability, dangerousness, and dirty appearance. While we cannot tell if the media cause members of the general public to develop negative stereotypes, it is clear that the portrayals in the media reinforce existing stereotypes.

There is some evidence that the extreme nature of the negative stereotype of the mentally ill found in earlier studies has given way to a more tolerant view of the mentally ill (Rabkin 1980). However, the most recent evidence suggests that negative stereotyping of the mentally ill may have increased (Phelan and Steuve 1997). The general public appear to be better informed about mental illness but they are not more likely to think of mental illness in the same way that they think of physical illness. When people become ill with a physical ailment, we do not blame the person for the illness, we do not construct negative stereotypes, and we hope they will obtain the high quality medical care they deserve. By contrast, the stereotype of mental illness includes the idea that the individual is personally responsible for his or her condition. We tell people to "get a hold of yourself" or to just "stop it!" When we think that people are responsible for their mental problems, we blame them and we have mixed or negative feelings about providing health care services because they do not "deserve" such help. This is why the medicalization process may be beneficial. To the extent that we have come to believe that mental and physical illness have the same basic causes (i.e., biological), we may blame the person less. In turn, this would lead to the reduction of stigma associated with the mental illness label. Medicalization will be discussed in the next chapter.

However, three characteristics continue to be stereotypically attributed to persons diagnosed as mentally ill; unpredictability, dangerousness, and lack of personal responsibility. The persistence of these stereotypes is illustrated by public reactions to the "insanity defense." There is a great deal of controversy about the legitimacy of this legal category. Critics charge that genuine criminals are "getting off" by pretending to be mentally ill, that too many people are eluding criminal responsibility by the use of this defense, and that dangerous people are returned to the street. These charges appear to be substantially inflated and to reflect the generalized negative stereotypes we have of persons who are mentally ill. How often do you think the insanity defense is used in criminal cases? In fact, the insanity defense is rarely used and, when used, rarely successful. Fewer than 0.2 percent of all felony cases involve the successful use of this defense. If this surprises you, perhaps you share some of the negative attributions about unpredictability, dangerousness, and responsibility that research shows is widespread.

On the other hand, these negative stereotypes seem to apply mostly to the category of the mentally ill in general. Personal exposure to mentally ill individuals changes these attributions considerably. Attributions of negative characteristics to specific individuals with whom the observer is familiar are very different. Depending on the amount of time spent with the person, the social distance between the observer and the person, and the education of the observer, the use of negative stereotypical descriptors can vary considerably. In general, the greater one's contact with a person diagnosed as mentally ill, the greater one's acceptance of that person, and the more likely that one will not use negative stereotypes of the mentally ill to describe the person. While some studies suggest that no stigma at all attaches to "former mental patients" (Crocetti, Spiro, and Siassi 1974), other evidence more strongly suggests the persistence and importance of labels as they affect attitudes and behavior toward those who receive the mental illness label.

Labels still matter. They appear to affect the way in which others treat those with the label and they affect the way the labeled person thinks of him or herself (Link et al. 1991). You may recall from the previous chapter that one of Scheff's propositions is that people use public stereotypes of mental illness to interpret their own deviant behavior. Link and his colleagues (1987) have shown that when someone who believes mental patients are dangerous is informed that an individual is mentally ill, he is more rejecting simply because of the label. That is, people's general attitudes (stereotypes) about mental illness affect their reactions to specific individuals who are labeled as mentally ill, regardless of how deviant their behavior actually is.

REACTIONS TO BEING LABELED

Those who are labeled mentally ill are acutely aware of these negative evaluations. Link et al. (1987) have shown that when a person is given a psychiatric label, she or he anticipates personal rejection. This, in turn, leads to demoralization, a decline in work performance, and loss of income, strained interpersonal relationships, and withdrawal from participation in social activities. Of course such behavior only reinforces observers' expectations about mentally ill persons and leads to increased rejection and isolation. Labeled persons may go to great lengths to minimize the number of persons who become aware of the label by concealing it or withdrawing from activities, or they may attempt to educate people who are aware of the label. Unfortunately, these attempts to offset or prevent stigmatic consequences of the mental illness label do not appear to be very effective (Link et al. 1991).

Whatever the ultimate causes of psychological disorder, personal and social reactions to those who are labeled as mentally ill have extremely powerful effects on their lives. Estroff (1981) describes the lives of chronically mentally ill persons as separate and diminished compared to "normals." The people she studied had found that they would not be accepted in the normal world despite the fact that returning to normal is the therapeutic goal of their treatment. They developed elaborate ways of "making it crazy" to deal with rejection on the one hand, and dependence on the mental health treatment system on the other hand.

The chronically mentally ill, those whose symptoms are severe, obvious, and long-lasting, and who have spent considerable time in psychiatric treatment, display the most visible signs of their disorders and are also the persons most obviously affected by labeling (even controlling for the amount of deviant behavior). The chronically mentally ill, however, represent a small proportion of those who are formally diagnosed as mentally ill. There is little research on how labels affect those who are diagnosed with less serious forms of disorder. It seems clear that they are not subject to the same levels of rejection and hostility as the chronically mentally ill, but it is also likely that they are self-conscious about disclosing their disorders because they fear rejection. The stereotype of rejection because of mental illness that we carry around in our heads may lead us to be guarded about our own conditions.

WHY A NEGATIVE STEREOTYPE DEVELOPS

We don't know very much about how these negative stereotypes develop in the first place. Although the media do play a role, the stigma associated with mental illness goes much deeper. People seem to have a basic fear of losing control of their thoughts and behaviors. Part of the stereotype of mental illness is that it involves the total loss of control over one's actions. This is a scary prospect for those of us who believe that we do have control over our lives. Labeling people as mentally ill when they do not appear to be in control has the function of separating them from us. Since we all would like to believe that we have some control of our lives, keeping those who might threaten this belief away from us might seem desirable. Part of the public's attitude seems to stem from this fear of losing control. Public attitudes also reflect the culture in which we all live. As we grow up we learn values for behavior that reflect ideas about what is proper and what is not. We live in a culture that makes the individual responsible for his or her own behavior. We live in a culture that expects us to earn our own keep and one that approves of certain sexual behaviors (specifically, heterosexuality) but not others. When we observe persons who violate these types of norms and values, we (the general public) sometimes regard this deviant behavior as a sign of mental illness. It is especially important to understand that cultural norms affect everyone in the society. In other words, beliefs about mental illness and the characteristics of the mentally ill are broadly based. If the members of a society share standards for acceptable behavior and expect these standards to be a matter of personal responsibility, then people who are seen as violators of those norms will be subject to control by the wider society.

Most members of a society share common sentiments toward those who are labeled as mentally ill. Psychiatrists and psychologists, as members of the wider culture, carry these basic values with them into their professional work. Their job is partly defined by the general social concern with the control of deviant behavior. The questions we turn to now are: How do professionals label mental illness and what is the extent to which professional and public attitudes and beliefs affect one another?

PROFESSIONAL LABELS

Professional labels for types of mental illness do not exist in a vacuum. Rather, they are strongly influenced by the wider society in at least two ways. First, the psychiatric profession itself reflects general public attitudes about deviant behavior by the manner in which it defines and identifies psychiatric disorders. Second, the personal attitudes of professionals affect the diagnosis and labeling of mental disorder as well as its treatment.

Our definition of mental illness as "incomprehensible" deviant behavior raises the possibility that the labeling (diagnosing) of mental illness, even by professionals, might reflect public ideas about the types of behavior that are regarded as incomprehensible and/or deviant. If this is true, then we should find evidence that public attitudes and values are reflected in diagnostic categories used by psychiatric professionals. We might find evidence that individual professionals sometimes (or often) judge "symptoms" in terms of stereotypical ideas (i.e., public attitudes) about those who display such symptoms.

Arguments about professional bias in diagnosis and treatment are somewhat controversial. They are derived from research with historical and/or sociological orientations and are often hotly contested by biological and psychologically oriented professionals. Nevertheless, the accumulation of evidence suggests that the position to be taken here has some validity. We will not go as far as some researchers who totally reject the "medical" approach to mental illness treatment. We argue, simply, that at least part of the system by which labels for mental illness are derived reflects social processes related to the treatment and control of deviant behavior and not just value-neutral scientific standards. In other words, we argue that professional attitudes are partly explained by the attitudes of the general public.

There are two compelling reasons to make this connection. First, by definition, psychiatric disorders are disturbances of mood or behavior and we can only identify disturbance by comparison to normal, undisturbed mood and behavior. Normal equals socially acceptable. Therefore, the very existence of the psychiatric profession directly reflects the general concern with controlling socially unacceptable behavior. This makes a direct connection between public standards and the professional practice of psychiatry.

Second, psychiatrists and psychologists are people. Like others, they absorb values, attitudes, and biases about personal behavior as they grow up and as they experience the world. At the very least, it is difficult to keep such values and attitudes out of diagnostic decision-making. Psychiatric professionals do not generally hold the same severe and negative stereotypes of the mentally ill that the general public does. We would not expect to hear professionals express sentiments consistent with rejection and stigma. Yet, it used to be standard practice for professionals to place their desks in their offices in such a way that they would be able to safely escape a client who became agitated or aggressive. Such standard practice is both practical (perhaps) and reflective of stereotypes of dangerous behavior as a characteristic of mental illness. While it is unlikely that psychiatric professionals are conscious of how such practices reflect general cultural stereotypes, they may well be such a reflection. In other words, societal and cultural stereotypes may be consciously and unconsciously built into professional systems (i.e., institutional-ized). We need to examine the extent to which the system institutional-izes public attitudes.

THE CLASSIFICATION OF MENTAL DISORDERS

Skultans (1979) argues that mental disorders are diagnosed as disorder precisely because behavior or mood is disturbed. She argues further that we can only make this judgment (disturbed) by comparing observed behavior to the values and rules used to govern behavior in a particular society. This means that the behaviors professionals use to diagnosis mental illness will vary from society to society and within a given society over historical time. Townsend (1978), for example, shows that attitudes toward the mentally ill differ between American and German society. He showed two important things: Attitudes about mental illness held by psy-chiatric personnel and general publics were consistent within each coun-try, and attitudes differed between Americans and Germans (both the general publics and professionals).

It is certainly not the case that psychiatric disturbances are totally different in every country. Some forms of behavior are considered to rep-resent psychological deviance in every society. Moreover, differences that have been observed between diagnostic rates in different countries are often attributable to interpretation differences about the same behavior (Townsend 1978). In other words, psychiatrists in America and Germany may disagree on diagnostic categories simply because each country's psy-chiatrists pay closer attention to different symptoms. Townsend (1978) points out that, even when diagnosticians are using standard classifica-tion systems, the process of interviewing a client to obtain a list of symp-toms leaves room for interpretation that may explain how nonscientific biases creep into the diagnostic process.

Classification systems, in general, can be extremely useful for facil-itating scientific understanding and for developing effective ways of working with classified items. The scientific classification of plants and animals, for example, has been extremely useful for understanding the origin of biological species and for tracking environmental effects on life forms. Similarly, the scientific classification of physical illnesses has been extremely useful for understanding their origins and developing effective treatments. The first step in modern medical treatment is to obtain a diagnosis (or classification) that can be used to specify a likely effective treatment. We feel better when a doctor gives our discomfort a scientific-sounding label. We are confident that the diagnosis will lead to effective treatment.

Classification of psychiatric disorders, however, differs profoundly from classification of physical disorders. Although Sigmund Freud argued strenuously that psychoanalysis should not be practiced by physicians, historical accident placed psychiatry into the medical establishment (Gay 1988). One consequence of this placement was a kind of second-class citizenship for psychiatrists based, in part, on the absence of a classification (diagnostic) system for psychiatric disorders that was similar to the existing system for physical disorders. Therefore, American psychiatrists developed such a system (The Diagnostic and Statistical Manual—DSM). The problem with this system, however, is that it is based on the accumulated experience of psychiatric practitioners and not on scientifically validated observations. In other words, the system relies on unscientific and (possibly) value-laden observations by (largely) white, middle-class, male psychiatrists. Empirical evidence shows, for example, that symptoms of psychiatric disorder cannot be sorted into exclusive categories (Mirowsky and Ross 1989). That is, the classification system does not objectively sort signs and symptoms into consistent diagnostic categories. Whereas two physicians who are shown an identical set of physical symptoms would be expected to make the same diagnosis, the same cannot be said for psychiatric diagnoses. That is why psychiatric diagnoses are routinely challenged in court cases whereas physical illness diagnoses are usually not challenged. We recognize that psychiatrists can profoundly disagree about diagnoses.

Such disagreement, of course, does not necessarily mean that diagnosis reflects social value systems and, perhaps, general public attitudes toward mental illness. It does suggest, however, that such values can become mixed with other diagnostic criteria more easily than is the case for the diagnosis of physical illness.

The Diagnostic and Statistical Manual (DSM) of the American Psychiatric Association represents the diagnostic "bible" of American psychiatry. The original and continuing motivation for the first edition in 1952 and subsequent revisions was to formalize and standardize the professional labeling of mental disorder. The manual reflects the official (American Psychiatric Association) professional attitude toward mental illness. The DSM defines mental disorder as a "... clinically significant behavioral or psychological syndrome or pattern that occurs in a person and that is associated with present distress (a painful symptom).... In addition, this syndrome or pattern must not be merely an expectable response to a particular event.... Whatever its cause, it must currently be considered a manifestation of a behavioral, psychological, or biological dysfunction in the person. Neither deviant behavior, e.g., political, religious, or sexual, nor conflicts that are primarily between the individual and society are mental disorders, unless the deviance or conflict is a symptom of a dysfunction in the person, as described above" (Spitzer and Williams 1987, xxii).

Prior to the first edition of the DSM, a number of competing classification systems existed. Each was based on a different set of psychiatric causal assumptions. The DSM classification system was created by gathering groups of distinguished psychiatrists together, asking them to make a list of disorders they agreed existed, and then asking them to describe sets of associated signs and symptoms. Clinical experience, research studies, and theoretical expertise were employed to develop the diagnostic system. The DSM is now in its fourth version and, with each successive version, its authors argue that the classification system becomes more scientific, valid, and objective. At the same time, however, the system is characterized as descriptive, atheoretical, and nonexclusive. The creators of the DSM system, realizing that there are many ways of explaining disordered behavior, aim to describe clusters of signs and symptoms rather than follow a specific explanation for how disorders arise. The hope is that practitioners with differing approaches will be able to use the classification system because it describes symptoms no matter how they were produced. This, of course, opens the door to subjective, value-laden interpretations of "symptoms". The system is atheoretical because it does not try to explain how symptoms occur. Although we would like to know if a person's pain results from a bacterial infection or an injury, the psychiatric approach is to simply describe the problem as "pain." In other words, the DSM system does not aim to explain the sources of observed disorder. Finally, the DSM is nonexclusive. This means that individuals may share common symptoms but be diagnosed as suffering from different disorders. It also means that the classification of the disorder (diagnosis) is subject to bias and interpretation. If symptoms can be shared among several types of disorder, for example, deciding which disorder is present depends on the professional's judgment about other distinguishing symptoms.

There are a considerable number of persons who regard DSM claims to scientific accuracy, validity, and objectivity as unfounded or questionable (Mirowsky and Ross 1989b; Kirk and Kutchins 1992). Critics claim that the diagnostic system is based on unverified assumptions (particularly assumptions about the role of genetic and biochemical processes and brain structure) as causal agents. Moreover, some critics have even raised the question, "Is there such a thing as mental *illness?*" In other words, are psychological disorders illnesses in the same sense as physical disorders?

We will briefly review the structure of the "objective" diagnostic process in order to show some of the ways in which "subjective" values can enter into the evaluation process. These subjective values reflect public perceptions and attitudes such as those we described in the first part of this chapter.

The diagnostic process for psychological illness has the same structure that we are familiar with for diagnosing physical disorder. That is, we seek the help of a medical authority (physician/psychiatrist) because of some dis-ease. We describe what is bothering us, the psychiatrist asks additional questions about our symptoms, does some tests, and attempts to reach some conclusions about what diagnostic category our symptoms fit. The DSM manual, for example, lists a series of questions related to depression, such as: Have you ever had a period of two weeks or longer when you lost your appetite? Have you ever had a period of two weeks or longer when you slept too much? These questions reflect expert opinion concerning the signs and symptoms of depression. In principle, a psychiatrist must ask each potential patient the same set of questions and the patient must answer these in a particular way in order for the psychiatrist to reach a diagnostic decision. A diagnosis cannot be made if the patient does not answer the questions in a certain way or does not have enough of the symptoms that have been established as the minimum criteria for diagnosis. Thus it is possible for a person to have quite a few of the symptoms of a mental illness but, if they only have three symptoms where four are required by DSM standards, they cannot be diagnosed as even "a little depressed." They can only be said not to be depressed.

Let's take a closer look at the DSM system. In particular we will review some of the diagnostic categories included in the latest version of the DSM (DSM-IV) in order to develop an impression of the extent to which the system reflects general social values about normal and deviant behavior. In addition, we will discuss some categories of disorder that have been recently added to or dropped from the official list. If the DSM reflects categories of social deviance, then it also ought to change in ways that correspond to changes in the public perception of problem behaviors.

DISORDERS USUALLY FIRST DIAGNOSED IN INFANCY, CHILDHOOD, OR ADOLESCENCE

This category of disorders includes mental retardation, learning disorders, attention deficit and disruptive behavior disorders, and elimination disorders. We can see that some categories such as mental retardation might clearly stem from biological conditions, but attention deficit disorders are clearly labeled as behavioral. The symptoms used to categorize attention deficit disorder/hyperactivity include: failure to finish things he or she starts, easily distracted, often acts before thinking, needs a lot of supervision, runs about or climbs on things excessively, has difficulty staying seated. Clearly the identification of these symptoms requires interpretation and judgment. How does one measure acting before thinking, for example? It should also be somewhat apparent that many of these disorders can only be defined in reference to specific social role expectations, such as the role of student (including the expectation to sit still).

DELIRIUM, DEMENTIA, AND AMNESTIC AND OTHER COGNITIVE DISORDERS

This category consists largely of disorders with clear biological origins, particularly brain tissue abnormalities. Persons with Alzheimer's disease and delirium and dementia due to general medical conditions are classified here.

SUBSTANCE-RELATED DISORDERS

This grouping of disorders includes alcohol dependence and abuse, amphetamine dependence and abuse, caffeine-related disorders, cannabis-related disorders, cocaine-related disorders, hallucinogen-related disorders, inhalant, nicotine, opoid, Phencyclidine, sedative, and polysubstance-related disorders. Apart from difficulties related to the existence and detection of "dependence," this set of disorders is clearly descriptive of behavioral deviance. For example, alcohol dependence is described as "... a pattern of pathological use for at least a month that causes impairment in social or occupational functioning." The pattern is established by the need for daily use of alcohol, inability to cut down or stop consumption, binges, etc. Impairment is established by observations of violence while intoxicated, absence from work, loss of job, and legal difficulties.

SCHIZOPHRENIC DISORDERS

This category includes schizophrenia, schizophreniform disorder, schizoaffective disorder, delusional disorder, and brief psychotic disorder. This category of disorders contains types of disturbance that are most nearly similar to the more stigmatic stereotypes of mental illness held by the general public. There are "bizarre" delusions, hallucinations, and incoherence. This category most nearly corresponds to the idea of mental disorder as incomprehensible behavior. These disorders are commonly attributed to organic/biological processes. Note, however, that it is the behavioral manifestations of the disorder that bring these conditions to the notice of psychiatric professionals. Recent studies of the prevalence of disorder in the community (Kessler et al. 1994) clearly show that even among those who could be diagnosed as schizophrenic, only slightly more than one-half are currently receiving treatment. One way to interpret this finding is to suggest that until such behavior is interpreted as psychiatric deviance, it is possible for individuals to function in the community. Until the collection of symptoms is labeled as mental illness, even very strange behavior and thought processes are not regarded as disorder.

MOOD DISORDERS

This category includes depressive disorders and bipolar (manic-depressive) disorders. The essential characteristic of these forms of disorder is prolonged emotional highs and lows, or just one of these. Symptoms of depression include poor appetite, difficulty sleeping or falling asleep, loss of interest or pleasure in usual activities, loss of energy, feelings of worthlessness, and so on. (Symptoms of mania are the opposite.) These symptoms must be prolonged (say more than two weeks).

ANXIETY DISORDERS

This category includes panic disorder, specific phobias (fears), obsessions and compulsions, and post traumatic stress disorder (which we will also discuss later). Anxiety is either the dominant symptom or the experience associated with a particular thing, event, person, or place. The condition of anxiety or phobia must be prolonged and distressing to the individual in order to qualify for diagnosis. It has been noted that there is considerable cultural variation in the expression of anxiety (Gallagher 1994). This suggests that both levels of arousal and the way it is displayed affect the interpretation of what such feelings mean. In other words, the sociocultural context is crucial for diagnosing anxiety-related disorders.

SEXUAL AND GENDER DISORDERS, EATING DISORDERS, SLEEP DISORDERS, IMPULSE-CONTROL DISORDERS, ADJUSTMENT DISORDERS, AND PERSONALITY DISORDERS

This is a set of categories that includes sexual dysfunction, sexual desire disorders (e.g., sex addiction), exhibitionism, fetishism, sexual masochism, sadism, voyeurism, gender identity disorders, anorexia nervosa, bulimia, insomnia, narcolepsy, nightmare disorder, kleptomania, pyromania, antisocial personality, narcissistic personality, and dependent personality disorders. The psychosexual disorders are clearly categories of behavior deviance. The criteria for diagnosis simply involve confirmation of the deviant behavior. An antisocial personality is explicitly defined in terms of violations of widely accepted norms and values. Symptoms include: failure to conform to social norms with respect to lawful behavior, irritability and aggressiveness, impulsivity, deceitfulness, recklessness, and lack of remorse.

Although there are more categories and hundreds of specific diagnostic conditions described in the DSM, those just described provide a good overview of the range of conditions that are subject to psychiatric diagnosis. It should be perfectly clear that most of the disorders described can only be defined by reference to community or public standards of normality and socially acceptable behavior. It should also be clear that making a connection between public standards of behavior and psychiatric problem identification does not in any way invalidate the psychiatric enterprise. The problems that bother people are real and people are genuinely relieved when professional assistance can ease their distress. Our point is simply that the definitional scope of psychiatry is strongly related to general community standards of acceptable behavior.

HOW CHANGES ARE MADE IN THE DSM

The DSM manual has undergone several modifications since its initial publication in 1952. In each subsequent version categories have been added and removed. Both the reasons that categories were added or dropped and the way in which decisions were made illustrate the normative basis for mental disorder definition. Revisions of the DSM are prepared by committees of eminent psychiatrists and psychologists who collate input from other psychiatric professionals and the research literature to evaluate the adequacy of current classification categories. This review process has resulted in the deletion of homosexuality as a psychiatric category, for example. It has also resulted in the inclusion of post traumatic stress disorder, and the delay of inclusion of self-defeating personality disorder.

Homosexuality as a diagnostic category was removed from the DSM in 1980 as a result of a social and political process (Conrad and Schneider 1980). Its removal followed the emergence of the gay liberation movement and gay rights organizations and a more tolerant public attitude toward sexual differences. (This is not to say that there is no longer significant homophobia among the general public or psychiatrists, but simply more general tolerance.) Gay activists began a systematic challenge to existing professional views of homosexuality in the early 1970s that was supported by some members of the American Psychiatric Association (APA). Partially as a result of these political activities, and partially because of a desire not to appear to be agents of social control, proposals for dropping homosexuality as a diagnostic category were presented by official APA decision-making bodies. The matter was formally put to a vote of the membership of the APA in 1974 and was accepted. Although this was actually a drawn out, emotional, and contentious process, the point to be emphasized here is the way the diagnostic system is subject to modification over time because of shifts in behavior standards and tolerance, not just advances in scientific research.

Post traumatic stress disorder was added to the DSM in 1980. This diagnostic category refers to the development of certain symptoms of distress, "following a psychologically traumatic event that is generally outside the range of usual human experience" (APA 1980, 236). Traumas

outside the usual range include rape or assault, military combat, natural disasters such as floods and earthquakes, man-made disasters, and
experiences of terrorism, for example. It was the aftermath of the
Vietnam war, however, that provided the impetus for the introduction of
this diagnosis into DSM. Vietnam war veterans began a strong campaign
for the recognition of some sort of post combat disorder that legitimated
the psychological reactions experienced by these veterans. Although the
eventual definition of post traumatic stress syndrome was broadened to
include a wider range of experiences, the political activities of Vietnam
war veterans and sympathetic psychiatrists were most central to the
adoption of this diagnostic category (Scott 1990). Again, this political
process demonstrates the close relationship between attitudes among the
public and professionals.

The diagnostic category of self-defeating personality disorder does
not appear in any version of the DSM (except as a proposed diagnosis in
need of further study). Rather, it was proposed for inclusion in 1984. Its
acceptance was deferred and it is unlikely that it will be adopted. This
type of disorder is characterized by avoidance of success (i.e., turning
down promotions) and frequent involvement in abusive or unsatisfactory
relationships. The proposal to include this diagnostic category was
strongly contested by the APA Committee on Women and allied groups.
They argued that the diagnosis would be differentially made for women.
Further, they suggested that it would be misused especially as a way of
blaming women as victims of spouse abuse and other forms of violence. It
was also argued that the diagnosis could be made if a woman in the labor
force gave up a promotion or transfer because it interfered with family
life. The set of criteria proposed for use in diagnosis of self-defeating personality disorder strongly resemble sets of behaviors and cultural values
related to violations of the traditional social definition of "female." As a
result of objections, the APA Board of Trustees voted not to include this
category in the DSM-III revision. Subsequent empirical work suggests
that it is probably not a meaningful category (Kass et al. 1989). Here
again, we find evidence for the close relationship between social norms
and professional diagnostic categories. In this case, the organized concerns and perceptions of women, reflecting a set of newer social values,
directly affected the scope of behaviors defined (or, not defined) as psychiatric conditions.

THE OBJECTIVITY OF DIAGNOSIS

The correspondence between general social norms of behavior and
deviance and psychiatric categories does not necessarily mean that a useful diagnostic system cannot be developed. It does make it highly unlikely

that any single causal explanation (e.g., biological, psychological, or socio-logical) will account for all forms of disorder that can be identified. The question we now address is whether the system for determining diagnoses for psychiatric illness works the same way that the system works for phys-ical illnesses. In particular, we are interested in learning the degree to which diagnosis itself is free of biases possessed by psychiatrists them-selves. One test of this question would be to see if persons with identical symptoms but otherwise some differences, say in gender or race, are equally likely to be diagnosed with the same illness. In principle, they should be. For physical illnesses, little red dots, fever, and loss of appetite might always indicate measles. This will be true for men and women, boys and girls, white people and Asians. Moreover, any physician who reads these symptoms will immediately make the same diagnosis.

This does not appear to be true for psychiatric diagnoses. For exam-ple, Loring and Powell (1988) sent a description of one set of symptoms reported by a patient to psychiatrists and requested that they make a diagnosis. The descriptions did differ in terms of the gender and race of the person who was said to experience the symptoms but did not differ in the presentation of symptoms. The psychiatrists who evaluated the symptoms, using DSM criteria (they said), did not agree on a diagnosis. Rather, diagnosis depended on the gender and race of the patient *and* the gender and race of the psychiatrist. For example, white male psychia-trists were most likely to make a diagnosis when the case described a white male but were much less likely to agree on a diagnosis when the case was female or nonwhite. Black psychiatrists also tended to make the diagnosis for blacks more than whites. When neither the race or gender of the case was revealed, diagnoses did not appear to vary by character-istics of the psychiatrist. This result suggests that information that psy-chiatrists have personally gathered about differences between men and women and blacks and whites affect their clinical judgments. In short, beliefs and attitudes that reflect psychiatrists as members of the general public affect their professional decision making. In an earlier study, Young and Powell (1985) found that nonrelevant criteria, such as obesity of the client, affect the likelihood of a diagnosis. In this study Young and Powell systematically altered a photograph of a middle-aged woman so that she appeared to be at an ideal weight, slightly overweight, or obese. Obese women were much more likely to be diagnosed with a psychiatric problem. Moreover, female mental health workers were more likely to diagnosis disorder among obese women. The age and weight of the eval-uator also had effects on the likelihood of a diagnosis.

Further evidence of professional bias might be found in the distrib-ution of diagnoses by socioeconomic and gender categories and differ-ences in treatment modalities (i.e., who gets hospitalized, who receives drug treatment). The view of psychiatry as an institution for the social control of deviant behavior and the maintenance of dominance by higher status groups is consistent with the patterns of diagnosis and treatment actually observed. Although it could be plausible to argue that specific disorders might be more prevalent among men or women or blacks or whites or among lower or upper social classes, the evidence of diagnostic bias discerned in studies such as those by Loring and Powell and Young and Powell suggest that cultural values and attitudes that professionals bring to diagnostic evaluations affect decision making.

SUMMARY

At the beginning of this chapter, we described an overblown stereotype of mental illness to suggest that public notions of mental illness and the mentally ill often result in prejudicial, negative impressions of persons labeled as mentally ill. We saw that public stereotypes reflect general cultural and social attitudes toward certain forms of deviant behavior. A characteristic of a stereotype is that it is applied to persons uncritically, that is, without reference to the actual characteristics of the labeled individual. The stereotype, perhaps, tells us more about the state of knowledge of the observer than about the person observed. If, however, the general public typically holds negative and often inaccurate views of the mentally ill, surely mental health professionals do not. Professional attitudes should differ strongly from the stereotypical conceptions of the public and attitudes should be more realistic. In fact, the general public and psychiatrists seem to agree about some of the causes of mental illness but they disagree on the description of individual characteristics. In particular, the general public holds an image of mentally ill persons that emphasizes their unpredictability, their dangerousness, and their lack of personal responsibility. Psychiatric professionals do not seem to hold these views.

The relative absence of stigmatic attributions by psychiatrists compared to the general public suggests that psychiatrists might not be affected by public values and attitudes. Indeed, psychiatrists make use of an elaborate diagnostic system intended to eliminate personal bias and provide for the scientific classification of mental illness. Our analysis, however, clearly reveals that it is in the nature of psychological disorder that the behaviors we identify as disorder represent forms of deviant behavior defined by general social standards. Therefore, we should not be surprised to find a close relationship between public definitions of deviant behavior and psychiatric definitions (although psychiatric definitions are much differently described and organized). This is what we found. While professionals are less likely to harbor negative, stereotypical views of persons diagnosed as mentally ill that characterize general public attitudes, they are not divorced from the attitudes and values of the general public. All of this merely illustrates the social nature of psychiatric definition and the linkage between the general social system and the specific social institution of psychiatry/psychology. Informal labeling done by family, friends, neighbors, etc. may mark an individual for rejection, hostility, and even punishment. Formal labeling (diagnosis) is intended to avoid all of these negative consequences but does indeed mark behavior as deviant and in need of social control. This theme will be developed further in the next chapter, which explores the social process that converts "bad" behavior into "sickness."

11

MEDICALIZATION OF DEVIANT BEHAVIOR AND MENTAL ILLNESS

In the previous chapter we outlined the current classification system (DSM) for defining psychiatric disorders and described its relationship to community norms and values. We suggested that the system reflects a combination of public and professional attitudes toward the origins of deviant behavior and how it should be controlled. The classification system was developed in a medical context by medical professionals. In this chapter we ask the question: Why are psychological disorders defined as illness and managed as medical problems?

Consider the following:

> "Catherine Benincasa was a woman of about twenty-six ... she ate almost nothing ... the presence of even a mouthful of food in her stomach caused her to vomit, and after a while she simply refused. Warned that by such eating habits she was bringing about her own death, Catherine shot back that eating would kill her anyway so she might as well die of starvation and do as she wished in the meantime." (Bell 1985, 23–24)

Now consider that a diagnosis of anorexia nervosa is made when all of the following statements are true:

1. The person refuses to eat enough to maintain at least the minimal normal weight for her age and height, and her body weight is 85 percent or less of what is expected.
2. The person has intense fear of gaining weight or becoming fat, even though she is far underweight.
3. The person denies the seriousness of the low weight or has a distorted sense of the body; for example, believing she is too fat even though she is underweight.

4. The person misses at least three consecutive menstrual periods because of her low weight (Diagnostic and Statistical Manual of Mental Disorders 1994).

If we apply the diagnostic criteria of the DSM to the description of Catherine Benincasa, we might reasonably conclude that she is suffering from anorexia nervosa.

In fact, no such diagnosis was ever made. Catherine Benincasa is otherwise known as Saint Catherine of Siena, co-patron saint with Francis of Assisi of all of Italy and this description of her eating problems was given in 1373 or 1374. Her refusal to eat, although alarming even to her religious superiors, was, in fact, part of the perception of her holiness, which led to her canonization as a saint. One woman's anorexia is another's sainthood (Bell 1985).

Catherine Benincasa *was not* mentally ill. At the time she lived, there was no concept of mental illness. Her behavior was recognized as deviant but interpreted as symbolic of her holiness. Catherine Benincasa was perceived to be engaging in an alarming set of behaviors. She was warned and, indeed, ordered by her religious superiors to cease this behavior. She experienced delusions and hallucinations. Still, those around her did not see her as ill or disordered.

Now consider this: John Hinckley, the man who attempted to assassinate President Ronald Reagan in 1981, was committed to a mental hospital. It was determined that he suffered from a mental illness and his crime was an action that he could not control. It was a consequence of his illness. The redefinition of this "crime" as "illness" illustrates an important characteristic of the contemporary social reaction to the deviant behavior we associate with mental disorder: the tendency to explain such deviant behavior as illness. Between the time when Catherine Benincasa lived and the present, we have clearly altered the way we interpret deviant behavior. Today Catherine would be diagnosed as anorexic and in 1373 John Hinckley would have been labeled as a criminal.

Mental problems today are commonly explained using a bio-medical model. That is why we are so comfortable using the term illness to describe the class of deviant behaviors that we view as incomprehensible. Despite the belief in a bio-medical model, however, psychiatrists have been unable to establish a reliable biological basis for most mental disorders. Yet it is clear that we increasingly think of mental disorder as biologically based.

This chapter will explain how we have come to think of psychological deviance as illness. We will see why we are so comfortable using the term "illness" to describe such deviance. The essence of this argument is that deviant behavior that was once defined as immoral, sinful, or criminal is now increasingly defined as illness and treated as a health problem (Conrad and Schneider 1992). Since the sociological perspective concentrates on the notion of controlling deviant behavior, the societal reaction to disorder as illness can be described as the social control of deviant behavior. Our problem becomes one of explaining why the control of this behavior occurs in a medical context.

We will first review some elementary ideas about the nature of deviant behavior and its control and some ideas about illness as a form of deviance. We will then explain exactly what we mean by the medicalization of deviance and how it affects the way we control deviant behavior. Next we will discuss the medicalization of madness and test the social control of deviance explanation by examining differences in incidence and prevalence of mental illness by social class and differences in treatment by social class. If we find differences in the distribution of mental illness by social class, it suggests that medicalization functions as a form of social control of deviant behavior. Finally, we will revisit the question of whether mental disorder should be viewed as deviant behavior or as biological dysfunction.

DEVIANT BEHAVIOR AND ITS CONTROL

Deviant behavior can be broadly defined as behavior that violates norms and role expectations, especially violations that are disapproved (Palmer and Humphrey 1990; Clinard and Meier 1994). Labeling theorists specify that behavior is deviant when other people react to and label the behavior as such but normative standards are also used to make an evaluation. Among the general categories of behavior usually designated as deviant are: crime, prostitution, homosexuality, mental illness, suicide, alcoholism, and drug use. The definitions of specific deviant behaviors change over time and vary across different social systems and within subcultures. As we will see in the next chapter, both the idea that mental disorder reflects illness and the types of behaviors that fit the categories of mental illness have also changed.

Violations of behavioral standards (whether actual or perceived) are usually met with attempts to control them. From some perspectives the reason for controlling behavior is the threat such behavior poses for the stability of the social system. For others, the reason for controlling deviant behavior is related to the maintenance of positions of social advantage and dominance. In this latter perspective, those in most favored positions define deviance as behavior that threatens their dominance and they seek to control such deviance to protect their positions. Of course, most deviant behavior is controlled by reducing its likelihood of occurrence. Specifically, the process of socialization results in the internalization of rules of behavior that mostly keep us from behaving in socially unapproved ways. Our behavior is also controlled by informal social sanctions in which people who know one another control behavior through verbal expressions of displeasure, reprimand, praise, or criticism. Evoking guilt or shame, withholding rewards, or administering punishments are also means for obtaining behavioral conformity.

Deviant behavior is also controlled more formally by specific social institutions such as the criminal justice system, religious institutions, the State, and the medical system. Formal methods of control involve organized systems that monitor behavior and sanction its violation. This is most clearly seen within the criminal justice system where the police detect deviant behavior and the courts decide the severity of the deviant behavior and the appropriate punishment.

ILLNESS AS DEVIANT BEHAVIOR

The idea that the medical system may also function as a mechanism of social control is more subtle. To understand how the medical system can function as an institution of social control, we need to understand how illness can be regarded as a form of deviance. Parsons (1951) has argued that the social system operates successfully only when everyone in that system does their "job." That is, because social systems are complex, the system depends on all its members fulfilling the expectations for the roles they occupy. When each of us acts successfully in our roles as spouse, parent, and worker (for example), then the social system works smoothly. Since roles are collections of norms, failure to fulfill roles fits the definition of deviance. One way in which individuals can fail roles is when they lose the capacity to perform them—when they become sick (Gerhardt 1989). Thus, illness can be conceived as a form of deviance because it interferes with one's ability to fill role expectations. The medical system becomes a mechanism for the social control of deviance because its job is to limit the extent of this deviance (by treatment) and to restore the capacity of individuals to fulfill their normal roles (i.e., cure the illness).

Clearly this type of deviance seems different from say, criminal behavior. Why? One big reason is our understanding of who (or what) is responsible for the deviance. Specifically, we believe that individuals *are not* responsible for the deviance associated with illness but that individuals *are* responsible for criminal deviance. John Hinckley was judged to be "not guilty" or not responsible for his action because of his illness. As a manifestation of his illness, his attempted assassination of the president represented a behavior that he was not responsible for committing. Based on our assumption of where responsibility lies, we try to control the deviance using a therapeutic approach (when individuals are not responsible) or punishment (when individuals are held responsible).

In modern societies most deviance is treated in one of two ways—by punishment or therapy/treatment. We tend to see these forms of reaction as separate in intent based on the perceived moral context of the deviance (Rotenberg 1978). Crime violates moral restraints and brings forth punishment (or correction) and coercive control. Illness is morally neutral and brings forth a more compassionate use of therapy and treatment. Societal reactions to deviance are thus bound up in attributions of cause, individual responsibility, and seriousness.

Punishment and treatment are not always complete opposites. Szasz (1994), for example, argues that treatment can disguise punishment. Treatment in a mental hospital, he argues, consists of the coercive control of the treated person's liberty, property, and life. Indeed, Szasz has gone so far as to argue that there is no such thing as mental "illness," but that there are problems of living that we regard as illness. According to him, the deviance represented by these problems is thought to be best controlled under the guise of therapy and treatment though it really constitutes "cruel compassion" or punishment.

But our concern is not to decide the validity of this argument. Today the dominant societal reaction among psychiatric authorities is to treat mental disorder as illness. We are careful to say "dominant" and "among psychiatric authorities" because there are minority views and differences in the use of the illness model for defining and reacting to mental disorder. Often members of the general public think of mental disorder as something that a person can control. Public stereotypes often include the notion that the disturbed person is responsible for his or her state of mind. If so, then the person's behavior ought to be punished (coercively controlled) rather than treated therapeutically. Should John Hinckley be in prison or a mental hospital?

On the other hand, if mental disorder is regarded as a form of illness, then the correct model of control is to use treatment and therapy to restore the person to "normal" functioning. This therapeutic model dominates the professional view of mental disorder and from a sociological view represents the medicalization of deviant behavior.

THE MEDICALIZATION OF DEVIANT BEHAVIOR

Over the past 250 years, the way that our social system has responded to deviant behavior has shifted from informal to formal (particularly legal and medical) forms of social control (Horwitz 1990). Even though most deviant behavior is still embedded in informal social situations and controlled at the informal level, there has been a perceptible shift in the involvement of formal institutions of social control. Donzelot (1979), for example, argues that an informal alliance has developed between medical authorities and women in households. Women report many forms of deviant behavior to medical authorities in the guise of concern for the health of household members. The result is that medical authorities are provided with a window into the family through which they can "police" the behavior of family members. Child neglect or child abuse would be examples of behavior in households that we feel it is appropriate for formal authorities to police and physicians or other medical personnel are often the first to detect evidence of such behavior.

In the case of deviant behavior that we now regard as mental illness, the shift that occurred involved changing the locus of responsibility for control of deviance from the family to a formal organization and the interpretation of deviance as a medical concern. Peter Conrad and Joseph Schneider (1980, 1992) have been principally responsible for developing this argument.

Medicalization has its roots in the general development of Western society and its social history. As we know, Western societies have become increasingly rationalized as a result of the scientific revolution, industrialization, etc. One upshot of this historical evolution has been the "secularization" of social control. That is, behaviors that were once regarded as violations of religious strictures and, therefore, properly controlled by religious institutions have come to be defined as secular violations that are controlled by the state, by the criminal justice system and, increasingly, by the institution of medicine.

The medical model became effective at explaining illness and producing workable treatments in the last half of the 1800s and, as it became effective, it also developed a high degree of legitimacy in the eyes of the public (Starr 1982). Moreover, in the United States the way physicians are organized has led to the development of very high esteem and authority for physicians. We trust physicians and accord them wide discretion in how they practice medicine, even when they don't really have good explanations for illness, such as mental illness. Therefore, to understand the fact that medicalization occurs, we have to appreciate the tremendous cultural authority and legitimacy of the enterprise of medicine.

Mental illnesses do not have the same symptomatic characteristics as physical illnesses. While we have reliable and unbiased ways of determining whether a person has kidney disease, we do not have the same ability to distinguish mental diseases (Mirowsky and Ross 1989). This ambiguity of diagnostic criteria, though it makes us more skeptical of the effectiveness of physicians to deal with mental illness, also facilitates the incorporation of various forms of "bad" deviant behavior into the "sickness" realm. Because diagnostic criteria are ambiguous, it permits one to argue that some particular form of deviant behavior represents a disorder even if the diagnostic criteria for that new disorder are similarly ambiguous.

THE MEDICALIZATION PROCESS

Let's look at how the medicalization process works and then discuss its benefits and drawbacks.

According to Conrad and Schneider a five-stage sequential model can be used to describe the medicalization process (though the model never works exactly as described in real life).

1. Definition of the Behavior as Deviant   In almost every case, the behavior that becomes medicalized is already regarded as deviant. This is an important feature because it validates the search for a way to control the behavior. Medicalization can be seen as one way to deal with social problems created by the existence of deviant behavior.

2. Prospecting: Medical Discovery   Medicalization is a political process. Because specific behaviors are already recognized as deviant, it is likely that there are pre-existing ways of dealing with it. Medicalizing the particular form of deviant behavior, therefore, requires a rationale for incorporating it under the umbrella of medicine. The first step in this process is the public "discovery" of a link between the deviant behavior and the scope of medical practice. This is typically accomplished by describing research that creates such a link and making a proposal that the discovered link justifies a medical claim for jurisdiction. Since medicine as a social institution has attained such a high level of prestige and legitimation, these claims are treated seriously by the general public.

3. Claims-Making: Medical and Nonmedical Interests   Once a link between the deviance and medical interests has been established, it becomes necessary to actively promote the recognition of the problem in medical terms so that its discovery can be legitimated in the public arena. Simply asserting that a form of deviant behavior has been shown by research to be a medical problem does not, in itself, result in acceptance of this claim. Rather, the claim must emerge from the professional research literature into a wider political arena.

The first step in this emergence is generally a period of claims-making to the general public and legislative and administrative authorities. The case must be made that the deviant behavior is significant, worthy of a social response, and that it is a medical problem. In part this claim is made by convincing professional organizations such as the American Psychiatric Association or the American Medical Association to endorse the view that the behavior reflects a genuine medical problem. Any special interest groups that take up the cause lend weight to the argument. It must also be seen that there is some public demand to address the problem. Thus, nonmedical groups can be mobilized to promote the medical perspective. Groups such as associations for children with learning disabilities, self-help groups, etc., can become advocates of the medical perspective and they can demand official action. Although Conrad and Schneider do not emphasize it, these claims are not necessarily unopposed by others who may disagree with the attempt to define the problem in medical terms. Although part of the problem is to get people and institutions to see the medical content of the problem, there are also other groups in the social system that may have an interest in not accepting the medical content of the problem. For example, those in the criminal justice system may not wish to see criminals avoid punishment by having their behavior redefined as illness. The insanity defense is a good example. Defining homelessness as a mental health problem is similarly controversial. For medicalization to succeed, a convincing claim must be established. Once this convincing claim has been established, the next step can occur.

4. Legitimacy: Securing Medical Turf Although it is not always necessary for formal political bodies such as Congress or state legislatures to officially authorize the medical system as the legitimate system to achieve control over some deviant form of behavior, it helps. For example, the insanity plea must be officially recognized and defined at the state or federal level of government. Defining child abuse as a mental health problem would similarly require official certification before medical authorities would be free to take control over this type of behavior. To the extent that the claim for medical jurisdiction is officially accepted by the political system, medical authorities obtain legitimation for their claims. As the examples above suggest, however, this acceptance may not be permanent or complete. Drunkenness is a good example of this outcome. Control over this form of behavior is claimed simultaneously by the criminal justice system and the medical system. Depending on who gets there first, drunkenness will be labeled as a crime or a mental health problem (alcoholism).

5. Institutionalization of a Medical Deviance Designation To the extent that the deviant behavior is recognized to be within the legitimate scope of medicine, its status as a medical issue can be better secured if the medicalized behavior is incorporated into standard classification systems such as the Diagnostic and Statistical Manual (DSM). Taking its place among already certified forms of disorder "institutionalizes" the behavior within the general medical system. General practitioners (not just early advocates and claims-makers) now make use of the designation because it is "officially" available. This diffusion to the general range of practitioners often assures that new cases will be identified and increases the stake that the entire profession has in the designation.

As the profession commits resources to the management of the new "illness," the illness becomes institutionalized. Outreach programs, special treatment regimens, and specialized organizations can arise that further entrench the medical claims within organizational forms.

This process, then, results in the transformation of deviant behavior into illness and medicine, as a social institution, becomes the exclusive or a dominant institution for the control of the particular form of deviant behavior. While it is possible that medicalization occurs because a particular form of deviant behavior really is caused by bio-medical processes, this is actually not relevant to the process. What matters is that medical authorities have succeeded in convincing the general public and appropriate political actors that the medical claim is valid. As we have also seen, it is not even necessary for medicine to have an effective explanation of cause or an effective "cure."

BENEFITS OF MEDICALIZATION

What are the benefits of the medicalization process? As we have mentioned, medicalization is not a totally negative process amounting to the control of behavior that is judged by some to be unacceptable. Medicalization has a number of benefits.

Humanitarian Response to Deviant Behavior   Control through medical means may be a kinder, gentler form of social control of deviant behavior. Medical treatment/therapy is contrasted with punishment (despite what Szasz argued).

Destigmatization   As a form of sickness, mental illness will be seen less as a motivated form of deviance to be punished and more as a form of physical illness for which the sufferer is not responsible. The person is allowed to enter the sick role, the problem is treated therapeutically, and the stigma of the mental illness label is reduced.

Optimistic Medical Model   The medical model is optimistic and encourages the idea of recovery and rehabilitation.

COSTS OF MEDICALIZATION

Yet medicalization also has costs.

Discouraging Understanding of Social Conditions That Lead to Disorder   One of the reasons the social causation of mental illness is controversial is because we think of madness as an individual phenomenon. Although environmental causes for physical illness are well known (i.e., exposure to asbestos, smoking), we still regard individuals as sick and we treat each occurrence of illness as an individual event. We could reduce individual cases of lung cancer most effectively by limiting smoking in general. However, the logic of medical treatment puts more focus on the individual. The result is that we spend much less money trying to prevent people from smoking than we do on medical techniques to deal with the consequences of smoking.

One of the central themes of this book is that there are social causes of disorder. If we find that some amount of women's depression can be explained by inferior economic and household conditions related to the social organization of gender, then treating this depression solely as an individual medical problem is clearly inadequate.

Cloaking the Imposition of Values and Biases in the Neutrality of Medical Terminology For example, until 1980 homosexuality was regarded as a mental illness. Then psychiatrists voted to eliminate the diagnosis based largely on changing public attitudes about homosexuality. The classification of homosexuality as a mental illness reflected biases and values that were hidden by the claim that homosexuality was a mental illness because it really was a physical disorder. In the period before the American Civil War, runaway slaves were thought to suffer from a condition called, "drapetomania." The notion that a slave would leave his or her situation was thought to be so irrational that the departing slave had to be suffering from some type of disorder.

Harmful Treatments Provided by Medical Techniques Some examples of potentially harmful treatments are lobotomy, psychoactive drugs, ECT (electroconvulsive therapy). Lobotomy consists of the surgical removal of a portion of the brain. The "therapeutic" result of this surgery is that the person's behavior is much more docile and less disturbing. Substantial changes in personality, memory, etc. often accompany the behavioral changes. Psychoactive drugs are extremely powerful substances. Prolonged use typically causes side affects such as tardive dyskinesia, a loss of muscular control, particularly of facial muscles. ECT is designed to simulate the effect of an epileptic seizure by electrically disrupting brain activity. In the short term, this treatment often reduces signs of depression and anxiety. However, it is rarely effective as a long-term cure and its effect on behavior is not understood. Although the side effects of each of these treatments may also be regarded as "acceptable" risk, they do constitute a potential drawback to the medical treatment of behavioral deviance.

THE MEDICALIZATION OF MADNESS

The medicalization process described by Conrad and Schneider (1980, 1992) depicts an historical process in modernized societies. The growing complexity and interdependence of modern life makes the social control of deviant behavior of all types a matter of necessity. As a consequence, we would expect that institutions of social control would expand in size and develop in complexity. Advances in the effectiveness of medical treatment and the expansion of medical authority have made the medical care system into a powerful institution of social control. Recall that some sociologists define illness as a form of deviance. Thus, defining deviance as illness places control of such deviance under the auspice of the medical treatment system.

In the cultural history of madness, the notion that madness has organic causes has always existed, even if it was not always the dominant explanation. As we shall describe in the next chapter, however, during the late eighteenth and early nineteenth centuries madness became associated with illness and physicians became responsible for its care and treatment. This occurred without explicit evidence for a biological link but it satisfied the growing need to control deviant behavior and the preference for "enlightened" and humane forms of treatment.

Finally, recall that we have defined madness as behavioral deviance that is not elsewhere classified or that appears incomprehensible to us. Such behavior can now be classified as illness and made comprehensible by asserting that it is caused by biological malfunction. Given the cultural authority of the medical establishment and its claim to understand and offer treatment for mental "illness," it is not unreasonable to accept the definition of madness as illness and physicians (psychiatrists) as sources of treatment.

THE PREVALENCE OF MENTAL ILLNESS IN THE GENERAL POPULATION

The medicalization of deviance argument contains the further implication that deviance will be more frequently observed among persons in lower social class positions because deviance is defined by those in higher social classes. We turn next to an examination of the distribution of mental illness in the general population in order to evaluate the validity of this proposition.

Departures from normal behavior represent symptoms that are used to classify deviance no matter what name the deviance is subsequently given. In the case of managing deviance defined as mental illness, issues of social control are raised. It makes sense, then, to examine the distribution of mental illness across the general population as one way to gauge the occurrence of the various forms of deviant behavior. Moreover, we can also examine differences in the way such illness is treated as a function of social position. Earlier in the chapter we mentioned that some authors regard the mental health system as a means for maintaining status differences within society. From this perspective we should observe differences in the amounts of mental illness and differences in methods for responding to (treating) mental illness that are related to differences in social status. (We will examine social bases for differences in treatment in the next section.)

How wide-spread is mental illness in the general population? The most recent estimate is that close to 30 percent of people between the ages of fifteen and fifty-four would report enough symptoms during the past year to qualify for an official (DSM) diagnosis if they were to be evaluated by a psychiatrist (Kessler et al. 1994). Over a lifetime the same study found that nearly 50 percent of the population would report at least one diagnosable disorder.

The results reported by Kessler et al. (1994) are based on a careful survey of the population of the United States. The survey used a special questionnaire that was designed to assess symptoms of mental illness, which, if the person described them to a psychiatric professional, would result in a diagnosis of mental illness. The results tell us that there is a widespread incidence of the types of deviant behavior and thought patterns that professionals would regard as mental illness. However, they do not mean that all of these people are ill, nor is there any indication that having particular sets of symptoms results in incapacity (inability to fulfill role obligations). Rather, the survey uncovered substantial amounts of these types of deviance. Only about 40 percent of those persons who report any lifetime symptoms of a mental illness also report receiving some form of professional help for their problems. As Scheff (1984) asserted, most deviance is unrecognized. Even among persons with substantial numbers of symptomatic episodes and severe forms of disturbance, fewer that 50 percent obtained mental health treatment.

It may be helpful to look at some numbers that will give you a sense of the types of disorder identified in this survey and their frequency of occurrence. Table 11-1 provides values representing the percentage of cases in the Kessler et al. (1994) study for reports from respondents that they experienced the appropriate symptoms to qualify for specific disorders sometime during their life and/or in the twelve months prior to the interview.

The last line in the table shows that almost 50 percent of adults have experienced symptoms consistent with one of the measured disorders in their lifetime and almost 30 percent in the last year. The numbers also show that psychoses such as schizophrenia, delusional disorders, and schizophrenic-like disorders are relatively rare. They are

Table 11-1   The Prevalence of Psychological Disorder in the U.S. Population

Disorder	Ever in Lifetime	Past 12 months
Major depressive episode	17.1%	10.3%
Manic episode	1.6	1.3
Dysthymia	6.4	2.5
Any affective disorder	19.3	11.3
Panic disorder	3.5	2.3
Social phobia	13.3	7.9
Simple phobia	11.3	8.8
Generalized anxiety disorder	5.1	3.1
Any anxiety disorder	24.9	17.2
Alcohol abuse without dependence	9.4	2.5
Alcohol dependence	14.1	7.2
Drug abuse without dependence	4.4	0.8
Drug dependence	7.5	2.8
Any substance abuse	26.6	11.3
Antisocial personality	3.5	—
Nonaffective psychoses (including schizophrenia)	0.7	0.5
Any disorder measured in survey	48.0	29.5

Source: Table adapted from Kessler et al. 1994.

reported by only 0.7 percent of respondents over a lifetime and one-half of one percent over the past twelve months. Since most stereotypes of madness are based on the characteristics of persons diagnosed as schizophrenic, the relative rarity of this disorder suggests that public perceptions of mental illness do not reflect the reality of the frequency of various disorders.

The most frequently experienced disorders are substance abuse disorders, depression, and phobias. While these are defined as illnesses, of course, it is easy to see substance abuse as an example of deviant (perhaps criminal) behavior that becomes classified as illness. Similarly, phobias (exaggerated fears of places, things, or social settings) and deep feelings of sadness might be seen as inappropriate (non-normative) reactions to circumstances rather than as illnesses. The finding that 48 percent of the general adult population reports a lifetime mental disorder seems very high until we see that most of this disorder is not the type that we stereotypically and negatively associate with the popular conception of madness (i.e., the psychoses). This is not to say that the disorders that are experienced are any less distressing, but it indicates that the high levels of illness are related to the categories of deviance we could as easily define as some other form of deviance. If alcohol and substance abuse problems were defined as criminal deviance, for example, lifetime rates of disorder would be 21 percent and twelve month rates would be 18 percent.

THE SOCIAL DISTRIBUTION OF MENTAL ILLNESS

Epidemiological studies of the distribution of mental illness consistently document differences in the prevalence and incidence of mental illness based on social class, age, gender, marital status, urbanicity, and race/ethnicity. Given that we characterize mental illness as deviant behavior, these general findings make it necessary for us to consider the possibility that defining deviant behavior as illness serves as a means of social control. In such a case we would expect that differences observed in epidemiological studies would reflect existing social status differences. In addition, we would expect there to be differences in the way in which deviance would be treated (i.e., punishment or therapy).

The earliest epidemiological studies of mental illness (Faris and Dunham 1939; Hollingshead and Redlich 1953; Srole et al. 1962) all observed differences in the rates of psychiatric disorder by social class, gender, and ethnicity.

In the introduction to the Faris and Dunham work, Ernest W. Burgess (1939) perfectly captured the notion that deviance is related to illness and to social organization in his summary of the study: "Cases of mental disorders ... show ... a pattern of distribution previously shown for such other kinds of social and economic phenomena as poverty, unemployment, juvenile delinquency, adult crime, suicide, family desertion..." (ix–x). Faris and Dunham interpreted the differences in rates of disorder that they found in different areas of the city (Chicago) as being due to personal disorganization arising from maladjustment in social relations. Poverty, unemployment, minority status, and types of housing were each shown to be related to different rates and types of mental disorders.

Hollingshead and Redlich (1953) designed their survey of New Haven, Connecticut, to test the possible relationship between the class system and mental illness. They obtained information about two thousand psychiatric patients under treatment and compared their social class standing to the proportions of those classes in the general population. They found that psychiatric disorders (those treated) were most likely to be found among the lower two of the five social classes they defined. They also found that disorders among lower-class patients were more likely to be those defined as psychoses while in higher classes disorders were more likely to be neuroses (including depression). They also noted differences in treatment methods that appeared to be associated with class. Those in the lowest classes were most likely to be treated organically (drugs, surgery, shock) or to receive custodial care with no treatment. Those in the highest classes were most likely to receive psychotherapy (psychoanalysis, counseling, talk therapies). We will return to the issue of treatment differences shortly.

Srole and his colleagues (1962) were the first to attempt a systematic population sample (albeit of a small part of one city, Midtown Manhattan). Moreover, they surveyed the population of the neighborhood concerning psychiatric symptoms rather than relying on the use of identified psychiatric cases as had Faris and Dunham and Hollingshead and Redlich. By their methods of tabulating symptoms, Srole et al. found only 18.5 percent of the surveyed population to be completely symptom-free. They estimated further that approximately 23 percent of their sample were impaired in terms of daily functioning by their symptoms while the remainder showed some symptoms but were not significantly impaired by those symptoms. The study also observed differences in rates of impairment related to socioeconomic status (the higher the status, the lower the rate), by gender, and by marital status, by ethnicity (national origin), religion, and age. Perhaps the most provocative finding of this study was the high rate of untreated disorder. Among those rated as impaired by their disorders, only 35.5 percent had ever been psychiatric patients. Finally, they also found that treatment availability and use varied in such a way that, "... those most in need of such services had by far the least access to them" (Srole et al. 1978, 469). This observation reproduced the one made by Hollingshead and Redlich in New Haven that persons in lower social classes were least likely to be treated, and when treated, received the least "humane" forms of treatment. The significance of this observation for us is the implication that these differences in treatment arise from the use of mental health services as a form of social control (punishment) of deviant behavior within lower status groups and its use as therapy/treatment among higher status individuals.

Finally, the most contemporary and careful epidemiological studies (Robins and Regier 1990; Kessler et al. 1994) continue to document both high levels of disorder in the community and low rates of psychiatric treatment. They also document socioeconomic, gender, age, marital status, and ethnicity/racial differences in rates of disorder and the application of treatment modalities. In general they find more depressive and anxiety disorders among women and more substance use disorders among men. The older one becomes and the higher one's social class or socioeconomic status, the lower the rates of disorder.

DEVIANT BEHAVIOR OR BIOLOGICAL DYSFUNCTION?

The preceding section establishes two important characteristics that require our attention in order to complete our discussion of the medicalization of deviance. First, there are differences in the incidence and prevalence of psychiatric disorder that depend on one's social status. Second, the likelihood of receiving treatment and the type of treatment received depend on one's social status. The argument that has been made in this chapter suggests that both of these observations support a "social control" perspective in which certain forms of behavioral deviance (especially those associated with lower-class culture) require the intervention of social control institutions (i.e., medicine) in order to minimize disruption of social life and threats to status-dominant groups. On the other hand, the same facts could be explained by arguing that persons in lower status positions are simply more susceptible to behavioral disorders or drift down to lower social statuses as the result of their constitutional (biological) inability to function at higher levels. In this case, the control of deviant behavior would be oriented toward treatment of illness and the deviance is "unmotivated" like all physical illness. These contrasting positions are known as the social causation and the social selection arguments. They are relevant here because we are exploring the notion that deviance is medicalized (a social process) and the contrary position that illness is being appropriately treated by the medical system because it has a constitutional, biological basis.

The community surveys of Midtown Manhattan (Srole et al. 1962), the ECA studies reported by Robins and Regier (1990), and the results reported by Kessler et al. (1994) all indicate that there is substantially more psychiatric disorder in the community than is officially treated. The same thing is often true for physical illness. We suffer with colds until they get better and we go to work or school when we feel ill rather than go to the doctor.

Thus, one question we might ask is, "What factors affect whether and how one is treated?" In this instance we may point to the well-known differences in access to medical care that occur because of the ability to pay or the possession of medical insurance. Although federal programs such as Medicare and Medicaid have increased lower-class access to medical care, this care is often inferior to that used by higher status persons.

Access to psychiatric care follows the same general pattern. From this perspective, access to treatment would not appear to be related to the social control of deviance because those without insurance or the ability to afford health care (the poor and marginally employed), would represent groups of which we would expect the greatest amount of deviant behavior that required control. We would expect lower-class persons to be more likely to be treated (regardless of ability to pay) because treatment would be synonymous with control. The difference may be explained by considering the two forms of social control response we described earlier: social control as punishment and social control as treatment/therapy (Horwitz 1990). Social control as punishment is delivered to lower-class persons, while control as treatment is provided to higher-status individuals.

To say this another way, there is substantially more deviant behavior in the community than is officially controlled. However, its control is based on two responses. For higher-status persons a therapeutic response is most likely and its availability draws higher-status people to treatment. On the other hand, for lower-status persons, treatment is more likely to take more coercive, punishment-like forms and so utilization is less likely even when we control for financial access. The earliest findings substantiating this claim come from the New Haven studies of Hollingshead and Redlich (1953). They reported that higher-status individuals with disorders were most likely to receive psychotherapy (talk therapy) and lower-class persons most likely to receive organic (drug and surgery) therapies. Since talk therapies are less coercive, such treatment can be considered to be a positive form of social control while invasive therapies such as drugs and surgery come closer to being forms of coercive social control. Data compiled by the U.S. Department of Health and Human Services show that "blacks and American Indians had much higher rates of admission than other racial and ethnic groups to State and county mental hospitals and non-Federal general hospitals.... Differences also occurred in the diagnostic distributions of blacks and whites, with schizophrenia somewhat more common among blacks, and affective disorders, among whites" (Rosenstein et al. 1987, 73). Moreover, this same report finds that admissions to public mental hospitals, where poorer patients are more likely to be admitted, are also more likely to be involuntary and stays in these types of hospitals tend to be longer than in other types of facilities (i.e., private hospitals). These findings are consistent with the notion of punishment in the sense that Szasz (1994) raised it earlier in the chapter, as deprivation of liberty and movement or "cruel compassion."

At the same time epidemiological studies find that the incidence of more severe forms of psychiatric disorder, such as schizophrenia, are higher in lower socioeconomic groups. Thus, the relationship between treatment with drugs, surgery and confinement, and social class may simply reflect differences in the rates at which serious mental illnesses arise in different social class levels. This explanation, however, cannot be used to account entirely for the systematic channeling of persons into different forms of treatment. For example, Robins and Regier (1990, 347) report that, "People with different types of disorder are handled in different kinds of institutions." Significantly, 80 percent of persons with antisocial personality disorder, drug abuse/dependence and alcohol abuse/dependence disorders who are institutionalized, reside in prisons and not psychiatric or long-term care facilities. In other words, behaviors that can be defined either as criminal or medical are consistently channeled into the prison system for "correction" or punishment rather than into the mental health treatment system. The tendency to channel this behavior to the criminal justice system appears to be related to low income and minority racial status. Such channeling shows that behaviors such as substance abuse are not completely medicalized. It also shows that as a society we continue to be ambivalent about how to deal with such deviance. Since many people consider such behaviors as drug abuse to be a matter of personal responsibility, the "appropriate" response to such deviance is punishment and coercion.

SUMMARY

In this chapter we have considered the medicalization of deviance as a process that helps us to explain why some forms of behavioral deviance are defined as mental "illnesses." We argued that mental illnesses can be described effectively as deviant behavior and that social systems develop a number of different ways to deal with this deviance. Historically the role of medicine as a form of social control has grown to the point that we now define many forms of deviant behavior that used to be called criminal (for example) as forms of biological disorder.

Defining deviance as a form of illness has some benefits. Illness is not assumed to be within the control of individuals and, therefore, the societal response tends to be therapeutic and helpful. On the other hand, to the extent that persons are thought to be responsible for their deviant behavior, the response is punitive and coercive. Today, we consider the social response to mental illness to be enlightened precisely because disorders are attributed to biological processes, which keeps us from blaming and punishing those who suffer from disorder.

At the same time, however, the potential to use the medical system as a means for controlling deviant behavior in a kindly guise must also be addressed. Surveys of psychiatric disorder in the community and in institutions suggest that there may be some basis for this view as well. In modern societies, employed, married, high socioeconomic status members of society enter psychiatric treatment voluntarily whereas involuntary commitments are disproportionately reserved for marginal members of society such as the unemployed, unmarried, divorced, and powerless. The use of hospitalization, surgery, and drugs is highest among persons utilizing the public mental health service system rather than private (and more expensive) treatment systems.

When we recognize mental disorders as examples of deviant behavior that are socially defined as illnesses, much about the detection and treatment system becomes clear. Societal reactions to deviant behavior vary between punishment and treatment/therapy and the way we regard mental disorders reflects these alternate modes of social control as well.

We pointed out that the contemporary reaction to deviant behavior as mental illness has emerged from an historical process related to industrialization, urbanization, and the growing interdependence of social systems. In the next two chapters we will provide an historical review of the changes in the societal reactions to mental disorder that will show the correspondence between the societal conceptions of the causes of mental disorder and institutional/organizational forms of response.

THE HISTORY OF SOCIETAL REACTIONS TO MENTAL ILLNESS

The history of societal reactions to mental disorder is the history of changes in societal perceptions of the meanings and origins of deviant behavior that, in turn, affect the ways in which societal responses to such deviant behavior are organized. The same can be said about cultural differences in the meaning of deviant behavior. While all cultures recognize deviant behavior within their societies, they do not all define this deviance in the same way or "treat" it in the same way.

In this chapter we will provide a cultural and historical summary of the ways in which the symptoms of deviant behavior have been interpreted and we will provide ample illustration of the importance of the social context for understanding the social control of deviant behavior. We will first review evidence from different cultures that shows the relativity of definitions of mental disorder. Then we will trace the history of European-American responses to the type of deviant behavior we now regard as mental illness. This will bring us to a description of the current mental health system in the United States in the next chapter.

DEFINITIONS OF DEVIANCE AND SOCIETAL RESPONSES ACROSS CULTURES

All cultures recognize some forms of deviant behavior and have developed specific ways to deal with deviance. In fact, there is a remarkable similarity (although there are differences as well) in the descriptions of deviant behaviors across cultures. We might discover that self-starvation is almost universally perceived to be unusual, dangerous, and troubling. We would also find, however, numerous ways of explaining why such self-starvation occurs and how a social system should deal with it.

Cultures vary in their ideas about the relationship between mind and body and, hence, in their beliefs about the degree to which physiological processes are related to mental processes. Cultures also vary in the degree to which abnormal behavior is explained as the result of inner- or outer-directed forces. In some cultures demons or ghosts or germs can invade individuals and cause their symptoms while in other cultures individuals bring on their own symptoms through sinful living or by placing themselves in league with demonic forces.

In another sense, however, there is remarkable consistency in the conceptualization of psychic disorders across cultures. Every culture has noted types of deviant behavior that are not considered comprehensible by ordinary rules of conduct and explanation. Although this deviant behavior is sometimes interpreted positively (e.g., as a sign of sainthood), it is most often evaluated negatively.

COMMON EXPLANATIONS

Four general explanatory approaches can be seen in surveys of cultural experiences with mental disorder.

First, there are explanations that connect the loss of vital substances from the body to mental disorder. The loss of one's soul, an imbalance of bodily humors, biochemical imbalances, and genetic disorders share this explanatory approach despite widely different elaborations of how the loss of vital substance affects mental states.

Second, there are explanations that connect the presence of foreign bodies to mental disorder. Possession by demons, Satan, germs, social stressors, or the presence of toxic chemicals share this approach in which the explanation of disorder stems from some invasion of an otherwise healthy individual.

Third, there are explanations that connect violations of cultural and social taboos to mental disorder. In these instances, mental disorder is viewed as either an internal or external punishment for unacceptable behavior. In some cultures, gods punish sinful behavior. The violation of moral tenets can cause confusion and guilt and in some cultures conflicts between components of the mind (id, ego, superego) result in disturbed behavior.

Fourth, there are explanations that connect the malevolent actions of others to an individual's suffering. Victims of witchcraft, child abuse, or social labeling may demonstrate behavior that is regarded as a sign of mental disorder.

As the list above suggests, "modern," "scientific" explanations for psychiatric disorder can be seen as new versions of old and varied themes. This is not to suggest that modern scientific theories are simply restatements of nonscientific theories but we do note the commonalities among explanations that are used to explain otherwise incomprehensible deviant behavior.

These general explanatory themes also contain assumptions about the importance of personal responsibility as a factor in the development of disorder. Losses of vital substance suggest conditions that are not under the control of the individual. Similarly, the presence of foreign bodies and victimization by malevolent forces lean away from assigning personal responsibility to the victim. On the other hand, violation of taboos, moral transgression, and internal struggles with social standards all suggest personal responsibility.

We can develop two general expectations about the societal responses to psychological disorder from these considerations. First, the "treatment" approach will be consistent with the assumed causes and, second, it is possible that alternate theories of causation can exist simultaneously so that within a given society there may also be alternate ways of explaining and dealing with disorder (e.g., genetic, psychological, and social).

What follows now will be a brief cross-cultural review of conceptualizations of mental disorder that should allow us to see the specific ways in which the four generic explanations we outlined actually appear. This will be followed by a more detailed description of the historical changes in the explanation and treatment of disorder in European and American society. This will permit us, finally, to consider the relationship between the explanation of disorder and societal responses to disorder.

The names of disorders, the number of disorders, and the specific description of signs and symptoms that identify specific disorders will vary across cultures and historical periods. However, in most instances the descriptions that follow are based on behaviors such as: "confusion of intellect, extreme fickleness of mind, agitation of the eyes, unsteadiness, incoherence of speech, mental vacuity ... feelings of voidness in the head, noises in the ears, hurried respiration ... anxiety ... intoxicated condition of the mind ... incoherent talk, laughing, singing ... irritability..." (Rao 1975, 634–635). In short, they are conditions that we recognize today as also being symptoms of psychiatric disorder (even if we give them more scientific-sounding names).

NON-WESTERN DEFINITIONS AND SOCIETAL RESPONSES

Among aboriginal Canadians such as the Eskimos, Cree, Ojibwa, and the Tlingit a variety of factors were said to cause disturbance. Most frequently, disorder was attributed to supernatural causes. Disease was related to the violation of taboos, to witchcraft malevolence, to demon possession, or intervention by harmful demons or spirits, and to soul loss (Margetts 1975). Treatments also varied depending on the specific causal explanation. Thus, magic was sometimes used, herbal preparations were employed, physical devices and regimens designed to recapture the soul were used, and strategies to drive out spirits were invoked.

In Arab countries traditional religious healers commonly believed that there were three causes of disease: the evil eye, evil-doing (which includes the presence of foreign substances), and demonological possession (Baasher 1975). A millennium ago, mental illness was divided into five categories that reflected its origins: those who are born mentally ill, those disturbed by burnt bile, those touched by ghosts, spirits, or Satan, those overcome by passionate love, and a group of "sane insane" with defective judgment, incompetence in management, and disturbances of temperament. Treatment, again, was linked to the presumed causes of mental disorder and included religious, drug, and purification cures.

In West Africa mental illnesses were often attributed to the evil works of enemies or the influence of spirits. Some African cultures conceive of mental disorder as a collective, community attribute. They engaged in community-wide activities such as community-wide dancing and confessions that were intended to prevent disorder. They sought to keep ancestors happy to prevent ancestral unhappiness from affecting the living. There was often little stigma attached to disorder and those displaying symptoms were simply tolerated within their communities (Lambo 1975).

In traditional Indian society, mental disorder was related to disequilibrium among the humors (Rao 1975). In early Indian medicine, disorder was a sign of possession by a demon or revenge by the spirits of the dead. Remedy lay in prayers, incantations, and the use of amulets. Demon possession implied that when a person fell ill, a magician rather than a physician should be called. However, other disorders were recognized as organic and were treated with drugs. In the Ayurvedic system insanity was distinguished by cause as: insanity caused by bodily humors, insanity produced by mental humors, insanity produced by a combination of bodily and mental humors, and insanity produced by external agents such as gods or demons.

In traditional Chinese culture insanity was related to imbalance between yin and yang, the two great antithetical life forces: positive and negative, dark and light, male and female, etc. Imbalance occurred because of infringement of natural law by the individual. Chinese culture puts tremendous importance on one's devotion to family (living and dead) and to proper conduct. Violations that caused imbalance in family or work also caused imbalance of yin and yang and led to insanity (Veith 1975).

These brief descriptions of conceptions of the cause of mental disorder are certainly not meant to be inclusive. Rather, the point is simply to illustrate the dual observations that insanity is universally recognized and that there are diverse, yet consistent ideas about what causes insanity. The characterization of causes, moreover, does not reflect the complexity of cultural conceptions of disorder nor the historical variations in these concepts within cultures. We will use Western culture to trace processes of change in more detail.

DEFINITIONS AND SOCIETAL RESPONSES IN EARLY WESTERN CULTURE

Among the early Greeks (eighth century B.C.) mental life was externally caused (thoughts came to one from the outside), interactional, and accessible to public view (Ducey and Simon 1975). Mind and body were not distinguished and mental disturbance was considered comprehensible as the outcome of competing external demands. Man's passionate involvement in life sometimes caused conflicts between impulses to action that created tensions leading to disorder. The individual Greek suffered the anguish of these competing tensions and the embarrassment of losing face within the community. Treatment involved refocusing attention on other matters and reestablishment of an equilibrium with the community.

This early historical conceptualization, however, changed substantially by the time of Plato (429–347 B.C.). Moreover, and of importance to us, these changes can be linked to changes in the definition and treatment of mental disorder. Between the time of Homer and Plato, Greek society underwent substantial change. Tribalism as a form of social organization was replaced by the notion of the City-State; the idea of the individual as an independent actor developed; rational, scientific thinking replaced "mythological," magical thinking; and morals and laws were viewed as human and not divine in origin. These changes are often cited as the major contributions of Greek civilization to our own civilization. They are said to mark the early transition to modern life and ways of thinking, especially the appreciation of scientific thought, the active role that man plays relative to nature, and the creation of a distinction between one's mind and body.

As a result of these changes, the conception of mental illness changed also. Mental life originated from within the individual. Mind and body were separate; people had more responsibility for their actions. Mental disturbances arose from inner conflict rather than from external events and forces. Finally, therapy was directed toward creating personal insight within the individual. In many ways, these ancient Greek conceptions about mental life are similar to our present ideas.

The Greeks of Plato's time felt that mental illness had several causes that explained the variety of ways in which persons acted when disturbed. Some forms of disorder were thought to be identical to physical illness—a brain disease that resulted in false perceptions of the world.

Some forms of disorder were caused by imbalances among bodily fluids (humors). Mental illness was a "black bile" problem.

Four types of mental illness were recognized. Prophetic madness and poetic madness were considered positive forms of insanity that were related to creativity while erotic madness and ritual madness were considered negative because they disturbed the individual's ability to participate as a productive citizen.

When Rome replaced Greece as the dominant Western society, there was, again, a shift in the way mental processes and behaviors were understood. Initially Roman culture did not recognize mental disorder as an entity in itself. Rather, it was recognized that some individuals became violence-prone without discernible explanation and such behavior was countered with reciprocal violence. While humeral or demonic influences brought about such behavior, derangement as a separate phenomenon was not recognized.

As Roman society matured, however, mental disorder became recognized as illness and was viewed as having an internal, physiological, and psychological basis. Individuals were held responsible for their own mental states, which resulted from the emotional turmoil of life. Madness was both a natural, human reaction to life and a manifestation of disease. Its treatment, therefore, was intended to be therapeutic rather than punitive. Isolation from excessive stimuli in quiet surroundings, exposure to art, music, and dramatic performances was often recommended. Care involved sympathetic and supportive personnel. Medical treatment of mental diseases consisted in the use of vapors, baths, diet, and certain drugs and compounds intended to restore humeral balance. Greek and Roman conceptions of mental illness reflect the ideas of substance loss, invasion by foreign bodies, victimization, and moral violation—the four general categories we identified in our survey of other cultures. The legacy of the Greek and Roman periods that is with us today is the distinction between mind and body that supports both a psychological and a biological explanation for mental disorder.

THE MIDDLE AGES

The legacy of Greece and Rome was, however, largely lost during the Middle Ages in Europe. The church, rather than the state or medical authorities, became the dominant social institution that defined abnormal behavior. Individuals could be possessed by the devil, for instance. As a result of possession, observed deviant behavior was not a personal responsibility. Correcting the problem required exorcism of Satan. Human beings, as vessels, were passive victims of larger forces related to good and evil, innocent victims of natural processes. Throughout the Middle Ages, disturbed people rarely had any special provisions made for them. They were largely looked after by their families or the community or, sometimes, allowed to wander the countryside (Porter 1987). Disturbed behavior appears to describe some "court fools" and town fools. Undesirable occupations such as grave digger were sometimes occupied by such persons. The mentally disturbed were simply part of the texture of life, neither subject to cure nor care although sometimes the beneficiaries of exorcism. Note here that disturbed behavior is present in society but its origins in the natural order and man's passive role in that order limited the societal response to such behavior.

This situation began to change in the mid-1400s. At the end of the Middle Ages, there were theological and social changes that profoundly altered the definition, explanation, and treatment of mental illness. The Catholic Church, under pressure from heretical views that led to the Protestant Reformation, began to interpret possession by Satan in a slightly different context. The individual so possessed was no longer a victim but a welcoming host for evil. The Church rescinded its earlier official declaration that witches were innocent victims of Satan. The witch herself became responsible for sinful and unlawful behavior. Some of this behavior resembles what we define as mental illness today. The Church, then, provided one impetus for a change in the conception of responsibility for mental disorder. If witches and others possessed by satanic forces had been seen as innocent victims of external forces, they were now viewed as having made an active pact with the Devil. Hence, they were personally responsible for their condition and subjected to coercive control (like being burned at the stake). Although this perspective did not hold out the prospect of cure (except by burning or drowning), it did relocate responsibility from external to internal, personal factors.

Szasz (1970) suggests that the behaviors that were associated with witchcraft are directly comparable to the behaviors we associate with mental illness today. He argues that the Inquisition, designed to identify and eliminate witches, and the contemporary mental health system, designed to identify and cure the mentally ill, are both institutional mechanisms intended to control deviant behavior and create scapegoats for institutional failings (the corruption of the medieval church or the destructiveness of modern capitalism).

Porter (1987), though unwilling to go as far as Szasz, does suggest that sometimes the behavior that we associate with madness was used to identify witches.

Most important, there is a shift from a world view in which individuals are passive life forms in a greater drama of Good versus Evil to a view of individuals as more responsible and independent agents. Rotenberg (1978) argues that Protestantism carries with it the notion that the individual bears responsibility for his or her fate. In consequence, states of mental disturbance are reflections of personal characteristics rather than the result of broad collective religious drama. Rotenberg suggests that the "Protestant ethic" includes the idea that change is possible, change whose object is to become one of the elect. By this ethic even the deviance associated with mental illness is subject to change. To be sick is to be among the damned; to be healthy is to be among the elect.

These theological changes were also related to social, economic, and political changes occurring at the same time. The Catholic Church of the late Middle Ages was the central religious, political, and economic institution in Europe. Changes in the religious interpretation of satanic possession were reflections of changes in the political and economic position of the church, however. By the late Middle Ages, commercial activity across Europe had reached a stage where the conservatism of the Church and its participation in economic activities were increasingly perceived to be counterproductive. This perception of the role of the church began to nurture a sentiment for separating the church as a religious institution from economic and social institutions.

Although this historical transition was quite complicated, for us its meaning is that individuals were increasingly held to be personally responsible for their deviant behavior, the behavior could be changed by personal effort, and control of deviant behavior became a general social concern rather than a strictly religious matter.

INDUSTRIALIZATION, ENLIGHTENMENT, AND THE NEED FOR ORDER

Foucault (1965) suggests that this transition is marked by what he calls the "Great Confinement." From about the middle of the seventeenth century, Foucault argues, the control of deviance became an increasing concern of the secular state. In an age when reason was becoming a dominating theme, unreason became a target of social management. The great confinement was characterized by an unselective "rounding up" of deviants of all kinds, from criminals to the physically handicapped to the poor to the mentally disturbed. Although the great confinement did not proceed in the same fashion or to the same extent throughout Europe (Scull 1993), its symbolism is clear. Problem populations were defined as those persons in the population who were not contributing to the economic and social well-being of the state. An increasingly complex and interdependent social system, based on a new definition of rationality, required the effective participation of all its members. The deranged simply constituted one class of deviants whose behavior required regulation in the service of the larger social system. As control of the state shifted from the church to secular political authorities, the charitable religious view of the victimized poor shifted to one in which deviance was viewed as a personal choice.

The gradual shift to a market economy, the importance of individual wages to family survival, the transition from paternalistic order to a capitalist social system, and an increased dissatisfaction with nonsystematic responses to social deviance represent social changes that provide the context for the subsequent history of the definitions and treatment of mental disorder.

In the early stages of the great confinement and other efforts to control rootless individuals, confinement brought together criminals, the mad, the ill, and the poor. No differentiation of types of deviance were made. In France and England, it was not until the mid to late 1700s that separate facilities intended to deal exclusively with the needs of the mentally disordered were established. In the early stages of the great confinement the object of confinement was just that, physical limitation and removal from daily life. As a consequence, places of confinement were not designed to be therapeutic. Conditions in such places were abysmal. Investigators reported unchecked filth, crowding, abuse, and disease. In this period the lunatic was someone who had lost his reason and, therefore, his humanity. As such he (or she) could be treated as a beast; beaten, shackled, abused.

At the same time, this view of the insane marked a change in the general social understanding of insanity. The explanation for insanity shifted from an emphasis on demonic possession and trafficking with the Devil to a view in which the madman represented a defective human being. This shift, initially entailing confinement, eventually led to attempts to restore and improve the lot of the mad. The idea that the insane could be restored is consistent with a medical view of insanity.

In the short term, this shift resulted in an examination of confinement facilities, a separation of different types of deviants, and a more humane view of the purpose of separation of the mad from the general population. The protestant ethic of personal responsibility and personal restoration provided an intellectual prod for the development of "therapeutic" approaches to the mentally disturbed. Reform movements aimed at improving living conditions in places of confinement and approaches to restoration and treatment led to the development of specialized facilities for the care and cure of the mad. By the end of the 1700s, the asylum as a place of refuge and care began to take hold within European societies. By 1850 this shift was completed (Scull 1993).

Clearly the shift in the treatment of the mad was related to changes in the economic and political landscape. These historical changes redefined the causes and treatment of madness as they also redefined man's relationship to his labor, his family, and himself. Deviance is explicitly recognized and differentiated, and increasingly becomes an institutional responsibility of the state. The unreason of madness, its essential incomprehensibility, represented a particular target for a society that based human actions on the use of reason.

The new emphasis on reasoning about the unreasoning led to the development of systematic, scientific explanations for the origins of madness. Chief among these, of course, was the medical/organic model. Moral management based on the enlightened understanding of human behavior and Romantic notions of the stress of urban, industrial life in comparison to rural, agricultural life legitimated "humanitarian" approaches to care. Both of these general approaches emphasized the notion of recovery and restoration. The medical explanation emphasized organic, noncontrollable causes while the moral model emphasized personal transgression and controllable causes of disorder.

In turn, treatments were clearly (and rationally?) based on causal theories. Medical causation models suggested the use of drugs, physical restraint, and surgery as therapeutic options while moral models emphasized kindness, reason, humane treatment, and education in moral life as options (Porter 1987).

THE GROWTH OF LARGE PUBLIC HOSPITALS

In the United States, between 1820 and 1875, Americans created an extensive network of public mental hospitals structured to perform two functions: to provide restorative therapy for curable cases and custodial care for incurable and indigent patients (Grob 1985). Thus, by the 1820s the insane were distinguished from other types of deviants and a positive, therapeutic approach dominated the way in which the societal reaction to this deviance was organized.

The explanation for mental illness that existed at that time combined moral and medical perspectives. Moral lapses and weaknesses produced physical disorders. The illness, itself, was physical. Lesions of the brain were the immediate cause of disorder. Moral lapses such as intemperance, overwork, domestic difficulties, excessive ambition, and faulty education were antecedent causes. "Mental illness was the inevitable consequence of behavior that represented a departure from accepted social norms" (Grob 1985, 3). Mental illness was a somatic disease that followed from the violation of the natural laws that govern human behavior. We see here an explicit linkage between behavioral deviance and illness.

This view of mental illness was not intended to result in punitive responses. Moral lapses and violations, consistent with the Protestant ethic's emphasis on personal salvation, were regarded as correctable. Moral transgression occurred because of defects in the individual and an inability to resist the temptations and pressures of an urban, industrial society. "If derangements of the brain and nervous system were the consequences of environmental pressures that led people to violate the natural laws governing behavior (thus leading to lesions of the brain), it followed that a change of environment could lead to a reversal of improper physical development" (Grob 1985, 4).

Treatment was thus moral in nature. Restoration of moral (nondeviant) behavior was expected to reverse the effects of moral failure (i.e., physical effects). The components of moral treatment consisted first in removing individuals from the environmental sources of their disturbance. Hospitals were established in rural settings far from the madding crowds. Special diets, tonics, laxatives, and drugs were employed in an effort to cleanse the system and control abnormal behaviors. Various mechanical devices were developed to restrict physical movement or to provide shocks to the physical body in order to activate or reactivate moral behavior. Religious instruction and carefully supervised forms of recreation were also used.

Reports suggest that this approach was often successful (Grob 1985). Apparently if patients responded to treatment relatively quickly, they could be expected to recover. That is, their behavior became more socially normative. On the other hand, some patients did not respond to the treatment and remained in the hospital. Over time, these retained (long-term) patients became the majority population of the hospitals and the utility of treatment became secondary to custodial maintenance. After 1900, chronic patients dominated mental hospital beds. By the 1930s, 80 percent of available beds were used for chronic patients.

MODERN MEDICAL AND PSYCHOLOGICAL EXPLANATIONS

Other societal developments, however, were also continuing to affect the definition and treatment of psychological disorder. The emergence of effective physical medical techniques, the development of psychoanalytic approaches, and the improved understanding of genetics that occurred in the late nineteenth and early twentieth centuries altered conceptions about the relationship between disordered behavior and its treatment.

The practice of medicine as a relatively effective and safe enterprise is a modern development. Prior to the 1870s or so, physicians did not have effective understanding of most illnesses. Treatments were pragmatic and not scientifically related to physiological causes. The germ theory of disease, the use of antiseptic techniques, better and more systematic physician training, and more scientific research in this period radically changed the quality of medicine and abetted the emergence of the profession of medicine and its high prestige. It also encouraged a view of mental disorder as a principally physical disorder and fostered the creation of the medical specialty of psychiatry. In contrast to moral theories in which sin leads to physical damage, the new medical model emphasized the primary causal role of physical defects and disease processes. While deemphasizing the role of the environment, it retained a focus on the individual but removed much personal responsibility. The success of medical practices also provided physicians with the legitimacy to "medicalize" deviant behaviors.

Psychoanalysis suggests yet another causal pathway to madness. Psychoanalysis maintains that the development of the mind can be affected by interactions with the environment. The mind itself contains the seeds of conflict between the impulses of the individual and the requirements of social systems. Civilization and its discontents include the inevitable conflict between individual desires and collective (social) needs. The resulting strain of this conflict can lead to mental disorder. In psychoanalysis we see the assignment of responsibility to the individual (although other persons and institutions contribute). Psychoanalytic and other developmental explanations for disorder suggest that violations of taboos and loss of vital substance (the failure to develop a mature psyche) should be invoked to explain mental disorder. Here the mind as a component of the individual—rather than physiological defects—causes mental illness.

By the 1940s theories of disorder representing the loss of vital substances (genetics, brain lesions), the presence of foreign bodies (stress of life), and violation of taboos (moral explanations and psychoanalysis) coexisted in the United States. Treatment modalities showed equal variations. Large public mental hospitals still dominated the institutional treatment of disorder. However, they were increasingly criticized as warehouses for the poor and unwanted (the chronic patients beyond moral cure). Moreover, psychiatrists and physicians, trained in modern medical techniques, eagerly developed surgical and biochemical treatments for mental illness that used the short-term hospital as a model. Psychoanalysis was conducted in the private offices of therapists on an outpatient basis.

The medical model developed in the latter part of the nineteenth and twentieth centuries has proven to be extremely effective for dealing with physical disorder, particularly infectious diseases. This success has been translated into widespread authority and power by practitioners of modern medicine (i.e., doctors). As mental disorder was folded under the authority of doctors, the prominence of biological explanations for mental disorders also rose. However, it was not until the 1940s that the medicalization of mental disorder expanded as a result of discoveries about the extent of behavioral disorder in the general population.

THE END OF THE HOSPITAL ERA

By the 1940s mental hospitals had become dumping grounds for the unwanted. The vast majority of residents of these hospitals were long-term chronic patients believed to be beyond help. While the conditions in these hospitals aroused humanitarian and economic concerns (most hospitals were publicly financed), it was the realization that mental disorders were widespread in the general population that led to the next historical change in the societal response to mental disorder.

In the history that we have provided in this chapter, the mental disorders we have been discussing represent the types that we would define today as schizophrenia, manic depression, paranoia, and other forms of extreme "psychotic" behavior. Only the most disturbed persons with behavior that we would easily regard as incomprehensible were subject to the type of control and treatment we have described thus far. In this sense, public and professional perceptions of the mentally ill were probably fairly close.

By the 1940s, however, the list of behavioral disorders began to expand. Freud's approach to psychiatric disorder highlighted a set of conditions that we familiarly call the *neuroses*; that is, disorders in which a person's ability to function is impaired but which rarely cause them to "lose touch" with reality. The problems of daily living increasingly came to be defined under the medical/psychiatric rubric. For the first time a very wide range of behaviors came under the scrutiny of psychiatric practitioners. And, while there might be no doubt that these behaviors caused distress, their definition as mental disorders was new.

In the 1940s the first large-scale medical and psychological screening of the general population took place as a result of the manpower needs of World War II. These screenings revealed that many volunteers and recruits were not emotionally fit to enter the army. While a certain amount of psychotic behavior was identified, it was the sizable amounts of debilitating neurosis that caused the most profound changes in the societal reaction to mental disorder. While Freud elevated the neuroses to a culturally important status, it was their relative frequency in the population that led to a reconsideration of the definition of disorder and methods for treating it.

The needs of the military for soldiers resulted in the systematic collection of information about the physical and psychological status of recruits and volunteers. These exams revealed much higher levels of disordered behavior than had been previously recognized on the basis of the frequency of psychotic behavior. In addition, the treatment of psychiatric problems in war zones showed psychiatric professionals that such cases could be cured more readily than expected based on experiences with the chronic patients residing in mental hospitals. The range of conditions that could be defined as disorders was greatly expanded by the "discovery" of the neuroses.

The shift to this wider definition of mental disorders occurred because of the observation that external stress (e.g., combat situations) could cause disorder even in those who were otherwise deemed to be in good physical and psychological health. The subsequent stress models emphasized the relationship between environment and health and set off a search for environmental stressors. This search inevitably identified more deviant behavior and linked it to mental disorder or disease. In establishing the link between civilian sources of stress and distress, researchers went into the community for the first time (see Hollingshead and Redlich 1953; Srole et al. 1962). They found both stressors and departures from high levels of psychological well-being. The medicalization of deviance as we understand it was hastened by this shift in the definition of disorder to include milder forms of neurosis and the search for environmental causes.

The extension of the definition of disorder and the discovery of environmental causes for disorder also implied changes in the way such disorder should be treated. Long-term hospitalization was increasingly discredited by its "warehouse" nature and the absence of serious attempts at treatment. The discovery of extensive disorder among the general public meant that treatment needed to be changed. During World War II soldiers who experienced shell shock or battle fatigue were often quickly and effectively treated without hospitalization through brief therapy sessions. This suggested to psychiatrists that similar community-based models might be successful in civilian life and could be used to cope with the new larger case load.

THE SHIFT TO COMMUNITY-BASED CARE

By the 1950s when the treatment system began to make its most recent transition (the subject of the next chapter), the causes of disorder were felt to flow from organic disorder, environmental stressors, and individual developmental conflicts. The dominance of medical doctors as healers of psychological disorder, which occurred as part of the general increase in cultural authority of physicians, meant that all of these causes would be interpreted in physiological terms. In short, mental disorder became mental illness.

Less severe forms of disorder were found to be both widespread and treatable by simple, short-term techniques. The mental hygiene of the general public was increasingly the focus of attention rather than the smaller, less treatable group of psychotic patients drifting through life in the large public mental hospitals. This newly expanded list of psychological problems called for a new treatment model (i.e., societal response). This model was the community treatment model and its emphasis was on identification and quick resolution of the disorders of daily living. The transition from a hospital-based to a community-based treatment philosophy had other causes as well. However, the perceived need to deal with a much more wide-spread phenomenon than had been previously expected and an expanded list of treatable disorders must be counted as one of the causes of this transition.

Szasz (1970) and others (Laing 1967; Cooper 1971) immediately noted this medicalization of deviance. They argued that psychiatry had become a major institutional form for the social control of deviant behavior. Whereas the efforts to control, cure, or manage the mentally ill that occurred prior to the late 1940s were directed toward a small proportion of the population whose behavior was severely disordered, the new emphasis on "troubled" and "distressed" individuals suggested that almost anyone could require psychiatric help at some time of their lives. Indeed, community surveys estimate the incidence of disorder in a lifetime to be around 50 percent. By that estimate, every other person in the general population will experience a set of symptoms indicative of a mental disorder in their lifetime. Laing (1967) and others argue that this clearly demonstrates the expansion of psychiatry into a tool for social control. They would go even farther and argue that there is no such thing as mental "illness" at all, just modes of behavior that we define as deviant and seek to control.

In the context of this chapter, the important point about this expansion of identifiable disorders is the change in the institutional or societal reaction to mental illness that followed. Widespread but distressing rather than disabling problems require a system of treatment that relies on community care rather than long-term hospital care. The acute-care medical model fits perfectly. Psychiatrists had already staked their claim to the treatment of mentally ill persons and, given their training as physicians, it was natural for them to extend their responsibility to these newer forms of disorder. Just as you call a doctor to arrange an office visit for a minor physical ailment, it made sense that a similar system would work for psychological ailments.

The next chapter will describe the current community-based system of care in greater detail. Here we want to note that the changes in the definition and scope of mental disorders changed the societal response to disorder. Mental disorder became a medical disorder. The DSM system is intended to look and work just like the standard methods for classifying physical disorders. In this system, moreover, individuals are not held responsible for their disorder but by the same token they are obligated to accept medical treatment. Here we also see a possible reason for the discrepancies between general public and professional perceptions of the mentally ill. Professionals classify neurotic cases as mental illness while the public sticks with a perspective that clearly focuses on severe psychotic behavior.

SUMMARY

A broad historical view of the developments described here might yield the following formulation of the relationship between social processes and conceptions of mental disorder. Disorder went from being something that befell the person (demonic possession) to something that the person brought on by his or her actions (moral violation) and inner personality, and back to something that befalls the person (illness).

Just as we moved from a social system based on the cycles of nature to one based on the control of nature, views of illness went from being external processes to internal (and controllable) processes and back again to natural processes. Thus, deviance became a personal responsibility rather than the outcome of uncontrollable processes and then reverted to an uncontrollable but treatable phenomenon. The Age of Reason is the Age of Control and mental illness is especially the manifestation of lack of control or incomprehensibility. It is, therefore, the object of extended efforts at control because the existence of such deviance threatens social order (Sontag 1978).

Mental illness was traditionally defined in terms of the most severe, unpredictable, incomprehensible behaviors. However, in the last century this definition has expanded considerably to include problems of living and reactions to stressful life circumstances. This expansion of definition extends the areas of life in which we seek some form of control. This is what we have referred to previously as the medicalization of deviance. Since the great confinement in the late 1700s there has been a long-term effort to control behavior that is deemed to be disruptive or dangerous to social order. This concern for the effects of disorder on the social system was new. The assumed origins of disorder have fluctuated between explanations emphasizing organic, moral, psycho-developmental, and environmental causes. As each of these types of explanation gained ascendancy in a particular historical period, we witnessed a corresponding change in the philosophy of treatment. When moral violation caused brain lesions, moral treatment healed such lesions. When psycho-developmental explanations were in vogue, psychoanalysis and talk therapies dominated. When the definition of disorders was expanded to include neurotic conditions, the biological control of deviant behavior rose to prominence.

13

The Challenge of Community Mental Health

The United States is in the midst of a major debate about the community-based treatment of mental illness and the deinstitutionalization of the mentally ill (Carling 1995). The media, social researchers, and mental health system advocates are pointing to issues such as the "failure of deinstitutionalization" and the need for "asylum" (Wasow 1986; Zipple, Carling, and McDonald 1988; La Fond and Durham 1992), the growing crisis of homelessness among people with mental disorders or "madness in the streets" (Isaac and Armat 1990), the poor or low quality of community programs (Torrey, Wolfe, and Flynn 1988; Isaac and Armat 1990), and the continued emphasis on maintenance rather than rehabilitation and reintegration (Kirk and Therrien 1975; Rose and Black 1985; Anthony and Blanch 1989).

It has been suggested that the above issues are being raised because the mental health field is currently undergoing a "paradigm shift" with regard to people with severe disabilities. According to Carling (1995), we have moved from a period of institutional and facility-based thinking in which people were seen as patients, through an intermediary phase in which these individuals were seen as service recipients needing comprehensive community support services, to a current worldview in which disabled persons are viewed as citizens with disabilities, but who share with all other citizens the potential for, and the right to, full community participation and integration.

This chapter will briefly review the history and development of community mental health care in the United States to understand its current status and why we may be on the verge of still another change in the definition of and treatment for mental disorder. We will also review the critique of community-based treatment, the impact of community care on the family, and some alternative treatment approaches that have recently developed.

Roots of Community Care

In the second half of the twentieth century there has been a significant shift in treatment patterns toward the community-based treatment of the mentally ill. The deemphasis of hospital-based treatment, the opening of psychiatric wards in general hospitals, the development of social work programs as part of psychiatric care, the creation of community-based living arrangements, vocational training programs, and the development of outpatient and aftercare programs constitute meaningful steps in the transition from the hospital-based treatment of mental disorders (Brand 1967).

A number of factors led to the emergence of the community mental health system. Most significant among these were the poor state of most public mental hospitals in the 1950s, the availability of psychotropic drugs, the economics of custodial care, the realization that there was a great deal of untreated mental illness among the general public, legal requirements for treatment in appropriate settings, and new philosophical orientations to mental health treatment.

THE STATE OF PUBLIC MENTAL HOSPITALS

In the decade following the end of World War II, the inpatient population of state mental hospitals grew enormously. Moreover, this overcrowding drew the attention and concern of politicians at the local, state, and national levels (Wilson and Kneisl 1992). In 1948 Albert Deutsch published *Shame of the States*, a sensational report that exposed the terrible conditions that existed in mental hospitals. The report documented severe underfunding of hospitals, use of untrained caretakers, deplorable sanitary conditions, degrading treatment, physical abuse, the general absence of psychiatric treatment, and very high mortality rates in U.S. public mental hospitals. It became apparent that for most mentally disordered individuals, the act of admission to a mental hospital was the end of the road. Once admitted to the mental hospital, most remained there for the rest of their lives, forgotten and forsaken. In 1961 Erving Goffman published his book, *Asylums*, which argued that "total" institutions such as mental hospitals created demoralized, dependent, helpless patients who could not survive outside of institutional structures. Moreover, Goffman suggested that the hospital actually played a counter-therapeutic role.

THE AVAILABILITY OF PSYCHOTROPIC DRUGS

In the 1950s, psychiatric treatment was revolutionized by the discovery of psychotropic drugs such as Thorazine, Haldol, and Elavil. These drugs seemed to control the most bizarre behavior, hallucinations and delusions, and other disturbing cognitive states. These drugs were widely and quickly adopted. Their effectiveness was taken as an indication of the essential accuracy of biochemical explanations for disorder and they facilitated arguments for deinstitutionalization. If these new drugs could control bizarre behavior and thoughts, then there was less need to confine mentally ill persons. Although there is some controversy as to whether the discovery and use of psychotropic medications caused declines in hospital populations, there can be no doubt that they sustained hospital discharges and shortened hospital stays dramatically (Gronfein 1985). Additionally, the advent of these medications sustained the developing community-based treatment model by suggesting that the use of medications made mental illness akin to any other chronic disorder.

THE ECONOMICS OF CUSTODIAL CARE

Increases in the patient census at virtually all public mental hospitals, the expense of maintaining large hospital complexes and their staff, and the long-term stays of patients began to be identified in the 1950s as a growing fiscal burden for the states. Although the cost of maintaining a patient in a mental hospital was relatively very low compared to costs in general hospitals, such expenses were increasingly scrutinized by state legislatures. Against a backdrop in which advocates of community-based care were promising that such care would be inherently less costly than institutional care, states became less and less willing to provide funding for large mental hospitals. Moreover, as legal decisions compelled states to raise the quality of care in such institutions, states chose to deinstitutionalize patients rather than to incur the enormous expenses that would have been mandated in order to provide acceptable treatment and care to the large number of hospital-based patients.

MENTAL ILLNESS IN THE GENERAL COMMUNITY

During World War II, almost two million adult men (approximately 17 percent of enlistees) were found unfit for military service because of psychiatric problems. This rate of undetected mental disorder was alarming to most observers. Early epidemiological studies such as those conducted by Faris and Dunham (1939) and Srole et al. (1962) affirmed this high rate of untreated disorder. Advocates for community-based treatment were able to argue that such treatment would be more humane than hospitalization and it would extend psychiatric services to unserved persons in the community. As the scope of the public health movement accelerated during the 1950s the inclusion of mental illness within that movement added to the attractiveness of developing community-based treatments.

LEGAL REQUIREMENTS

During the 1960s and 70s, the judicial branch of the government also played a role in shifting care into the community. Three major lawsuits in 1975 resulted in decisions by a federal court that spurred community care and deinstitutionalization as a judicial mandate. The cumulative effect of these decisions was to add a legal rationale to the already existing impetus to decrease state mental hospital populations. In the first case, popularly known as the "Willowbrook Consent Decree," the court specified that the inpatient mental hospital population be reduced significantly, that community placements be created and implemented, and that patients be placed in the "least restrictive setting." In the second case (*O'Connor v. Donaldson*), the U.S. Supreme Court asserted that states could not confine to mental hospitals people who were not dangerous and who were capable of surviving alone or with others in the community. The final case (*Dixon v. Weinberger*) determined that involuntarily committed patients not only had the right to placement in the least restrictive setting but that alternative facilities to the hospitals must be created for those patients who did not require confinement (Rose and Black 1985). The principle of treatment in the least restrictive environment, the costs of improving hospital facilities to meet judicial mandates, and the decline in forced commitment each contributed to the need to provide community-based services.

NEW PHILOSOPHICAL ORIENTATIONS TO TREATMENT

During the first half of the twentieth century, psychiatrists and psychologists developed a number of treatment techniques such as psychoanalysis, behavior modification, brief situational therapies, and family therapy that did not rely on the hospital as a component of treatment. Coupled with the distrust of hospital care, the need to treat persons in the least restrictive environment, and the advent of psychotropic medication, mental health specialists began to envision a philosophy of treatment that kept a client as close to his or her community as possible. In other words, an orientation developed among psychologists and psychiatrists that patients were best treated by disrupting their daily lives as little as possible consistent with their need for treatment. Rather than removing a person from familiar faces and routines, it was felt that retaining as many of these interpersonal relationships and routines as possible was most therapeutic.

DEINSTITUTIONALIZATION

The confluence of these factors resulted in two major shifts in the care of the mentally ill. First, large numbers of institutionalized patients were released from hospitals—deinstitutionalization. Second, a system of community-based services was developed to serve both this old clientele and a newer clientele consisting of community-residing persons who represent those in the general public who show signs of disorder but are otherwise untreated.

On the surface, this process has been highly successful. In 1955 there were 560,000 resident patients in public mental hospitals and by 1983 this number had fallen to 120,000. Hospitals today are fewer, smaller, and better staffed. Lengths of stay have been reduced from years to days. There has been a corresponding growth in the number of persons receiving services from community-based mental health services showing that persons who were previously unserved are now being treated. We turn, then, to a description of the detailed history of the community mental health system.

THE COMMUNITY IDEAL

As a large number of hospital patients became ready for discharge, the need to develop supportive mental health services in the community became apparent.

In 1955, the Joint Commission on Mental Illness and Health (a collaborative effort by the American Psychiatric Association and the American Medical Association) was created. The task of this group was to evaluate the conditions and needs of the mentally ill clientele in the United States and to make recommendations to Congress in order to develop a national mental health program. The Commission issued its report in 1961. The landmark recommendations of the group called for the following:

- A shift from institutional to community-based care
- A more equitable distribution of mental health services
- A focus on preventive services
- Consumer participation in both the planning and delivery of mental health services
- Recruitment and training of laypersons as mental health paraprofessionals

- The education of an increased number of mental health services professionals
- Public support of research
- Shared federal, state, and local funding for the construction and operation of community-based mental health care centers (Wilson and Kneisl 1992)

The philosophy of the last recommendation was that treatment should be available to and provided for mentally ill patients in their own local communities as far as possible. The process of deinstitutionalization was beginning. The aim of this movement was to reduce the number of mental patients in state hospitals by 50 percent over a two-decade time period (Minkoff 1978). It was believed that deinstitutionalization and community treatment would aid the mentally ill to live in the community and lead relatively normal lives.

The recommendations by the commission set in motion what has come to be known as the "third revolution" or turning point in psychiatric care. The first revolution was the notion of treatment rather than incarceration, punishment, or isolation for the mentally ill (1800–1900), while the second was the emphasis on intrapsychic causes of mental illness (courtesy of Sigmund Freud and the invention of psychoanalysis, 1900–1950). The "third revolution" was the community mental health care movement. The focus of the movement can be summarized from the following quote:

> The objective of modern treatment of persons with mental illness is to enable the patient to maintain himself in the community in a normal manner. To do so, it is necessary (1) to save the patient from debilitating effects of institutionalization, (2) to return him to home and community life as soon as possible, and (3) thereafter, to maintain him in the community as long as possible. Therefore, aftercare and rehabilitation are essential parts of all service to mental patients, and the various methods of achieving rehabilitation should be integrated in all forms of service. (Joint Commission on Mental Illness and Health 1961)

John Kennedy, then president of the United States, appointed a committee to study the recommendations of the Joint Commission and in February 1963 called for "a bold new approach" to the prevention and treatment of mental illness in which mental health services would be integrated with community life. The Congress responded by passing the Community Mental Health Centers (CMHC) Act in October 1963 to support the establishment of mental health centers in the local community. This legislation authorized 150 million dollars in federal funds. The funds were to be matched by state funds over a three-year period and used for the construction of comprehensive community mental health centers. In order to qualify for federal funding, each CMHC was mandated to provide five essential services (see Table 13-1).

Table 13-1   Essential Community Mental Health Services

1963	1975	1981
In-patient care: 24-hour hospitalization for any person in the community requiring around-the-clock care	Five essential services mandated in 1963, plus:	Out-patient care
Out-patient care: Psychiatric treatment for clients living at home	Follow-up care: Ongoing programs for community residents after discharge from a mental health facility	Partial hospitalization
Partial hospitalization: Treatment programs for clients not requiring around-the-clock care; day treatment programs allowing clients to maintain jobs during the day and return to the hospital at night	Transitional services: Living arrangements for persons unable to live on their own but not requiring hospitalization, or newly discharged from a mental health facility and requiring assistance in adjusting to living on their own	24-hour hospitalization and emergency care
Emergency care: 24-hour emergency services	Services for children and adolescents: Mental health diagnostic treatment, liaison, and follow-up services for children and adolescents	Consultation and education
Consultation and education: With professionals or community groups in schools, health clinics, churches, courts, law enforcement agencies, etc.	Services for elderly: Mental health diagnostic treatment, liaison, and follow-up services for the elderly	Screening services
	Screening services: Assistance to courts and other agencies to screen persons referred to mental health agencies	
	Alcohol and substance abuse services: Programs geared toward prevention, treatment, and follow-up in alcohol and substance abuse	

CHARACTERISTICS OF COMMUNITY MENTAL HEALTH SERVICES

As the term suggests, community mental health services refer to all activities undertaken in the community for the maintenance of mental health and the treatment of mental illness.

The first characteristic that distinguished CMHC care from the more traditional mental health services was its emphasis on practice in the community, as opposed to practice in institutionalized settings.

A second characteristic of the orientation was its emphasis on a total community or population rather than on individuals. The community was geographically defined in terms of a "catchment area" or mental health service area and was used to describe the population to be served by a particular CMHC. Typically, a catchment area included between 75,000 and 200,000 individuals. These segments were considered to be small enough to assure that the range of services needed could be provided.

A third dimension was its emphasis on disease preventive and health promotive services. This was in sharp contrast to the medical model and mainly therapeutic intervention methods used in earlier institutional settings.

The CMHC approach emphasized the comprehensiveness of services and their continuity. This meant that CMHCs would provide the full spectrum of mental health needs in the community. In addition, CMH caregivers would assume the responsibility for helping mental health clients move from one service program to another, and monitoring and coordinating their moves as well. Comprehensiveness of services included direct as well as indirect services, such as consultation with family and other members of the mentally ill person's social network, and general public education through the mass media, for example.

The CMHC focus was on short-term therapy and crisis intervention as opposed to costly long-term therapy or hospitalization.

An interesting feature of the CMHC was that, for the first time, the mental health field was opened wider to nonmedical professionals (e.g., psychologists and social workers), and nonhealth professionals (e.g., teachers, clergy, and social scientists) (Satin 1994). In addition, CMHCs encouraged the tapping of new sources of personnel such as nonprofessionals (i.e., community representatives who had limited formal training but were able to play useful roles in the community due to acquired skills and life experiences). In doing so, CMHCs asserted that mental health professionals were not the sole providers of services (a threat to the dominance and control of psychiatrists), or the sole source of information about the mental health needs of the community. This feature also emphasized the commitment of CMHCs to the concept of "community control," which focused on the fact that a CMHC was meant to operate with and on behalf of the community. Finally, the CMHC approach stressed the need to identify sources of stress within the community and not just within the individual (e.g., the impact of major plant closings or community-wide disasters).

Overall, the CMHC concept asserted the following:

- Services should and would be available when and where needed.
- Medical services would be integrated with other human services.
- The aim would be to enhance the positive and reduce the negative effects of life experiences.

THE IMPLEMENTATION OF CMHC

Passage of the 1963 legislation resulted in the transformation of the National Institute of Mental Health (NIMH), a research and training-oriented institute within the National Institute of Health, into an organization that was responsible for a third function, service. The CMHC program made the NIMH the administrator for a federally subsidized treatment system for the mentally ill.

From 1963 through the late 1970s, the discharging of mentally ill persons into the community escalated, eventually lowering the number of state and county psychiatric hospital populations by close to 80 percent. The growth of CMHC and aftercare services followed much more slowly because the CMHC Act did not work as planned. Some of the states and local municipalities could not match the federal funds needed to implement and sustain the services. Many others, and especially those in poor, rural areas, were unable to generate enough funds through their service fees. As a result, the program and many services, e.g., aftercare programs, and public and mental health education and consultation did not always develop as planned.

Even then, the "dumping," as it is referred to by critics of deinstitutionalization, of mentally ill hospital patients into community facilities, streets, and neighborhoods continued. Communities were not prepared to receive the patients who were discharged. Community attitudes toward the mentally ill were extremely negative. Mental patients were stigmatized, feared, and mocked for their conditions and behavior. In addition, financial support to provide housing and other facilities to the discharged population was lacking. Communities resisted and protested against the development of any housing or treatment facilities for the mentally ill in their own neighborhoods. It is alleged that, unwelcomed and scorned, many former patients found life outside the institution frightening and undesirable. Inadequate community services combined with an unfamiliar and hostile environment made mental health progress limited and difficult, and many patients found themselves caught up in "the revolving door" phenomenon in which most discharged patients were admitted and readmitted into mental hospitals and institutions, some within a few months of discharge. Many advocates for the rights of the mentally ill began to argue that the needs of the mentally ill population were better served by mental institutions than in the community. Community services were neither comprehensive nor coordinated. If this were not enough, the costs to the states of maintaining public mental hospitals did not decline in sync with declines in hospital populations. Between court-ordered mandates to increase the level of care in institutions and continued maintenance and personnel costs, mental health services actually became more costly, with the Federal government paying for the new CMHC system, while the states continued to pay for the older hospital system.

By the beginning of the 1970s it was apparent that there were many problems in the community mental health centers plan. Problems were reported by most states. Significant issues involved the lack of adequate resources for aftercare of mental patients and the lack of coordination between local and state agencies involved in CMHC care. In addition, the community-based system had concentrated what resources it had on the treatment of the "worried well," those clients who experienced mild to moderate problems that were most readily treated in contrast to the chronic and severely mentally ill client. In most cases, the result was a disorganized and uncoordinated variety of services, crisis centers, and mental health clinics whose primary function was to provide and monitor medication, and provide emergency services through social service departments.

REFOCUS ON THE CHRONIC PATIENT

In the face of this critical assessment of the CMHC program, in 1975 the U.S. government amended its original 1963 legislation. The new legislation not only reemphasized the five essential services mandated earlier, but added seven additional mental health service requirements (refer to Table 13-1).

In 1977, President Carter established a twenty-member president's commission on mental health to reassess mental health needs. The 1978 report advocated strengthening the community mental health care system and community support systems. The other recommendations included the following:

- The continued phasing-out of large public hospitals
- Improving the delivery of services to underserved and high risk populations such as minority groups
- Establishing national insurance that included coverage for mental

health, and encouraging private insurance carriers to include coverage of mental health issues

- Providing financial support to increase the numbers of mental health professionals, especially those working with minorities, children, and the elderly
- Developing advocacy programs for the chronically mentally ill
- Protecting the rights of all persons who needed mental health services
- Increasing support for all research related to mental health and illness
- Establishing a center within the NIMH whose primary focus would be on primary prevention
- Providing public health education to the public in order to enhance their understanding of mental health issues
- Centralizing the evaluation efforts of all governmental agencies that were concerned with mental health

In 1977, the National Institute of Mental Health began a new program called the Community Support Program (CSP). This program involved the concept of "comprehensive community support systems" (Turner and Tenhoor 1978), and shifted the focus of interest from extending treatment to mild cases of disorder to dealing with the multiple and difficult needs of severely disabled, chronically mentally ill young adults. From the beginning the CSP program worked directly with state mental health agencies to promote "decentralized, debureaucratized care and force a systems view on community mental health" (Mosher and Burt 1994). The ten elements of the CSP program are listed below:

1. Identify the population—whether in the hospital or the community—and reach out to offer appropriate services
2. Provide assistance in applying for entitlements
3. Provide crisis stabilization services in the least restrictive setting possible
4. Provide such psychosocial rehabilitation services as goal-direction, rehabilitation, evaluation, transitional living arrangements, socialization, and vocational rehabilitation
5. Provide such supportive services of indefinite duration as living arrangements, work opportunities, age and culturally appropriate daytime and evening activities
6. Provide medical and mental health care
7. Provide backup support to families, friends, and community members
8. Involve concerned community members in planning, volunteering, and offering housing or work opportunities

9. Protect client rights, both in the hospital and the community

10. Provide case-management services to assure continuous availability of appropriate forms of assistance (NIMH 1981)

Some of the existing service deficiencies that prompted the CSP program were identified by Turner and Tenhoor (1978) as follows:

- Inadequate definition of service system goals
- Fragmentation and lack of coordination among service agencies
- Lack of a systematic approach to funding community-based services
- Lack of commitment by "mainstream" agencies to serve the mentally ill population
- Lack of effective community organization and advocacy

In response to the problems mentioned above, a federal contract was signed with nineteen state mental health agencies to create community support programs whose main focus would be on discharged state psychiatric hospital patients. States were encouraged to develop community support systems (CSS). NIMH defined the CSS as "a network of caring and responsible people committed to assisting a vulnerable population to meet their needs and develop their potentials without being unnecessarily isolated or excluded from the community" (Turner and Tenhoor 1978, 329). The service components listed above (starting on page 183) were to be developed within each community based on existing economic, political, and treatment resources.

In 1980, the Community Mental Health Systems Act was passed. It was designed to implement the recommendations of the president's commission (described earlier). For example, it authorized continued funding of community mental health centers, the development of ambulatory care and preventive care units, and services for high risk populations. Another objective of the act was to coordinate the two-tiered mental health system that had evolved since the 1963 mandate in which the severely mentally ill continued to reside in state institutions, while those with lesser disabilities used CMHC services.

The programs authorized by the revised act were to begin in 1982. Before they could get started, the role of the federal government in mental health shrank. The 1980 Community Mental Health Systems Act was repealed in 1981. The repeal bill moved the authority, allocation of funds, and administration of mental health programs from the NIMH to the states. Each state received a block grant to cover mental health services. The scope of services mandated for CMH centers were reduced to five essential services (see Table 13-1). As of 1984, federal funding for CMHC centers and mental health delivery programs was stopped. At present the continued existence of CMH centers and the quality of services depend on state support, private funding, and earned revenues.

DEINSTITUTIONALIZATION AND COMMUNITY MENTAL HEALTH—PERSISTENT PROBLEMS AND CURRENT ISSUES

More than three decades after the onset of deinstitutionalization and the advent of community mental health care services, large numbers of the severely or chronically mentally ill receive little or no psychiatric treatment. Many are incarcerated in jails or remain homeless on the streets, others are housed in boarding or nursing homes in conditions scarcely better than the "back wards" of the state mental hospitals from which they were supposedly rescued. It is apparent that the community health care movement has fallen far short of its mission, even though its advent appealed to virtually everyone involved in redesigning the mental health system, including the general public. Why and how did such a universally supported movement fail, or has it not been a failure after all?

While deinstitutionalization resulted in the discharge of thousands of hospitalized mental patients, community-based treatment was simply not available for many of them. By 1975 the goal of reducing state mental hospital inpatient population had been achieved (Comptroller General 1977). The process of discharge continued through the late 1970s.

According to Morgan (1993), the chief reason for the speedy closure of old state mental hospitals in the late 1970s and through the 1980s, was spurred by a desire to improve the provision of services to the mentally ill. There was yet another reason—an attempt to reduce costs. Research conducted by Ryan, Ford, and Clifford (1991) between 1978 and 1988, suggests difficulties in transferring hospital financial resources to community-based service organizations. Rose and Black (1985) maintain that a document by the Legislative Commission on Expenditure Review (LCER) in 1975 indicated that, even though more than 50 percent of inpatient beds in state psychiatric hospitals were vacated by 1973–74, only 6.5 percent of the state hospital resources were reallocated from these settings to outpatient CMH care. While state psychiatric facilities continued discharging mentally ill populations into communities, they were not simultaneously reallocating their budgets so that state mental health funding did not follow patients from facility to community.

In their original agenda, public officials saw deinstitutionalization as a way to significantly reduce state mental health budgets. As planned, significant savings would be made from the cancellation of plans to build new, or update older state mental hospitals. Closing existing hospitals would result in significant savings that would be directed to the less expensive CMHC services. The plan also included transforming some of the larger state hospitals into centers for the long-term and combined care of all chronic diseases, including mental illness. State and local governments, however, were unable to pay for the implementation of the new programs. The federal government could not or did not provide the necessary financial support for the full development of the CMHC care program. As a result, hospitals were not closed, and CMH centers did not grow fast enough.

The problems that emerged were twofold: Many of the mentally ill continued to be treated within the institutional setting and then discharged into the community where grossly inadequate services were all that existed. Rehospitalization rates began to accelerate—many mentally ill patients discharged from institutions soon returned to them, unsupported and unserved in the community. Civil liberty laws, however, kept many of these severely ill mental patients from being maintained within hospitals. This trend of hospitalization—discharge and rehospitalization— increased expenditures that government officials had hoped would be controlled and decreased due to deinstitutionalization. In a report by the U.S. Comptroller General (1977, 24), the following was noted: "State and local agencies administering programs that serve or can serve the mentally disabled—have not provided financial or other support needed to help mentally disabled persons (1) avoid unnecessary admission or readmission to public institutions, (2) leave such facilities, or (3) receive appropriate help in communities."

An issue encountered in the concept of deinstitutionalization was distinguishing between availability, accessibility, and appropriateness of services, even in those cases where services did exist. The matter of creating community-based services was seen as the ability to provide appropriate services. The criteria for deciphering what was appropriate generally went unexplored (Rose and Black 1985). In addition, the CMHC care system was developed primarily to meet the needs of the acutely mentally ill. Basically, this system was set up to focus on those mentally ill individuals who suffered from short-term mental illnesses that would respond to medication, counseling, and other social services—an acute care treatment model. By making services available in the community, however, CMHCs assumed that adequate care would also be provided to mentally ill patients requiring more than short-term services. As a result, a large number of mentally ill individuals went without adequate or appropriate services. Even for acutely ill mental patients, services were fragmented and uncoordinated, and there was a general lack of aftercare programs and follow-up. In other words there was a general lack of comprehensiveness and continuity of care (a goal of CMHC). In place of the state hospital's centralized care, the continuity of care for patients in the community was fragmented, uncoordinated, and inadequate.

The CMHC movement was also, in part, a reflection of the antipsychiatric movement. As psychiatrist Fritz Freyhan points out, CMHC was committed to a "new myth of social curability" (1980, 406). In the nineteenth century, psychiatrists claimed tremendous therapeutic powers within institutions. The CMHC movement transferred some of the power and hegemony of psychiatrists to the community. The advent and increased belief in the power of psychotropic drugs and psychoanalytic techniques carried the domination of psychiatrists within mental institutions into the federally funded community system, however. The CMHC's mandated services were limited and mostly clinical in approach, except for consultation and education. The shift from hospital-based care into CMHC programs was, therefore, only in the locus of mental health service delivery without actually being a shift in approach and intervention. With the medicalized approach to problem definition and solutions, psychiatrists defined appropriate services for client needs in the community (Rose and Black 1985). This transfer of clinical services into the community was often described as the creation of "institutions without walls."

Mosher and Burti (1944) point out that the psychiatric orientation has reinforced the practice of maintaining disturbed people on neuroleptic drugs. These drugs led to a new problem—tardive dyskinesia (TD)—an impossible-to-hide physical disfigurement, as well as other substantial side effects which required additional treatment. It is estimated that nearly 5 percent of the mentally ill population develop tardive dyskinesia and as many as 80 percent of patients on psychotropic medications report some degree of unpleasant side effects. Most psychotic patients continue to be treated with these neuroleptic drugs even though sufficient research exists to show that many patients can be treated without these drugs and that the long-term outcome is no better today than before these drugs were introduced.

During the period of heightened deinstitutionalization, questions were rarely raised about what was happening to those mentally ill patients who had been discharged. Questions were also seldom raised about where patients were being sent or actually went. The concept of the "least restrictive setting" simply assumed that mental hospitals were the most restrictive and that any other setting was better. Evidence indicates that a large number of patients were placed in private for-profit nursing homes, while others were placed in intermediate care facilities, licensed adult-homes, or in single-room occupancy (SROs) or "welfare" hotels in which a patient rented a room from a landlord.

The most progressive of community residences were halfway or three-quarterway houses and other transitional facilities. These settings were believed to be therapeutic in themselves—"therapeutic communities." In actuality many of these facilities were "mini-institutions," "candy-coated hospitals," and "living room jails," that were grossly under-serviced. So the discharged went from "total institutional control to the least restrictive alternative, to halfway independence to assisted independence" (Howie the Harp 1995). The practice of community placement began to be known as reinstitutionalization.

More dramatic was the growing number of dirty, weird-looking faces on city streets, living in deteriorating neighborhoods (Talbott 1979). As discussed earlier, CMHC was set up essentially for acute-care. In doing so, CMHC designers failed to take into adequate consideration the needs of the scores of chronically or severely mentally ill. Research indicates that as time went by the proportion of patients suffering from chronic mental illness served by CMHCs actually decreased.

A number of reasons were responsible for the decrease. First, CMHC did not offer programs and services tailored to the needs of the chronically mentally ill. Some programs existed but these were usually the least prestigious, had the fewest and least trained staff, and were generally viewed as undesirable but necessary services. The more progressive and better trained staff members of CMHCs rarely chose to work with the "chronics." Part of this attitude came from the belief that not much could be done with these mental patients or that chronic problems just did not get better. Consequently, many chronics were denied services or maintained in the community through drug treatments (Kirk and Therrien 1975). In practice, most chronic patients were often made to feel unwelcome—it was felt that their presence alone would drive away the "better" clients—those with less severe or acute problems.

In addition, CMHC and supplementary services in the community rarely acknowledged the world of poverty, social stigma and discrimination, inadequate housing, lack of family and social supports, unemployment, and other related problems that comprise the daily life of former mental patients. Under the rubric of community integration, many former patients and users of CMHCs continued to live without much contact with anyone in the community.

As the homeless population in the country has grown, so has the debate on its composition. While the issue of homelessness is an economic and social problem, it is estimated that 30 to 40 percent of the homeless (in shelters and on the streets) suffer from a mental illness.

In summary, the community mental health movement has been partially successful at best. The movement seems to have been successful in achieving three objectives:

■ Establishing mental health services in the community (Even in this respect, many fewer than the original 2,000 CMHCs have been built. As of 1991, only 672 of the original 761 CMHCs built were still in operation.)

- Providing indirect services to caretaking agencies
- Providing short-term treatment programs that were effective in acute mental illness cases

Less success has been achieved in some other areas:

- Building a community-based, coordinated system capable of meeting a wide variety of mental health needs of the community
- Optimal use of nontraditional sources of personnel
- Involving the community in developing and evaluating the CMHC program

Further, two other goals of community mental health were not achieved:

- Developing a concern for the total population
- Identifying and reducing community stresses

Analysis of NIMH data has also revealed three conclusions about deinstitutionalization and CMHCs:

- Out-patient care has not replaced in-patient care.
- Public institutions have not been replaced by community-based facilities.
- Private resources have not replaced public ones as funding sources for the care of the mentally ill.

CURRENT TRENDS IN COMMUNITY MENTAL HEALTH

In discussing the current state and the future of CMHCs, one must remember that it has only been two decades since the notion of a "community support system" (CSS) for the mentally ill was conceived. The fundamental idea of CSS was that most of the mentally ill could be treated in their own communities and that with community support, self help, and other basic resources needed for day-to-day living, they could lead productive lives in the community.

The CSS concept has led to several changes. The first change has been in the kind of clinical and other community support services being offered today. Day programs, psychosocial clubhouses, supported housing, supported employment, vocational training, and a number of services operated by consumers themselves, such as drop-in centers, now exist in many communities (Carling 1995). Overall, there has been a dramatic increase of new service models.

Another arena of change in community mental health has been

brought about by the growth of consumer advocacy and self-help groups, mostly led by families of ex-mental patients and many ex-mental patients themselves. The most powerful and largest among these groups is the National Alliance for the Mentally Ill (NAMI), which has 1,000 affiliates with membership of over 140,000 families nationwide. The NAMI is mainly composed of parent groups of ex-mentally ill or mentally ill children who have been frustrated by the system. Today, the NAMI and many other such groups have formed support groups, circulate newsletters, hold monthly meetings, and conduct legislative lobbying. It is predicted that the consumer advocacy movement will continue to grow and gain power. The rise of consumer and family advocacy groups is partially the result of the intended empowerment of these constituencies as part of the realization of community support programs. The other stimulus to the development of groups such as NAMI is related to the impact on families of treating family members in the community.

THE FAMILY AND COMMUNITY MENTAL HEALTH CARE

Families have traditionally been uninvolved in the care and treatment of their disordered members largely because of two factors: the belief by psychiatric authorities that families cause disorder, and the fact that treatment used to take place in institutional settings (Fisher, Benson, and Tessler 1990). Of course, treatment no longer occurs exclusively in hospitals and it is estimated that seventy-five percent of chronically mentally ill persons maintain some contact with their families while they live in the community (only about 25 percent live with their families).

Psychoanalytic and psychodevelopmental theories of mental illness often identify the family as a main cause of mental disorder. As such, the family is often viewed as a source of conflict rather than as a source of support and care. This view of the family's role in relation to the mental health of the patient being treated continues to be held by many mental health treatment personnel today. In such cases, even though mentally ill persons have considerable contact with their families, staff at mental health facilities are reluctant to involve family members in the treatment process or to encourage contact between the family and the client. Staff are often prohibited by confidentiality laws and by their beliefs about the causal role of the family from sharing information about their clients with family members. This is one source of frustration for families; they cannot get information on treatment progress or what they can do to help.

This negative view of the family, however, is one that is hard to sustain in the era of community-based care. First, as psychiatric illness has been medicalized, the role of the family as a causal agent becomes murkier. If disorders are biologically based, then family context cannot be a principal cause of the illness. Second, the number of persons treated for mental disorders in the community makes it impossible to blame the family since the family has become a major source of support and care. The greater role of the family in relation to the mental health of its members can be described in two ways: in terms of family reactions to the illness and in terms of family caregiving and consequent "burden."

FAMILY REACTIONS TO MENTAL ILLNESS

Families appear to go through a number of stages as they react to the family member who has been diagnosed with a mental illness (Tessler, Killian, and Gubman 1987). Not all families go through these stages and family reactions also depend on how disruptive and persistent the member's behavior is and whether the member resides with the other members of the family.

Families initially tend to normalize symptomatic behavior, then deny its seriousness. However, once the behavior is officially labeled, they react to its longer-term implications. These include the following:

- Faith in mental health professionals: Just as we place our faith in physicians treating other medical problems, most families are optimistic about the outcome of treatment by mental health professionals.

- Dealing with recurrent crises: In the meantime the family member repeatedly disrupts family life (clearly this characteristic varies with the seriousness of the disorder) and commands high amounts of attention. Both the treated family member and the family experience periodic crises related to the disorder and the family needs to cope with such crises.

- Recognition of chronicity: As time goes on, family members recognize that the client will not improve to the point of full recovery. They become pessimistic and this leads to loss of faith in the mental health system.

- Loss of faith in the mental health system: Family members blame the system for its failure to help their family member. This loss of faith is increased by the often disdainful and negative interaction of mental health personnel with family members.

- Belief in the family's expertise: As the family goes through the experiences of crises and long-term cycles of wellness and illness, they often find ways to cope with these cycles and this leads to a belief that the family can develop control mechanisms to handle the illness. However, this also leads to the realization that the disorder will require continued attention, so family members worry about the future. Mothers and fathers are the principal family members interacting with a mentally ill child and, as these parents age, they worry about the continued care of their disabled child.

There is not an exact sequence through which all families go, nor is it likely that families will react in these precise ways. Some families reject the ill member entirely and some get a great deal of satisfaction from their involvement. The stages families go through are similar to those that any family might experience as they adjust to the presence of a chronically ill or disabled member.

In the case of mental illness, however, families may need to deal with the needs of their ill member to a greater extent than is the case for physical illness. The reason for this is the comparatively poor state of community-based services for the mentally ill. Community mental health systems contain "holes" or "cracks" that represent inadequate and fragmented services (Tausig 1987). As a result, it often falls to families to attempt to provide care and services even if families are not very good at doing so. The family is a fall-back option when all else fails. When a client falls through the cracks somewhere, the family often becomes the arrival point of the fall. Thus, to some extent, the family reaction to its mentally ill member reflects their role as service providers by default.

The impact of mental illness on the family is typically described in terms of "burden." Studies suggest that between 55 and 75 percent of families perceive themselves to be burdened by their involvement with a disabled family member.

FAMILY BURDEN

Burdens on the family or specific family members can vary greatly both in terms of total amount and in terms of what aspects of the relationship is burdensome. As families adjust to the level of contact and the level of need of the disabled family member, they do this in the context of many years of exposure to the ups and downs of their family member and their own experiences.

Burden is frequently divided into two parts, *objective* burden and *subjective* burden. This allows one to distinguish between the care activities and behaviors one engages in directly for the benefit of the disabled member and the emotional and physical consequences of providing that care. The components of objective burden include the following:

- Financial burdens: Health care coverage for long-term mental illness is often not available or is insufficient to meet needs. As a result, it is not unusual for families to exhaust their own financial resources in efforts to find treatment and care for the disabled member.
- Time demands: It is also not uncommon for one person in the family to assume primary responsibility for tasks related to the ill family member's care. Primary caregivers (usually mothers) often give

up outside employment, assist the member with tasks such as dressing, eating, scheduling, transportation, money management, and social activities.

■ Disturbed domestic routines: When the disabled person lives with other family members, their behavior is often disruptive to family life. Unpredictable behaviors and crises can change family plans. Role relationships between other members of the household can also be disrupted. Spouse and children may resent the amount of time the disabled member requires.

■ Constraints on social and leisure activities: Reduced interactions with friends, neighbors, and other social contacts are frequent experiences.

Subjective burden describes the feelings that are generated by these objective burdens of care as well as physical conditions that can be attributed to care and management of disabled family members. In addition, family members have a great deal of worry and anxiety about the condition of their family member. These subjective reactions are related to high levels of distress among caregivers. We described the subjective burden of care in Chapter 8 as an example of non-normative role-related distress.

The community mental health movement and the community mental health system that has developed have enlarged the role of the family in the care of mentally disabled members. The involvement may be voluntary or involuntary and it may be a positive or a stressful experience for the family. For many families with a severely disabled member, the experience is highly negative. Moreover, families find little help from the formal system of care. As a result they often become involved in alternative forms of mental health treatment and care.

ALTERNATIVE FORMS OF COMMUNITY-BASED CARE

Whether families feel burdened by their involvement with mentally ill members or not, they and the disabled member do not limit their search for services to those offered by conventional public or private mental health care providers. Because families and individuals often realize that mental disorders are chronic, and because existing formal mental health services cannot be expected to be responsive to all the needs of the ill person, it is quite natural that alternate forms of community-based services are sought. These services can range from informal support groups for family members to unconventional and esoteric therapies based on a wide range of theories of illness cause and treatment.

A recent survey found that 34 percent of a random sample of American adults reported using at least one unconventional therapy in the past year (Eisenberg et al. 1993). Most of these users of unconventional therapies had sought treatment from medical doctors as well. Persons suffering from anxiety and/or depression were among the most likely individuals to seek out unconventional treatments (45 percent and 35 percent, respectively). They were most likely to use relaxation techniques, imagery, and self-help groups.

There are a wide variety of unconventional or alternate therapies available and some of these are even offered in conjunction with conventional therapies. Often these alternate therapies, however, are viewed as quackery, ineffective, or dangerous by conventional medical practitioners. A review of practices suggests that few are inherently dangerous. The worst case is that the treatment is ineffective.

Some of these therapies include the following:

- Imagery, a process that involves visualization intended to reduce anxiety, develop senses, or re-order associations
- Meditation, a self-directed process for relaxing the body and mind
- Hypnosis, yoga, and biofeedback, a process that uses instruments to monitor physiological processes and feed the information back to the person so he or she can learn to control the process
- Dance therapy (which has its own professional association and scholarly journal), music therapy, art therapy
- Prayer and mental healing
- Support groups for both families and persons with similar diagnoses

In addition to these therapies that do not involve any consumption of medicines, treatments using acupuncture, megavitamin dosages, Ayurvedic medicine (a traditional Indian medical system), homeopathic medicines, and naturopathic medicine (combinations of botanical medicines, dietary changes, traditional oriental medicine, and modern Western medicine) are also widely used forms of therapy.

The precise extent of use of each of these alternate therapies is unknown although their popularity is undeniable. These therapies represent alternate ideas about the causes and cures of illness but to consumers these alternatives represent possible relief from illness or the burden of care. While the conception of community-based mental health care originally meant the extension of hospital-based care into community-based facilities, we are only now beginning to realize that the concept of community is really much broader than the original notion that motivated the deinstitutionalization process. In some instances providers of traditional, conventional forms of psychiatric care have incorporated some of these unconventional treatments into their regimen of treatment resources. Many community programs now sponsor family support groups, social clubs, and promote self-help efforts for clients and their families. This is especially the case among those with chronic and severe forms of illness where the effectiveness of conventional treatments is subject to considerable uncertainty. One of the unforeseen consequences of the movement of services into the community has been the loss of professional medical dominance over the treatment process. In hospital-based settings psychiatrists were clearly in charge but today, in the community, there are many alternate types of mental health practitioners and many alternate forms of therapeutic intervention.

14

THE CONTRIBUTION OF SOCIOLOGY

While there may be those who revel in their madness, most people who have some form of psychological disorder feel that they suffer from that disorder. Every instance of psychological disorder is experienced by an individual as a personal trouble. Certainly every person who suffers from a disorder has a unique personal history and set of experiences that may be used to "explain" the origins of that personal trouble. Unhappy childhoods, bad breaks, mean mothers, and family histories of disorder can often be linked to current disorder. Yet, there are also likely to be experiences common to individuals that we can also identify and link to disorder. Thus, personal troubles may have roots in social conditions that create these common experiences. Personal troubles are related to social problems (Mills 1959).

In this book we have described these common experiences as the stresses and strains of normal everyday life that are the consequences of social stratification and social role configurations. One contribution of sociology to the study of psychological disorder is the recognition that social structures play a role in creating disorder. Moreover, we have also described the treatment of disorder as a socially organized response entailing social constructions of the meaning of deviant behavior and socially agreed upon means for treating (controlling) that disorder. That is the second contribution.

In this chapter we will discuss the value and limits of a sociological perspective for the understanding and treatment of mental disorder. Rather than simply summarizing or repeating the contents of the previous chapters, we will assume that we have made our point. There is a valid sociological explanation that can be made but, so what? We will begin our evaluation with a brief review of the value and limits of some

other explanations for disorder. We will then discuss the social and political implications of controlling deviant behavior and we will try to relate
what we have learned to the reality of emotional distress felt by individuals. The contribution of sociology will be gauged by the intellectual
sense it makes for understanding a social problem and by its helpfulness
in dealing with personal troubles.

OTHER EXPLANATIONS

At the outset of this book we explicitly excluded discussions of the bio-
logical/chemical/genetic, psychodynamic, cognitive, and behavioral explanations for disorder. This was not done because we believe these perspectives have nothing to contribute to the explanation of disorder, but
because such explanations are so widely familiar that the contribution of
a sociological perspective might be obscured if we tried to present these
different perspectives simultaneously. Nevertheless, we must now bring
these explanations back into our discussion to see the "fit" of a sociological perspective.

The current standard understanding of the causes of mental illness and methods for treating disorder reflect an approach that focuses on the individual as its object. This certainly seems appropriate
when the immediate objective is to relieve individual suffering. These
explanations for the origins of disorder stem from direct observations of
persons who seek care for their disorder. The perspectives derived from
such observations can be characterized collectively by the term *medical
gaze*. The medical gaze (Foucault 1973) regards disorder as pathological, individual-centered, and treatable. In other words, individual disordered behavior develops from the progression of some abnormal process
(either physical or mental) and can be either cured or managed. The
abnormal condition that develops is defined as an "illness" that requires
active "treatment" to restore a normal state. This is a practitioner's perspective, a clinical orientation that sees "cases" which require treatment.

What is common to these perspectives is the relatively peripheral
importance of social context as a source of distress and an emphasis on
individual characteristics as very important. There is a "... focus on prox-
imate risk factors, potentially controllable at the individual level..."
(Link and Phelan 1995). And, indeed, where the task is to directly help
people who are suffering, such an orientation seems appropriate. In clinical practice each of the perspectives that we regard as part of the medical gaze is employed to assess problems and treat them. As our previous
discussion of the community-based treatment of mental illness pointed
out, this results in a variety of treatment alternatives and the likelihood
that individual clients will experience interventions that reflect these dif-

fering explanations. Often these differing approaches are described as consistent with a biopsychosocial or multiple causation model.

Few persons concerned with mental illness would argue that social factors play no role in explanations for mental disorder. Few persons would argue that there is a single cause for all disorders. Despite the general acceptance of a multiple causation perspective, most mental health professionals clearly prefer or give more weight to some one specific explanation. "Mental health professionals differ considerably in viewing mental illnesses primarily as disease, as disturbances in the functioning of the personality, or as problems in living" (Mechanic 1989, 4). We need to briefly describe the components of this "bio-psycho-social" model.

THE BIOLOGICAL BASIS OF PSYCHOLOGICAL DISORDER

As we noted before (see especially Chapter 11), the biological explanation of the causes of mental disorder is widely accepted among mental health professionals and the general population. The "bio" part of the multiple causation model represents a perspective that is sometimes also called, "the medical model." It assumes that mental illness is a physical illness (Frazer and Winokur 1977) manifest in the brain (Lickey and Gordon 1991) as physical abnormalities, "... including loss of nerve cells and excesses and deficits in chemical transmission between neurons..." (Andreasen 1984, 221).

The brain is viewed as the organ of behavior and behavior is viewed as the complicated result of the actions and interactions of brain structures and chemical and electrical events within the brain. Abnormalities of behavior arise because of abnormalities in brain structure and/or chemical and electrical events. Abnormal behavior is a sign of illness with exactly the same meaning as any other symptom of physical illness, such as chest pains as a sign of heart disease. Mental illnesses should be considered physical illnesses. Because brain structure and function arise from heredity and developmental maturation, techniques for treatment are identical to those used to deal with other forms of physical malfunction. Hence, drugs and surgical interventions are the logical forms of treatment.

This causal explanation is often (but not exclusively) limited to illnesses described as mood disorders (depression, mania), schizophrenia, dementias (such as Alzheimer's), and anxiety disorders. These more severe forms of disorder appear to be responsive to drug therapy, though they are rarely cured by such therapy. Proponents of biological explanations cite the responsiveness of these conditions to drug treatment as evidence for the validity of their position. However, as Mirowsky and Ross (1989) point out, drug treatments may relieve symptoms without removing the cause of the symptoms as novocaine relieves the symptoms of toothache without removing the cause of the pain. Thus, the effectiveness of drugs in controlling symptoms cannot be used to prove that behavioral disorder is a direct function of biological disorder. Despite great advances in the understanding of genetics, brain chemistry, and the neurosciences in general, researchers remain largely unable to locate distinct genetic abnormalities or anatomical malfunctions that account for the appearance of mental disorders. It is a strong article of faith that such evidence is just over the research horizon.

The role of the environment (both social and material) is limited in biological models to the effects that such environmental factors have on the structure, development, and function of the brain. Accidents, infections, malnourishment, and the stress of everyday life may represent precipitating conditions for illnesses by affecting brain structure and functioning. The term *breakdown* has a direct physical meaning in which the "broken" brain defines mental illness (Andreasen 1984). Relatively speaking, biological explanations for mental illness strongly rely on the "bio" component of biopsychosocial multiple causation explanations for disorder. Psychological and social factors are consequences and causes of biological abnormalities but play no significant independent role in causing mental illness.

The widespread use of psychoactive drugs in contemporary psychiatric practice reflects the acceptance of biological explanations for mental disorder. The drugs have direct effects on chemical processes that co-occur with deviant forms of behavior. Despite misgivings about adverse side effects, many of those treated in this way report relief from symptoms. The biological approach for explaining psychological disorder fits neatly into the general medical model for explaining physical disorder. Such explanations do, however, rely on the belief that brain "diseases" arise as a natural biological process related to biological inheritance or environmental "triggering" of biological disorder. Disease is not related to independent personality or intellectual developmental factors nor to social contextual factors. These factors are either irrelevant entirely as causal factors or are regarded as consequences of brain anomalies. The "brain" and the "mind" are regarded as a single biological entity and, hence, only malfunctions of the brain underlie the observation of behavior and thought disorder.

As we discussed in reviewing the medicalization of deviance (Chapter 11), proponents of a biological explanation believe that the stigma of mental illness comes from the public belief that persons suffering from mental illness are somehow responsible for their disorder. By contrast, proponents argue that mental illness, as physical illness, should be regarded as an uncontrollable biological process that does not reflect moral failure (Andreasen 1984).

Though biologically oriented explanations for mental illness are accepted by many practitioners, the biopsychosocial model clearly aims to incorporate more factors into the explanation of disorder.

THE PSYCHOLOGICAL BASIS OF PSYCHOLOGICAL DISORDER

The "psycho" component of the multiple causation model refers to a wide variety of specific theories and therapies that can be traced to the influence of Freudian psychology. These theoretical approaches include psychoanalysis, non-Freudian developmental theories, and cognitive theories. They hold in common a belief that behavior can be explained by unconscious and/or conscious psychological processes rather than biological processes. For the most part, these theories accept a separation between the body and the mind. The mind develops and matures in stages and disorder can be traced to developmental failures that result from childhood trauma or other disruptions of developmental sequences. Therapy tends to rely on "talk" and is felt to be useful in treating cases of anxiety, phobia, obsessions, compulsion and some types of delusion, hallucination, and paranoia that are linked to schizophrenia.

Psychoanalysis was invented by Sigmund Freud during the period from the 1890s to the 1920s. This approach to the understanding of psychological disorder is based on the belief that human beings possess an instinctual (and therefore largely unconscious) set of psychological drives that they seek to fulfill through interaction with the external world. As the person normally matures, he or she passes through a set of developmental stages that mostly lead to a mature, adult balance between psychological needs and environmental sources of need satisfaction (including other people). Disorder represents failures to pass through this developmental sequence in proper form. Failure to master the demands of a given stage of psychosexual development results in distortions of the relationships between parts of the unconscious (id, ego, superego) that appear in adults as psychological disorder. Because these distortions occur within the unconscious, they cannot be resolved by conscious introspection. However, trained therapists can make use of techniques opening "windows to the soul" such as dreams, to uncover unconscious conflicts and then provide assistance for resolving these conflicts.

Psychodynamics is a more general term for theoretical perspectives that assume the existence of the unconscious as well as a developmental process of psychological/personality maturation. Data derived from Freudian psychoanalysis provide the basic elements for psychodynamic theories (Blum 1966; Saul 1980).

Psychodynamic explanations for the causes of disorder and its treatment are highly individualistic. Adult (or childhood) disorders are caused by very particular "injurious influences" that distort a child's psychological development so that disorder reflects the after-effects of these influences on individual personalities (Berzoff et al. 1996). Therefore, "... psychodynamic treatment ... requires an understanding of the particular, individual patient and an adaptation of the treatment to meet his particular and individual personality, problems and needs" (Saul 1980, 7). The objective of therapy is to discover the distorted patterns that have developed in the hope that conscious effort can correct them.

Psychodynamic explanations for disorder tend to see biological symptoms as consequences of psychological disorder. The mind often converts psychological problems into physical ones. The social environment plays a more direct causal role but solely as a source of proper or improper influence on psychological development. The approach is so intensely individual that data about the social distribution of disorder is rarely, if ever, amassed by practitioners of psychodynamic explanations.

Cognitive theories of psychological disorder represent a variety of additional approaches for explaining mental illness. They differ from developmental psychodynamic theories because they focus on current conscious thought processes. The basic premise of cognitive approaches to disorder is that disorder arises from errors and distortions in thinking that then lead to behavior that is inappropriate to actual conditions. The theoretical explanation has been likened to information processing errors in computers (Eysenck 1993). The approach has been used to explain and treat depression, anxiety, personality disorders, and obsessive-compulsive disorders. It is used to treat individuals, couples, and families.

Cognitive psychology assumes that individuals with mental disorders are suffering from the effects of distorted, exaggerated, mistaken, or unrealistic ideas (cognitions) about the world and the way that the world works (Freeman et al. 1990). These erroneous cognitions can result in anxiety and depression when they lead the individual to misinterpret situations and act inappropriately. As the individual recognizes the difficulties they are having, they can enter a self-sustaining cycle that reinforces the distorted patterns of thought and action.

Therapy is directed toward the recognition of where and how thoughts "went wrong" (Carmin and Dowd 1988). Patients learn to recognize automatic thoughts and underlying assumptions that they have learned over time and that operate to distort cognitions and create misperceptions of situations. The goal is to teach the client in this type of therapy how to change these automatic thoughts and assumptions so that more appropriate behavior will result.

Although misperceptions may be caused by biological, developmental, or learning factors, cognitive psychologists are not especially concerned with addressing the sources of distortion. Rather, they work with the current problem. It is also an individually focused approach although it is recognized that the immediate social environment (i.e., partner, family) can be both a source of distorted perceptions and a reinforcer of erroneous cognitions. Sometimes therapists must work with couples or families to affect the sources of erroneous cognitions. Thus, the model is social only in so far as it recognizes the possible influence of "family systems" and the possibility that errors in cognition may be learned.

THE SOCIAL BASIS OF PSYCHOLOGICAL DISORDER

The "social" component of the biopsychosocial model refers to the phenomenon of social learning and specifically to behavioral approaches to mental disorder. Behaviorist explanations for deviant behavior do not view deviant behavior as an outcome of either disease processes or psychological processes (Bandura 1969). Rather, behavior is a learned response in which the individual becomes conditioned to behave in a particular manner. Deviant behavior that can be regarded as a symptom of mental illness simply represents a learned behavior that departs from socially normative expectations. The individual becomes conditioned to act in a particular way in a particular environmental context. Sometimes such conditioned responses do not correspond to what others generally expect and the person's behavior is judged to be in need of modification.

Behaviorist explanations for deviant behavior specifically deny the role of conscious and unconscious psychological processes as well as biological/genetic factors as central to the production of behavior. At the same time, behaviorist approaches have found a niche in the biopsychosocial explanation of mental illness because the approach can be used to deal with specific problems in quick and effective ways. The therapeutic form of behavioral intervention is commonly called "behavior modification."

The basis of behaviorist explanations for disorder is the idea of conditioning in which a desired behavior is rewarded and, therefore, continues to be performed. In fact, it is not necessary for the reward to remain in order for the behavior to be produced. After the behavior-reward relationship has been reinforced, the behavior will continue whenever the conditions associated with the behavior are present even without the reward. Behavioral deviance (including some of what we regard as symptoms of mental illness) is, thus, simply learned behavior that others find unacceptable.

This deviant behavior can be corrected by "disconnecting" the environmental stimulus from the conditioned behavioral response and associating a different (less deviant) response with the stimulus. Behaviorists do not believe that the "mind" exists except in so far as it processes information about the current environment and past experience. Rather, the basis of action is simply a set of learned behaviors that require little or no mental processing or psychological motivation.

Behaviorist techniques are often effective for dealing with specific behavioral problems such as phobias or object-related anxieties. For example, people who are afraid to ride elevators can be "treated" by a program of behavior modification that uncouples the association of elevators with scary feelings and couples elevators with pleasurable experiences. It is not uncommon in mental health group homes for "token economies" to be established in which group home residents are rewarded with "tokens" for behaviors such as cleaning their rooms, attending programs, and doing chores that help the group home run well and "teach" residents behavioral skills that can be useful to them outside the group home setting.

Behavioral approaches, thus, do not aim to "cure" individuals of disease nor to manage conscious or unconscious psychological mental processes. Rather, they deal with specific undesirable deviant behaviors without concern about possible biological and psychological causes. Treatment can be quick and very effective. Its limitation (among others) seems to be its narrow application to specific forms of deviant behavior and its inability to explain larger, more complicated kinds of human behavior. It is exclusively focused on the individual and his or her reaction to a given environmental stimulus. The individual is the exclusive focus of attention. In the multi-causal explanation for psychological disorder, behavioral (social) explanations account for some of the dysfunctional behaviors that arise from the societal reaction to disorder rather than the reaction to basic causes of disorder. The "social" component of the model does not represent a true sociological component. Rather, it fits a medical model focused on individuals as the vessels of disorder and the objects of treatment.

THE PLACE OF SOCIOLOGICAL EXPLANATIONS

Robert Fancher (1995) believes that none of the commonly used explanations for disorder (those that make up the biopsychosocial model) are either logically or empirically supported. Rather, he argues that there are "cultures of healing" that reflect specific disciplinary beliefs and biases about the causes of and cures for mental disorder. He believes there is no objective validation for any current causal explanation (in the biopsychosocial model) or therapeutic approach.

In fact, there are very few scientifically reliable studies of the success of the various causal explanations and therapies. While most theorists and practitioners will agree that no one explanation accounts for all cases of disorder and no therapeutic approach deals with all types of disorder, everyone has their preferred perspective. This is reflected not only in the creation of hyphenated (bio-psycho-social) models, but in the wide variety of therapeutic approaches to treatment. This is probably a good thing since it is also unlikely that we will ever find a "one-explanation-fits-all" solution.

One of the contributions of a sociological perspective on mental disorder comes from its ability to provide a plausible (and empirically evaluated) explanation for the causes of disorder. This explanation certainly reflects a sociological "culture" and would, therefore, be subject to criticism as narrowly focused and incomplete. However, the sociological explanation has been much better tested than the other explanatory cultures that Fancher (1995) criticizes.

In fact, the descriptions we have provided of a sociological stress process and the research that supports it can be used to make a substantial claim for a successful sociological explanation of mental disorder that goes beyond biopsychosocial models (Mirowsky and Ross 1989).

The essential insight of a sociological explanation for disorder is that the opportunities and constraints of everyday life, which are created by one's positions in social hierarchies and the roles one assumes, can be used to predict levels of distress.

This is an explanation that sometimes seems illogical. How can really bizarre behavior and thoughts be attributed to structured inequalities? How can one person exhibit these signs of disorder while another sociologically identical person does not? The individual seems like an inevitable victim of social structure, with no personal responsibility or escape. And, finally, how can we treat a disordered individual if the explanation for the disorder is gender discrimination?

But this is also an explanation that is very logical. Should we be surprised that a young, poorly educated, single mother, working in a boring job for low pay is depressed? Under these circumstances would it really seem logical to argue that her brain is broken or that her cognitions are distorted?

The key to understanding the contribution and place of a sociological explanation is to realize that people are simultaneously psychological and sociological beings (as well as, for example, economic, political, and religious beings). They have unique personal histories and experiences but they also share a surprisingly wide variety of histories and experiences. What is shared (say, experiencing racial discrimination) may lead directly to feeling of distress but it can also be filtered through the concrete reality of one's life so that discrimination can lead to demoralization, which can lead to distress. Individuals are usually not conscious of how status and role structures affect them. People just "are" and that's life. It ain't always fair. But this is an incorrect description. "Life" isn't the same for the people who hire maids as it is for the maids. It is not the same for men and women and it is not the same for poorly educated and well-educated persons. From an individualistic perspective these differences are not apparent. If we are who we are, then it doesn't matter how we got that way and there is no point in trying to change the way things are. Under such circumstances, explanations for psychological disorder that focus on each individual as a unique case might make sense. However, since we know that life chances do differ substantially, it no longer makes sense to explain people's feelings solely in terms of unique experiences. Link and Phelan (1995) call this "contextualizing risk factors." They argue that illness cannot be understood solely in terms of the most immediate precursors to illness. We must also understand the social context that created the immediate risk factors.

A few years ago there was a public broadcasting system documentary about depression. In one segment a young woman was being treated for manic-depression by a white-coated psychiatrist who was frustrated by the failure of his drug-based treatment and who was suggesting electroshock therapy as a next course of action. The woman resisted but you could see the strong pressure brought to bear by the psychiatrist in league with her husband. The introduction to the segment mentioned that this woman had been a nurse but had quit when she married. She also had two young boys and seemed to get no parenting assistance from her ex-marine husband. These "background" facts appeared to play no role in the psychiatric treatment of this woman. From a psychiatric perspective these conditions were not causes of disorder in any real sense; at most they triggered a biological reaction (manic-depression).

A sociological perspective would see things differently. The loss of an important source of identity (nurse), confinement to household tasks, and the strain of parenting would be regarded as important stressors relating directly to the disorder. It seems highly likely that changing these characteristics of the social setting would be important therapeutically. We need to know why this situation occurred. It is rare that a husband quits his job when he gets married, rare that he would stay home to raise his children, and rare that his wife would leave all childrearing tasks to him. Gender has a lot to do with why this unhappy woman is in treatment. So it doesn't seem likely that a treatment course that ignores these ideas would be effective and, sure enough, the medication is not working. After all, the medication did not restore her job, get her out of the house more often, or provide assistance with childcare.

This case does not reflect a bad job of psychiatric case work either. It reflects a perspective that simply does not recognize the importance of social arrangements as causes of disorder. Contextualizing the risk means relating this woman's distress not only to role loss and social isolation, but to the social forces that made *her* the likely marital partner to experience such role loss and isolation.

This illustration also allows us to suggest one way that the sociological perspective can be applied to individual treatment. The recognition of the sociological context as a possible causal risk factor can certainly influence treatment. While it may not be possible to change the general effects of gender stratification on this woman's distress, it would certainly be possible to change some of its specific consequences in her life.

If treatment is based on explanations for disorder and existing explanations are incomplete, then persons treated are not as likely to obtain relief as would persons treated by a more complete explanation. Based on commonly accepted criteria for scientific evaluation, sociological explanations are often better supported. This is not to say that they are the *only* correct explanation or the entire explanation but simply that they need to be part of any general explanation.

SOCIAL CAUSES OF PSYCHOLOGICAL DISTRESS

At the opening of this chapter we noted that individuals experience mental illness as a personal problem. We also described the biopsychosocial model as one that focuses on the individual and his or her problem. The previous section, however, clearly illustrates one reason we need to understand the social causes of psychological distress. Understanding personal troubles as partial reflections of social problems can help to improve individual treatment.

Sociological explanations implicate characteristics of broad social structure such as gender and socioeconomic differences as factors that affect well-being. The further implication is that changing these structural arrangements would alter the rates of disorder that can be attributed to social conditions. In turn, this implies a political process in which, for example, inequalities in income would be reduced in order to reduce rates of disorder that can be attributed to income inequality. The sociological contribution to the explanation of psychological distress also includes social policy implications.

In the arena of public health, innovations such as sanitary sewer systems, the creation of safe food supplies, and universal vaccination programs provide examples of extremely effective health interventions that treat no one but have a dramatic effect on health. That is, they prevent disease from occurring and thereby improve the health of everyone. Think about lung cancer. We know that many cases of lung cancer are caused by smoking cigarettes. The immediate cause of lung cancer is related to the destruction of lung tissue and the stimulation of cancerous tumors. This knowledge may be beneficial for devising a treatment for a lung cancer patient. However, if this individual never smoked, the probability of getting lung cancer would have been drastically lower. Never smoking might be regarded as an individual choice and, therefore, it would still be seen as part of an individualistic explanation for where lung cancer comes from (in this case, where it does not come from). But we also know that smoking is influenced by the availability of cigarettes, their cost, and their promotion by cigarette companies. If social (public) policies concerning the availability, cost, and advertising of cigarettes were directed toward the elimination or reduction of the use of tobacco products, this would certainly reduce the incidence of lung cancer. As it is, each person who gets lung cancer from smoking has a personal trouble but that trouble is also related to social policies about accessibility and availability of tobacco products as well as the social problem represented by deaths and incapacity from lung cancer. The "social cost" of smoking is considered to be enormous.

So are the social costs of mental illness. The treatment of mental illness is itself costly. Mental illness also affects worker productivity, job turnover, absenteeism, marital and family stability, parenting, and economic and social well-being. If the origins of mental disorder are regarded as individual, there is little that can be done from a policy perspective. Practitioners simply wait for patients to show up and then they treat them. But just as lung cancer rates can be reduced by preventive public policy measures, so can mental illness rates.

It may be easier to discourage cigarette smoking than to reduce threats to mental health status based on gender, race, education, or income, however. Changes in status systems and role configurations related to them often imply that someone will lose resources in order that someone gain. Changes in access to resources provoke efforts by those who might lose their relative advantage to resist that loss.

Contextualizing risk factors implicates basic conditions of social organization and so provokes substantial political questions that far exceed the scope of sociology as a discipline. Medical models are unlikely to see the importance of changing contextual risk factors because, of course, such models are partly defined by their lack of interest in contextual causes of disorder.

On the other hand, the sociological explanation for the causes of psychological distress can affect mental health services and the societal reaction to mental illness, in general.

SOCIETAL REACTIONS TO MENTAL ILLNESS

We need to address the question of the utility of the sociological perspective for improving direct clinical care and the organization of mental health services. Can sociological explanations for social problems have beneficial effects on personal troubles?

As we think about illness, our goal as treatment providers is the cure or management/care of that illness. This, of course, usually assumes a medical model in which pathological behavior is redirected along a preferred path. Incorrect cognitive assumptions, errant genetics, or deviant behavior call forth therapeutic actions to realign expectations and behavior. In turn, we assume, individuals feel better about their psychological selves and are happier and "healthier" if such a realignment occurs.

The irony here is that mental health treatment professionals do not agree about what outcomes they should expect for those treated. This is particularly true for the most "disabled" of mentally ill persons. In the vast majority of less serious disorders, the goal is the resumption of previous roles (as they were enacted prior to mental disorder). For more severe cases, a single goal for treatment is elusive, perhaps like treating chronic physical illness, it might be that of permitting the maximum participation consistent with the character of the disability (Mechanic 1989).

Community support programs and case management team approaches are built on the recognition of the importance of social context for treatment of disorder. These approaches for treating chronically disabled psychiatric patients try to account for financial, work, family, physical health, and social skill needs simultaneously. In doing so (whether they are successful or not) the approach recognizes that illness is not limited to its immediate physical and psychological symptoms even though the approach is individualistically focused.

Recognizing that societal reactions to deviant behavior play an important role in determining the content and meaning of "therapeutic" responses to symptoms of mental illness is an important insight of a sociological perspective. It permits a public discourse on mental illness that would otherwise not exist. The description of the medicalization of deviance, for example, clarifies much of the contemporary history of mental health treatment. The medicalization process has both positive and negative consequences and the recognition of these facets of medicalization permits more informed debate and policy making.

Mental illness and its treatment is a social construction and, as such, also reflects broader social values and processes. As we suggested that the social causation perspective requires the contextualization of risk, the societal reaction perspective requires the contextualization of treatment policy. We have argued that public and professional ideas about mental illness are related to one another. The contextualization of treatment policy means that mental health policy cannot be made without understanding the wider social, political, and economic contexts in which policy decisions occur. Such a clarification of the context in which policy is made does not, however, assure that insights from this perspective will find their way into actual decision making.

Research representing a social causation explanation for the causes of psychological distress and a social control of deviant behavior explanation for the structure of mental health services will not be automatically accepted simply because they are based on scientifically credible evidence. There is a process problem of converting knowledge itself into "knowledge application." Weiss and Bucuvalas (1980) argue that for knowledge to be applied, it must meet two tests. First, the knowledge must be evaluated as true (scientifically rigorous and consistent with experience) and second, it must be seen as useful (offering practical guides to action and changing current practices). Research and theory can and will be applied to real problems when that research and/or theory makes sense to people and when the research suggests ways in which they can act to take advantage of this new information. One of the purposes of this book has been to provide a clear presentation of the mental health research by sociologists in the past thirty years, so that its utility for understanding the real distress that people experience and the way that distress may be reduced can be assessed.

BIBLIOGRAPHY

American Psychiatric Association. *Diagnostic and Statistical Manual of Mental Disorders*. Washington, DC: American Psychiatric Association, 1952.

American Psychiatric Association. *Diagnostic and Statistical Manual of Mental Disorders*, 3rd ed. Washington, DC: American Psychiatric Association, 1980.

American Psychiatric Association. *Diagnostic and Statistical Manual of Mental Disorders*, 4th ed. Washington, DC: American Psychiatric Association, 1994.

Andreasen, Nancy C. *The Broken Brain: The Biological Revolution in Psychiatry*. New York: Harper & Row, 1984.

Aneshensel, Carol S. "Marital and Employment Role-Strain, Social Support, and Depression among Adult Women," in *Stress, Social Support and Women*, ed. Steven E. Hobfoll. Washington, DC: Hemisphere Publishing Corporation, 1986.

Aneshensel, Carol S., and Leonard I. Pearlin. "Structural Contexts of Sex Differences in Stress," in *Gender and Stress*, ed. Rosalind C. Barnett, Lois Biener, and Grace K. Baruch. New York: Free Press, 1987.

Aneshensel, Carol S., Ralph R. Frerichs, and Virginia A. Clark. "Family Roles and Sex Differences in Depression." *Journal of Health and Social Behavior*, 22, no. 4 (1981): 379–393.

Aneshensel, Carol S., Leonard I. Pearlin, and Roberleigh H. Schuler. "Stress, Role Captivity, and the Cessation of Caregiving." *Journal of Health and Social Behavior*, 34, no. 1 (March 1993): 54–70.

Aneshensel, Carol S., Carolyn M. Rutter, and Peter A. Lachenbruch. "Social Structure, Stress, and Mental Health: Competing

Conceptual and Analytical Models." *American Sociological Review*, 59, no. 2 (April 1991): 166–178.

Angrist, Shirley, Mark Lefton, Simon Dinitz, and Benjamin Pasamanick. *Women after Treatment: A Study of Former Mental Patients and Their Normal Neighbors*. New York: Appleton-Century-Crofts, 1968.

Anthony, E. James. "The Response to Overwhelming Stress in Children," in *The Child in His Family*, Vol. 8, ed. E. James Anthony and Colette Chiland. New York: John Wiley and Sons, 1988a.

Anthony, E. James. "Psychosocial and Psychiatric Disturbances in Children and Their Relation to Stressful Life Circumstances," in *The Child in His Family*, Vol. 8, ed. E. James Anthony and Colette Chiland. New York: John Wiley and Sons, 1988b.

Anthony, W. A., and A. K. Blanch. "Research on Community Support Services: What Have We Learned?" *Psychosocial Rehabilitation Journal*, 12, no. 3 (1989): 341–342.

Baasher, Taha. "The Arab Countries," in *World History of Psychiatry*, ed. John G. Howells. New York: Brunner/Mazel, 1975.

Baca-Zinn, M., and D. S. Eitzen. *Diversity in Families*, 3rd ed. New York: Harper Collins, 1993.

Baker, Dean B. "The Study of Stress at Work." *Annual Review of Public Health*, 6 (1985): 367–381.

Bandura, Albert. *Principles of Behavior Modification*. New York: Holt, Reinhart, and Winston, 1969.

Barnett, Rosalind C., and Grace Baruch. "Social Roles, Gender, and Psychological Distress," in *Gender and Stress*, ed. Rosalind C. Barnett, Lois Biener, and Grace Baruch. New York: Free Press, 1987.

Barnett, Rosalind C., and N. Marshall. "The Relationship between Women's Work and Family Roles and Their Subjective Well-Being and Psychological Stress," in *Women, Work, and Health: Stress and Opportunities*, ed. Marie Frankenhaeusen, Ulf Lundberg, and M. Chesney. New York: Plenum, 1991.

Barnett, Rosalind C., Lois Biener, and Grace Baruch. *Gender and Stress*. New York: Free Press, 1987.

Beiser, Morton. "The Etiology of Childhood Psychiatric Disorder: Sociocultural Aspects," in *Manual of Child Psychopathology*, ed. Benjamin B. Wolman. New York: McGraw-Hill, 1969.

Bell, Rudolph M. *Holy Anorexia*. Chicago, IL: University of Chicago Press, 1985.

Berzoff, Joan, Laura Melano Flanagan, and Patricia Hertz. *Inside Out and Outside In: Psychodynamic Clinical Theory and Practice in Contemporary Multicultural Contexts*. Northvale, NJ: Jason Aronson, 1996.

Billings, Andrew G., and Rudolf H. Moos. "Work Stress and the Stress-

Buffering Roles of Work and Family Resources." *Journal of Occupational Behaviour*, 3, no. 3 (July 1982): 215–232.

Blau, Peter M. *Inequality and Heterogeneity: A Primitive Theory of Social Structure*. New York: Free Press, 1978.

Blood, Robert O., Jr., and Donald M. Wolfe. *Husbands and Wives: The Dynamics of Married Living*. Glencoe, IL: Free Press, 1960.

Blum, Gerald S. *Psychodynamics: The Science of Unconscious Mental Forces*. Blemont, CA: Wadsworth, 1966.

Brand, Jeanne L. "The United States: A Historical Perspective," in *Community Mental Health: An International Perspective*, ed. Richard H. Williams and Lucy D. Ozarin. San Francisco, CA: Jossey-Bass, 1967.

Braverman, Harry. *Labor and Monopoly Capital: The Degradation of Work in the Twentieth Century*. New York: Monthly Review Press, 1974.

Brenner, Harvey. "Estimating the Social Costs of National Economic Policy: Implications for Mental and Physical Health, and Criminal Aggression," in *Achieving the Goals of the Employment Act of 1946—Thirtieth Anniversary Review*, Vol. 1. Washington, DC: U.S. Government Printing Office, 1976.

Breslau, Naomi, David Salkever, and Kathleen S. Staruch. "Women's Labor Force Activity and Responsibilities for Disabled Dependents: A Study of Families with Disabled Children." *Journal of Health and Social Behavior*, 23, no. 2 (June 1982): 169–183.

Brody, Elaine M. "Women in the Middle and Family Help to Older People." *Gerontologist*, 21, no. 5 (October 1981): 471–480.

Brody, Elaine M. *Women in the Middle: Their Parent Care Years*. New York: Springer Publishing Co., 1990.

Brown, George W., M. Bhrolchain, and Tirril Harris. "Social Class and Psychiatric Disturbance Among Women in an Urban Population." *Sociology*, 9 (1975): 225–254.

Brown, George W., and Tirril Harris. *Social Origins of Depression*. New York: Free Press, 1978.

Burgess, Ernest W. "Introduction," in *Mental Disorders in Urban Areas: An Ecological Study of Schizophrenia and Other Psychoses*, Robert E. L. Faris and H. Warren Dunham. Chicago, IL: University of Chicago Press, 1939.

Cain, G. G. "The Economics of Discrimination: Part 1." *Focus*, 7 (1984): 1–11.

Campbell, Angus, Philip E. Converse, and Willard L. Rodgers. *The Quality of American Life*. New York: Russell Sage, 1976.

Campbell, Karen E., Peter V. Marsden, and Jeanne S. Hurlbert. "Social Resources and Socioeconomic Status." *Social Networks*, 8, no. 1 (1986): 97–117.

Caplan, R. D., S. Cobb, J. R. P. French, R. Van Harrison, and S. R. Pinneau. *Job Demands and Worker Health*. Washington, DC: U.S. Department of Health and Human Services, 1975.

Carling, Paul J. *Return to Community: Building Support Systems for People with Psychiatric Disabilities*. New York: Guilford Press, 1995.

Carmin, Cheryl N., and E. Thomas Dowd. "Paradigms in Cognitive Psychotherapy," in *Developments in Cognitive Psychotherapy*, ed. Windy Dryden and Peter Trower. Newbury Park, CA: Sage, 1988.

Catalano, Ralph A., and David Dooley. "Economic Predictors of Depressed Mood and Stressful Life Events." *Journal of Health and Social Behavior*, 18, no. 3 (September 1977): 292–307.

Catalano, Ralph A., and David Dooley. "Health Effects of Economic Instability: A Test of Economic Stress Hypothesis." *Journal of Health and Social Behavior*, 24, no. 1 (March 1983): 46–60.

Chen, Edith, and Sidney Cobb. "Family Structure in Relation to Health and Disease: A Review of the Literature." *Journal of Chronic Diseases*, 12 (1960): 544–567.

Cleary, Paul D., and David Mechanic. "Sex Differences in Psychological Distress among Married People." *Journal of Health and Social Behavior*, 24 (1983): 111–121.

Clinard, Marshall B., and Robert F. Meier. *Sociology of Deviant Behavior*, 9th ed. Fort Worth, TX: Harcourt Brace Jovanovich College Publishers, 1994.

Cohen, Patricia, Jim Johnson, Selma A. Lewis, and Judith S. Brook. "Single Parenthood and Employment Double Jeopardy?" in *Stress between Work and Family*, ed. John Eckenrode and Susan Gore. New York: Plenum, 1990.

Cohen, Rosalie. "Neglected Legal Dilemmas in Community Psychiatry," in *Sociological Perspectives on Community Mental Health*, ed. P. Roman and H. Trice. Philadelphia, PA: Davis, 1974.

Conrad, Peter, and Joseph W. Schneider. *Deviance and Medicalization: From Badness to Sickness*. St. Louis, MO: Mosby, 1980.

Conrad, Peter, and Joseph W. Schneider. *Deviance and Medicalization: From Badness to Sickness*, Expanded ed. Philadelphia, PA: Temple University Press, 1992.

Comptroller General of the United States. *Returning the Mentally Disabled to the Community: Government Needs to Do More*. Washington, DC: Government Accounting Office, 1977.

Cooper, David Graham. *Psychiatry and Anti-Psychiatry*. New York: Ballantine Books, 1971.

Cox, Harold G. *Later Life: The Realities of Aging*, 2nd ed. Englewood Cliffs, NJ: Prentice Hall, 1988.

Crocetti, Guido M., Herzl R. Spiro, and Iradj Siassi. *Contemporary*

Attitudes toward Mental Illness. Pittsburgh, PA: University of Pittsburgh Press, 1974.

Deutsch, Albert. *Shame of the States.* New York: Arno Press, 1948.

Dohrenwend, Barbara S. "Life Events as Stressors: A Methodological Inquiry." *Journal of Health and Social Behavior,* 14 (1973): 167–175.

Dohrenwend, Bruce P., and Barbara Dohrenwend. *Stressful Life Events and Their Contexts.* New Brunswick, NJ: Rutgers University Press, 1981.

Donzelot, Jacques. *The Policing of Families.* New York: Pantheon Books, 1979.

Downey, Geraldine, and Phyllis Moen. "Personal Efficacy, Income, and Family Transitions: A Longitudinal Study of Women Heading Households." *Journal of Health and Social Behavior,* 28, no. 3 (September 1987): 320–333.

Ducey, Charles, and Bennett Simon. "Ancient Greece and Rome," in *World History of Psychiatry,* ed. John G. Howells. New York: Brunner/Mazel, 1975.

Durkheim, Emile. *Suicide.* New York: Free Press, 1897/1951.

Eaton, William W., Christian Ritter, and Diane Brown. "Psychiatric Epidemiology and Psychiatric Sociology: Influences on the Recognition of Bizarre Behaviors as Social Problems," in *Research in Community and Mental Health,* Vol. 6, ed. James R. Greenley. Greenwich, CT: JAI Press, 1990.

Eisenberg, David M., Ronald C. Kessler, Cindy Foster, Frances E. Norlock, David R. Calkins, and Thomas L. Belabanco. "Unconventional Medicine in the United States: Prevalence, Costs, and Patterns of Use." *New England Journal of Medicine,* 328, no. 4 (January 1993): 246–252.

Elkind, David. *Ties That Stress: The New Family Imbalance.* Cambridge, MA: Harvard University Press, 1994.

England, Paula, and L. McCreary. "Integrating Sociology and Economics to Study Gender and Work," in *Women and Work: An Annual Review,* Vol. 2, ed. A. H. Stronberg, L. Larwood, and B. A. Gutek. Newbury Park, CA: Sage, 1987.

Estroff, Sue E. *Making it Crazy: An Ethnography of Psychiatry Clients in an American Community.* Berkeley, CA: University of California Press, 1981.

Etzion, Dalia. "Moderating Effect of Social Support on the Stress-Burnout Relationship." *Journal of Applied Psychology,* 69, no. 4 (November 1984): 615–622.

Eysenck, Michael W. *Principles of Cognitive Psychology.* Hove East Sussex, UK: Lawrence Erlbaum, 1993.

Fancher, Robert. *Cultures of Healing: Correcting the Image of American Mental Health Care.* New York: W. H. Freeman, 1995.

Faris, Robert E. L., and H. Warren Dunham. *Mental Disorders in Urban Areas: An Ecological Study of Schizophrenia and Other Psychoses.* Chicago, IL: University of Chicago Press, 1939.

Feltey, Kathryn M. "Single Parents," in *The Encyclopedia of Marriage and Family*, ed. David Levinson. New York: MacMillan, 1995.

Fenwick, Rudy, and Mark Tausig. "The Macroeconomic Context of Job Stress." *Journal of Health and Social Behavior*, 35, no. 3 (September 1994): 266–282.

Fisher, Gene A., Paul R. Benson, and Richard C. Tessler. "Family Response to Mental Illness: Developments since Deinstitutionalization." *Research in Community and Mental Health*, 6 (1990): 203–236.

Foucault, Michel. *Madness and Civilization: A History of Insanity in the Age of Reason*, trans. Richard Howard. New York: Random House, 1965.

Foucault, Michel. *The Birth of the Clinic: An Archeology of Medical Perception.* New York: Vintage, 1973.

Fox, Mary F., and Sharlene Hesse-Biber. *Women at Work.* Palo Alto, CA: Mayfield Publishing Co., 1984.

Frazer, Alan, and Andrew Winokur. *Biological Bases of Psychiatric Disorders.* New York: Spectrum Publications, 1977.

Freeman, Arthur, James Pretzer, Barbara Fleming, and Karen M. Simon. *Clinical Applications of Cognitive Therapy.* New York: Plenum Press, 1990.

French, John R. P., Jr., Robert D. Caplan, and R. Van Harrison. *The Mechanics of Job Stress and Strain.* New York: Wiley, 1982.

Freyhan, Fritz. "The History of Recent Developments in Psychiatry." *Comprehensive Psychiatry*, Vol. 21, no. 6 (Nov/Dec 1980): 402–410.

Friedman, Robert M., Judith W. Katz-Leavy, Ronald W. Manderscheid, and Diane L. Sondheimer. "Prevalance of Serious Emotional Disturbance in Children and Adolescents," in *Mental Health, United States 1996*, ed. Ronald W. Manderscheid and Mary Anne Sonnenschein, U.S. Department of Health and Human Services Publication No. (SMA) 96-3098. Washington, DC: Superintendent of Documents, U.S. Government Printing Office, 1996.

Gallagher, Bernard, III. *The Sociology of Mental Illness*, 3rd ed. Englewood Cliffs, NJ: Prentice Hall, 1994.

Gay, Peter. *Freud: A Life For Our Time.* New York: Norton, 1988.

Gelles, Richard J., and Murray A. Straus. "Violence in the American Family." *Social Issues*, 35, no. 2 (1979): 15–39.

Gerhardt, Uta. "The Sociological Image of Medicine and the Patient." *Social Science and Medicine*, 29, no. 6 (1989): 721–728.

Glass, Jennifer, and Valerie Camarigg. "Gender, Parenthood, and Job-Family Compatibility." *American Journal of Sociology*, 98, no. 1 (July 1992): 131–151.

Goffman, Erving. *Asylums: Essays on the Social Situation of Mental Patients and Other Inmates.* Chicago, IL: Aldine Publishing Co., 1961.

Goldberg, Gertrude S. "The United States: Feminization of Poverty Amidst Plenty," in *The Feminization of Poverty: Only in America*, ed. G. S. Goldberg and Eleanor Kremen. New York: Greenwood Press, 1990.

Goldberg, Wendy A., Ellen Greenberger, Sharon Hamill, and Robin O'Neil. "Role Demands in the Lives of Employed Single Mothers with Preschoolers." *Journal of Family Issues*, 13, no. 3 (September 1992): 312–333.

Gove, Walter. "The Relationship between Sex Roles, Marital Status, and Mental Illness." *Social Forces*, 51 (1972): 34–44.

Gove, Walter. "The Current Status of the Labeling Theory of Mental Illness," in *Deviance and Mental Illness*, ed. W. R. Gove. Beverly Hills, CA: Sage, 1982.

Gove, Walter, and Michael R. Geerken. "The Effect of Children and Employment on the Mental Health of Married Men and Women." *Social Forces*, 56, no. 1 (1977): 66–76.

Gove, Walter, and Jeanette F. Tudor. "Adult Sex Roles and Mental Illness." *American Journal of Sociology*, 78, no. 4 (1973): 812–835.

Gove, Walter, Michael M. Hughes, and Carolyn B. Style. "Does Marriage Have Positive Effects on the Psychological Well-Being of the Individual?" *Journal of Health and Social Behavior*, 24, no. 2 (1983): 122–131.

Granovetter, Mark. *Getting a Job: A Study of Contacts and Careers.* Cambridge, MA: Harvard University Press, 1974.

Greenhaugh, Leonard, and Zehava Rosenblatt. "Job Insecurity: Toward Conceptual Clarity." *Academy of Management Review*, 9, no. 3 (July 1984): 438–448.

Greenstein, Theodore W. "Gender Ideology and Perceptions of the Fairness of the Division of Household Labor: Effects on Marital Quality." *Social Forces*, 74, no. 3 (March 1996): 1003–1028.

Grob, Gerald N. *The Inner World of American Psychiatry, 1890–1940.* New Brunswick, NJ: Rutgers University Press, 1985.

Gronfein, William. "Psychotropic Drugs and the Origins of Deinstitutionalization." *Social Problems*, 32, no. 5 (June 1985): 425–436.

Hall, Ellen M. "Gender, Work Control, and Stress: A Theoretical

Discussion and Empirical Test," in *The Psychosocial Work Environment: Work Organization, Democratization, and Health*, ed. Jeffrey V. Johnson and Gunn Johansson. Amityville, NY: Baywood Publishing, 1991.

Hall, Richard H. *Sociology of Work: Perspectives, Analyses, and Issues*. Thousand Oaks, CA: Pine Forge Press, 1994.

Heaney, Catherine A., Barbara A. Israel, and James S. House. "Chronic Job Insecurity among Automobile Workers: Effects on Job Satisfaction and Health." *Social Science and Medicine*, 38, no. 10 (May 1994): 1431–1437.

Hobfoll, Steven E. "The Ecology of Stress and Social Support Among Women," in *Stress, Social Support, and Women*, ed. Steven E. Hobfoll. Washington, DC: Hemisphere Publishing Corporation, 1986.

Hochschild, Arlie Russell. *The Second Shift*. New York: Avon, 1989.

Hollingshead, August B., and Frederick C. Redlich. "Social Stratification and Psychiatric Disorders." *American Sociological Review*, 18, no. 2 (April 1953): 163–169.

Holmes, Thomas H., and Richard H. Rahe. "The Social Readjustment Rating Scale." *Journal of Psychosomatic Research*, 11 (1967): 213–218.

Hong, Jinkuk, and Marsha Mailick Seltzer. "The Psychological Consequences of Multiple Roles: The Non-Normative Case." *Journal of Health and Social Behavior*, 36, no. 4 (December 1995): 386–398.

Horwitz, Allan V. *The Social Control of Mental Illness*. New York: Academic Press, 1982.

Horwitz, Allan V. *The Logic of Social Control*. New York: Plenum Publishing, 1990.

Howie the Harp. "Preface," in *Return to Community: Building Support Systems for People with Psychiatric Disabilities*, ed. Paul J. Carling. New York: Guilford Press, 1995.

Hughes, Michael, M., and Walter R. Gove. "Living Alone, Social Integration, and Mental Health." *American Journal of Sociology*, 87 (1981): 48–74.

Hurrell, Joseph J., Jr. "Machine-Paced Work and the Type-A Behaviour Pattern." *Journal of Occupational Psychology*, 58, no. 1 (March 1985): 15–26.

Irwin, Charles, Jr., ed. *Adolescent Social Behavior and Health*. San Francisco, CA: Jossey-Bass Inc., 1987.

Isaac, Rael Jean, and Virginia C. Armat. *Madness in the Streets: How Psychiatry and the Law Abandoned the Mentally Ill*. New York: Free Press, 1990.

Joelson, Lars, and Leif Wahlquist. "The Psychological Meaning of Job

Insecurity and Job Loss: Results of a Longitudinal Study." *Social Science and Medicine*, 25, no. 2 (1987): 179–182.

Joint Commission on Mental Illness and Health. *Action for Mental Health*. New York: Basic Books, 1961.

Kandel, Denise B., Mark Davies, and Victoria H. Raveis. "The Stressfulness of Daily Social Roles for Women: Marital, Occupational, and Household Roles." *Journal of Health and Social Behavior*, 26, no. 1 (March 1985): 64–78.

Karasek, Robert A. "The Political Implications of Psychosocial Work Redesign: A Model of the Psychosocial Class Structure," in *The Psychosocial Work Environment: Work Organization, Democratization, and Health*, ed. Jeffrey V. Johnson and Gunn Johansson. Amityville, NY: Baywood Publishing, 1991.

Karasek, Robert A., and Tores Theorell. *Healthy Work: Stress Productivity, and the Reconstruction of Working Life*. New York: Basic Books, 1990.

Karasek, Robert A., Bertil Gardell, and Jan Lindell. "Work and Non-Work Correlates of Illness and Behaviour in Male and Female Swedish White Collar Workers." *Journal of Occupational Behaviour*, 8, no. 3 (July 1987): 187–207.

Karasek, Robert A., Konstantinos P. Triandas, and Sohail S. Chandry. "Co-Worker and Supervisor Support as Moderators of Association between Task Characteristics and Mental Strain." *Journal of Occupational Behaviour*, 3, no. 2 (April 1982): 181–200.

Kass, Frederic, Robert Spitzer, Janet B. W. Williams, and Thomas Widigen. "Self-Defeating Personality Disorder and DSM-III-R: Development of the Diagnostic Criteria." *American Journal of Psychiatry*, 146, no. 8 (August 1989): 1022–1026.

Kessler, Ronald C., and William J. Magee. "Childhood Family Violence and Adult Recurrent Depression." *Journal of Health and Social Behavior*, 35, no. 1 (March 1994): 13–27.

Kessler, Ronald C., and Jane D. McLeod. "Sex Differences in Vulnerability to Undesirable Life Events." *American Sociological Review*, 49, no. 5 (October 1984): 620–631.

Kessler, Ronald C., and James A. McRae. "The Effect of Wives' Unemployment on the Mental Health of Married Men and Women." *American Sociological Review*, 47 (1982): 216–227.

Kessler, Ronald C., and Harold W. Neighbors. "A New Perspective on the Relationships Among Race, Social Class and Psychological Distress." *Journal of Health and Social Behavior*, 27, no. 2 (June 1986): 107–115.

Kessler, Ronald C., James S. House, and J. Blake Turner. "Unemployment and Health in a Community Sample." *Journal of Health and Social Behavior*, 28, no. 1 (March 1987): 51–59.

Kessler, Ronald C., J. Blake Turner, and James S. House. "Unemployment, Reemployment, and Emotional Functioning in a Community Sample." *American Sociological Review*, 54, no. 4 (August 1989): 648–657.

Kessler, Ronald C., Patricia A. Bergland, Shanyang Zhao, Philip J. Leaf, Anthony C. Kouszis, Martha L. Bruce, Robert M. Friedman, Rene C. Grosser, Cille Kennedy, William E. Narrow, Timothy G. Kuehnel, Eugene M. Laska, Ronald C. Manderscheid, Robert A. Rosenheck, Timothy W. Santori, and Max Scheiner. "The 12-Month Prevelance and Correlates of Serious Mental Illness (SMI)," in *Mental Health, United States*, ed. Ronald W. Manderscheid and Mary Anne Sonnenschein. Center for Mental Health Services. U.S. Department of Health and Human Services Publication No. (SMA) 96-3098. Washington, DC: Superintendent of Documents, U.S. Government Printing Office, 1996.

Kirk, Stuart A., and Herb Kutchins. *The Selling of DSM: The Rhetoric of Science in Psychiatry*. New York: Aldine de Gruyter, 1992.

Kirk, Stuart A., and Mark E. Therrien. "Community Mental Health Myths and the Fate of Former Hospitalized Patients." *Psychiatry*, 38, no. 3 (1975): 209–217.

Kohn, Melvin L., and Carmi Schooler. "Occupational Experience and Psychological Functioning: An Assessment of Reciprocal Effects." *American Sociological Review*, 38, no. 1 (February 1973): 97–118.

Kohn, Melvin L., and Carmi Schooler. *Work and Personality: An Inquiry into the Impact of Social Stratification*. Norwood, NJ: Ablex Publishing Corp., 1983.

Kohn, Melvin L., and Carmi Schooler. "Job Conditions and Personality: A Longitudinal Assessment of Their Reciprocal Effects." *American Journal of Sociology*, 87, no. 4 (1988): 1257–1286.

Kohn, Melvin L., Atsushi Naoi, Carrie Schoenbach, Carmi Schooler, and Kazimierz M. Slomczynski. "Position in the Class Structure and Psychological Functioning in the United States, Japan, and Poland." *American Journal of Sociology*, 95, no. 4 (January 1990): 964–1008.

Kornhauser, Arthur William. *Mental Health of the Industrial Worker: A Detroit Study*. New York: Wiley, 1965.

Kraut, Karen, and Molly Luna. *Work and Wages: Facts on Women and People of Color in the Workforce*. Washington, DC: National Committee on Pay Equity, 1992.

Kuhnert, Karl W., and Robert J. Vance. "Job Insecurity and Moderators of the Relation between Job Insecurity and Employee Adjustment," in *Stress and Well-Being at Work: Assessments and Interventions for Occupational Mental Health*, ed. James C. Quick, Lawrence R. Murphy, and Joseph J. Hurrell Jr. Washington, DC: American Psychological Association, 1992.

La Fond, John, and Mary L. Durham. *Back to the Asylum: The Future of Mental Health Law and Policy in the United States*. New York: Oxford University Press, 1992.

Laing, R. D. *The Politics of Experience*. New York: Ballantine Books, 1967.

Lambo, T. Adeoye. "Mid and West Africa," in *World History of Psychiatry*, ed. John G. Howells. New York: Brunner/Mazel, 1975.

Larocco, James M., James S. House, and John R. P. French Jr. "Social Support, Occupational Stress, and Health." *Journal of Health and Social Behavior*, 21, no. 3 (September 1980): 202–218.

Lennon, Mary Clare. "Sex Differences in Distress: The Impact of Gender and Work Roles." *Journal of Health and Social Behavior*, 28, no. 1 (September 1987): 290–305.

Lennon, Mary Clare. "Women, Work, and Well-Being: The Importance of Work Conditions." *Journal of Health and Social Behavior*, 35, no. 3 (September 1994): 235–247.

Lennon, Mary Clare, and Sarah Rosenfield. "Women and Mental Health: The Interaction of Job and Family Conditions." *Journal of Health and Social Behavior*, 33, no. 4 (December 1992): 316–327.

Lickey, Marvin E., and Barbara Gordon. *Medicine and Mental Illness: The Use of Drugs in Psychiatry*. New York: W. H. Freeman and Co., 1991.

Lin, Nan. "Social Resources and Instrumental Action," in *Social Structure and Network Analysis*, ed. Peter V. Marsden and Nan Lin. Beverly Hills, CA: Sage, 1982.

Lin, Nan, John C. Vaughn, and Walter M. Ensel. "Social Resources and Occupational Status Attainment." *Social Forces*, 59, no. 4 (1981): 1163–1181.

Link, Bruce. "Understanding Labeling Effects in the Area of Mental Disorders: An Assessment of the Effects of Expectations of Rejection." *American Sociological Review*, 52, no. 1 (February 1987): 96–112.

Link, Bruce, and Francis T. Cullen. "The Labeling Theory of Mental Disorder: A Review of the Evidence," in *Research in Community Mental Health*, Vol. 6, ed. James R. Greenley. Greenwich, CT: JAI Press, 1990.

Link, Bruce, and Jo Phelan. "Social Conditions as Fundamental Causes of Disease." *Journal of Health and Social Behavior*, Special Issue (1995): 80–94.

Link, Bruce, Mary Clare Lennon, and Bruce P. Dohrenwend. "Socioeconomic Status and Depression: The Role of Occupations Involving Direction, Control, and Planning." *American Journal of Sociology*, 98, no. 6 (May 1993): 1351–1387.

Link, Bruce, Jerrold Mirotznik, and Francis T. Cullen. "The Effectiveness of Stigma Coping Orientations: Can Negative Consequences of Mental Illness Labeling Be Avoided?" *Journal of Health and Social Behavior*, 32, no. 3 (September 1991): 302–320.

Link, Bruce, Francis T. Cullen, James Frank, and John F. Woznick. "The Social Rejection of Former Mental Patients: Understanding Why Labels Matter." *American Journal of Sociology*, 92, no. 6 (May 1987): 1461–1500.

Link, Bruce, Francis T. Cullen, Elmer Struening, Patrick E. Shrout, and Bruce P. Dohrenwend. "A Modified Labeling Theory Approach to Mental Disorders." *American Sociological Review*, 54, no. 3 (June 1989): 400–423.

Loring, Marti, and Brian Powell. "Gender, Race, and the DSM-III: A Study of Objectivity of Psychiatric Diagnostic Behavior." *Journal of Health and Social Behavior*, 29, no. 1 (March 1988): 1–22.

Lowe, Graham S., and Herbert C. Northcott. "The Impact of Working Conditions, Social Roles, and Personal Characteristics on Gender Differences in Distress." *Work and Occupations*, 15, no. 1 (February 1988): 55–77.

Margetts, Edward L. "Canada," in *World History of Psychiatry*, ed. John G. Howells. New York: Brunner/Mazel, 1975.

Marx, Karl. *Early Writings*, ed. and trans. T. B. Bottomore. New York: McGraw-Hill, 1964.

Matthews, Lisa, Rand D. Conger, and K. A. S. Wickerama. "Work-Family Conflict and Marital Quality: Mediating Processes." *Social Psychology Quarterly*, 59, no. 1 (March 1996): 62–79.

Mechanic, David. *Mental Health and Social Policy*, 3rd ed. Englewood Cliffs, NJ: Prentice Hall, 1989.

Menaghan, Elizabeth G. "Assessing the Impact of Family Transitions on Marital Experience," in *Family Stress, Coping, and Social Support*, ed. Hamilton I. McCubbin, A. Elizabeth Cauble, and Joan M. Patterson. Springfield, IL: Charles C. Thomas, 1982.

Menaghan, Elizabeth G. "Role Changes and Psychological Well-Being: Variations in Effects by Gender and Role Repertoire." *Social Forces*, 67, no. 3 (March 1989): 693–714.

Merz, C. Noel Bairey. "The Secondary Prevention of Coronary Artery Disease." *American Journal of Medicine*, 102, no. 6 (June 1997): 572–581.

Michello, Janet A. *Gender and Depression: An Evaluation of Social Role Explanations*. Unpublished Doctoral Dissertation, Department of Sociology, University of Akron, Akron, OH, 1989.

Miller, Joanne. "Individual and Occupational Determinants of Job Satisfaction: A Focus on Gender Differences." *Sociology of Work and Occupations*, 7, no. 3 (August 1980): 337–366.

Mills, C. Wright. *The Sociological Imagination*. New York: Oxford University Press, 1959.

Minkoff, K. "A Map of Chronically Mental Patients," in *The Chronically Mental Patient*, ed. J. Talbott. Washington, DC: American Psychiatric Association, 1978.

Mirowsky, John, and Catherine E. Ross. *Social Causes of Psychological Distress*. New York: Aldine de Gruyter, 1989.

Mirowsky, John, and Catherine E. Ross. "Psychiatric Diagnosis as Reified Measurement." *Journal of Health and Social Behavior*, 30, no. 1 (March 1989a): 11–25.

Mirowsky, John, and Catherine E. Ross. "Rejoinder—Assessing the Types and Severity of Psychological Problems: An Alternative to Diagnosis." *Journal of Health and Social Behavior*, 30, no. 1 (March 1989b): 38–40.

Mirowsky, John, and Catherine E. Ross. "Sex Differences in Distress." *American Sociological Review*, 60, no. 3 (June 1995): 449–468.

Moen, Phyllis, Julie Robinson, and Donna Dempster-McClain. "Caregiving and Women's Well-Being: A Life Course Approach." *Journal of Health and Social Behavior*, 36, no. 3 (September 1995): 259–273.

Morgan, Steve. *Community Mental Health: Practical Approaches to Long-Term Problems*. New York: Chapman and Hall, 1993.

Mosher, Loren R., and Lorenzo Burti. *Community Mental Health: A Practical Guide*. New York: W. W. Norton and Company, 1994.

National Institute of Mental Health. *A Network for Caring: The Community Support Program of the National Institute of Mental Health. Summary Proceedings of Four Learning Community Conferences on Manpower and Development Training. January 1978–November 1979*. Washington, DC: U.S. Department of Health and Human Services Publication No. (ADM) 81-1063.

New York Times. "Postal Service Expands Anti-Violence Plan." April 20, 1995, sec. A, p. 20.

New York Times. "The Downsizing of America." March 7, 1996, sec. A, p. 1.

Nunnally, Jum C., Jr. *Popular Conceptions of Mental Health: Their Development and Change*. New York: Holt, Rinehart, and Winston, 1961.

Ortega, Suzanne, and Jay Corzine. "Socioeconomic Status and Mental Disorders," in *Research in Community and Mental Health*, Vol. 6, ed. James R. Greenley. Greenwich, CT: JAI Press, 1990.

Palmer, Stuart, and John A. Humphrey. *Deviant Behavior: Patterns, Sources, and Control*. New York: Plenum Press, 1990.

Parsons, Talcott. *The Social System*. New York: Free Press, 1951.

Pearlin, Leonard I. "Sex Roles and Depression," in *Life Span Developmental Psychology: Normative Life Crises*, ed. Nancy Datan and Leon H. Ginsberg. New York: Academic Press, 1975a.

Pearlin, Leonard I. "Status Inequality and Stress in Marriage." *American Sociological Review*, 40 (1975b): 344–357.

Pearlin, Leonard I. "The Social Context of Stress," in *Handbook of Stress: Theoretical and Clinical Aspects*, ed. Leo Goldberger and Shlomo Breznitz. New York: Free Press, 1981.

Pearlin, Leonard I. "Role Strains and Personal Stress," in *Psychosocial Stress*, ed. Howard Kaplan. New York: Academic Press, 1983.

Pearlin, Leonard I. "The Sociological Study of Stress." *Journal of Health and Social Behavior*, 30, no. 3 (September 1989): 241–256.

Pearlin, Leonard I., and Morton A. Lieberman. "Social Sources of Emotional Distress," in *Research in Community and Mental Health*, Vol. 1, ed. Roberta G. Simmons. Greenwich, CT: JAI Press, 1979.

Pearlin, Leonard I., Joseph T. Mullan, Shirley J. Semple, and Marilyn M. Skaff. "Caregiving and the Stress Process: An Overview of Concepts and Their Measures." *Gerontologist*, 30, no. 5 (October 1990): 583–594.

Peterson, Richard R. "A Re-Evaluation of the Economic Consequences of Divorce." *American Sociological Review*, 61, no. 3 (June 1996): 528–536.

Phelan, Jo, and Ann Steuve. "Public Conceptions of Mental Illness in 1950 and Today: Findings from the 1996 General Social Survey Module on Mental Health." Presented at the *92nd Annual Meeting of the American Sociological Association*, Toronto, Ontario, Canada. August 9, 1997.

Porter, Roy C. *A Social History of Madness: The World Through the Eyes of the Insane*. New York: E. P. Dutton, 1987.

Rabkin, Judith G. "Determinants of Public Attitudes About Mental Illness: Summary of the Research Literature," in *Attitudes toward the Mentally Ill, Research Perspectives: Report of an NIMH Workshop*, ed. Judith G. Rabkin, Lenore Gelb, and Joyce B. Lazar. Washington, DC: U.S. Department of Health and Human Services, 1980.

Rabkin, Judith G., and Elmer L. Struening. "Life Events, Stress, and Illness." *Science*, 194 (December 1976): 1013–1020.

Radloff, Lenore. "Sex Differences in Depression: The Effects of Occupational and Marital Status." *Sex Roles*, 1 (1975): 249–265.

Rao, A. Venicoba. "India," in *World History of Psychiatry*, ed. John G. Howells. New York: Brunner/Mazel, 1975.

Reskin, Barbara F., and Shelley Coverman. "Sex and Race in the

Determinants of Psychophysical Distress: A Reappraisal of the Sex-Role Hypothesis." *Social Forces*, 63, no. 4 (June 1985): 1038–1059.

Reskin, Barbara F., and Irene Padavic. *Women and Men at Work.* Thousand Oaks, CA: Pine Forge Press, 1994.

Robins, Lee N., and Darrel A. Regier, eds. *Psychiatric Disorders in America: The Epidemiological Catchment Area Study.* New York: Free Press, 1990.

Rollins, Boyd, and Harold Feldman. "Marital Satisfaction Over the Family Life Cycle." *Journal of Marriage and the Family*, 32 (1970): 11–28.

Rosario, Margaret, Marybeth Shinn, Hanne Morch, and Carol Huckabe. "Gender Differences in Coping and Social Supports: Testing Socialization and Role Constraint Theories." *Journal of Community Psychology*, 16, no. 1 (February 1988): 55–69.

Rose, Stephen M., and Bruce L. Black. *Advocacy and Empowerment: Mental Health Care in the Community.* Boston, MA: Routledge and Kegan, 1985.

Rosenbaum, S., and B. Starfield. "Today's Children, Tomorrow's Youth." Paper presented at the National Invitational Conference on Health Futures of Adolescents. Daytona Beach, FL, 1986.

Rosenfield, Sarah. "Sex Roles and Societal Reactions to Mental Illness: The Labeling of 'Deviant' Deviance." *Journal of Health and Social Behavior*, 23, no. 1 (March 1982): 18–24.

Rosenfield, Sarah. "The Health Effects of Women's Employment: Personal Control and Sex Differences in Mental Health." *Journal of Health and Social Behavior*, 30, no. 1 (March 1989): 77–91.

Rosenfield, Sarah. "The Costs of Sharing: Wives' Employment and Husbands' Mental Health." *Journal of Health and Social Behavior*, 33, no. 3 (September 1992): 213–225.

Rosenstein, Marilyn J., Laura J. Milazzo-Sayre, Robin L. Macaskill, and Ronald W. Manderscheid. "Use of Inpatient Psychiatric Services by Special Populations," in *Mental Health, United States, 1987*, ed. Ronald W. Manderscheid and Sally A. Barrett. Rockville, MD: U.S. Department of Health and Human Services, National Institute of Mental Health, Division of Biometry and Applied Sciences, 1987.

Ross, Catherine E., and Joan Huber. "Hardship and Depression." *Journal of Health and Social Behavior*, 26 (1985): 312–327.

Ross, Catherine E., and Marieke Van Willigen. "Education and the Subjective Quality of Life." *Journal of Health and Social Behavior*, 38, no. 3 (September 1997): 275–297.

Ross, Catherine E., and Chia-Ling Wu. "Education, Age, and the Cumulative Advantage in Health." *Journal of Health and Social Behavior*, 37, no. 1 (March 1996): 104–120.

Ross, Catherine E., John Mirowsky, and Joan Huber. "Dividing Work, Sharing Work, and In-Between: Marriage Patterns and Depression." *American Sociological Review*, 48 (1983): 809–823.

Rotenberg, Mordechai. *Damnation and Deviance: The Protestant Ethic and the Spirit of Failure.* New York: Free Press, 1978.

Roxburgh, Susan. "Gender Differences in Work and Well-Being: Effects of Exposure and Vulnerability." *Journal of Health and Social Behavior*, 37, no. 3 (September 1996): 265–277.

Ryan, P., R. Ford, and P. Clifford. *Case Management and Community Care, Research and Development for Psychiatry.* London, 1991.

Satin, David G. "Introduction: Social Responsibility and Professional Vested Interests," in *Insights and Innovations in Community Mental Health: Tem Erich Lindemann Memorial Lectures*, ed. David G. Satin. Northvale, NJ: Jason Aronson Inc., 1994.

Saul, Leon J. *The Childhood Emotional Pattern and Psychodynamic Therapy.* New York: Van Norstrand Publishing Co., 1980.

Scheff, Thomas J. *Being Mentally Ill: A Sociological Theory.* Chicago, IL: Aldine Publishing Co., 1966.

Scheff, Thomas J. *Being Mentally Ill: A Sociological Theory*, 2nd ed. New York: Aldine Publishing Co., 1984.

Scott, Jacqueline, and Duane F. Alwin. "Gender Differences in Parental Strain: Parental Role or Gender Role?" *Journal of Family Issues*, 10 (1989): 482–503.

Scott, Wilbur J. "Post Traumatic Stress Disorder in DSM-III: A Case in the Politics of Diagnosis and Disease." *Social Problems*, 37, no. 3 (August 1990): 294–310.

Scull, Andrew. *The Most Solitary of Afflictions: Madness and Society in Britain, 1700–1900.* New Haven, CT: Yale University Press, 1993.

Selye, Hans. *The Stress of Life.* New York: McGraw-Hill, 1956.

Simon, Robin W. "Gender, Multiple Roles, Role Meaning, and Mental Health." *Journal of Health and Social Behavior*, 36, no. 2 (June 1995): 182–194.

Skultans, Vieda. *English Madness: Ideas on Insanity, 1580–1890.* London: Routledge and K. Paul, 1979.

Sontag, Susan. *Illness as a Metaphor.* New York: Farrar, Strauss, and Giroux, 1978.

Spitzer, Robert L., and Janet B. W. Williams. "Introduction," in *Diagnostic and Statistical Manual of Mental Disorders*, 3rd rev. ed., ed. American Psychiatric Association. Washington, DC: American Psychiatric Association, 1987.

Srole, Leo, Thomas S. Langer, Stanley T. Michael, Marvin K. Opler, and Thomas A. C. Rennie. *Mental Health in the Metropolis: The Midtown Manhattan Study.* New York: McGraw-Hill, 1962.

Srole, Leo, Thomas S. Langer, Stanley T. Michael, Price Kirkpatrick,

Marvin K. Opler, and Thomas A. C. Rennie. *Mental Health in the Metropolis: The Midtown Manhattan Study*, rev. ed. New York: New York University Press, 1978.

Starr, Paul. *The Transformation of American Medicine*. New York: Basic Books, 1982.

Stone, Robyn, Gail Lee Cafferata, and Judith Sangl. "Caregivers of the Frail Elderly: A National Profile." *Gerontologist*, 27, no. 5 (October 1987): 616–626.

Szasz, Thomas. *The Myth of Mental Illness: Foundations of a Theory of Personal Conduct*. New York: Hoeber-Harper, 1961.

Szasz, Thomas. *The Manufacture of Madness: A Comparative Study of the Inquisition and the Mental Health Movement*. New York: Harper & Row, 1970.

Szasz, Thomas. *Ideology and Insanity: Essays on the Psychiatric Dehumanization of Man*. Garden City, NY: Anchor Books, 1975.

Szasz, Thomas. *Cruel Compassion: Psychiatric Control of Society's Unwanted*. New York: Wiley, 1994.

Takeuchi, David T., and Russell K. Adair. "The Exposure and Vulnerability of Ethnic Minorities to Life Events," in *Research in Community and Mental Health*, Vol. 7, ed. James R. Greenley and Philip J. Leaf. Greenwich, CT: JAI Press, 1992.

Talbott, J. A. "Deinstitutionalization: Avoiding the Disasters of the Past." *Hospital Community Psychiatry*, 30 (1979).

Tausig, Mark. "Detecting 'Cracks' in Mental Health Service Systems: Application of Network Analytic Techniques." *American Journal of Community Psychology*, 15, no. 3 (June 1987): 337–351.

Tausig, Mark. "Microsocial Implications of the Macrostructural Distribution of Social Resources." *Sociological Focus*, 23, no. 4 (October 1990): 333–340.

Tausig, Mark, and Rudy Fenwick. "Gender Differences in the Causes of Worker Stress." Paper presented at *The International Conference on Social Stress*. Venice, Italy, 1992.

Tausky, Curt. *Work and Society: An Introduction to Industrial Society*. Itasca, IL: F. E. Peacock, 1984.

Terkel, Studs. *Working*. New York: Avon, 1972.

Tessler, Richard C., Lewis M. Killian, and Gayle D. Gubman. "Stages in Family Response to Mental Illness: An Ideal Type." *Psychosocial Rehabilitation Journal*, 10, no. 4 (November 1987): 3–16.

Thoits, Peggy A. "Multiple Identities and Psychological Well-Being: A Reformation and Test of the Social Isolation Hypothesis." *American Sociological Review*, 48, no. 2 (April 1983): 174–187.

Thoits, Peggy A. "Multiple Identities: Examining Gender and Marital Status: Differences in Distress." *American Sociological Review*, 51, no. 2 (April 1986): 259–272.

Thoits, Peggy A. "Gender and Marital Status Differences in Control and Distress: Common Stress Versus Unique Stress Explanations." *Journal of Health and Social Behavior*, 28, no. 1 (March 1987): 7–22.

Thoits, Peggy A. "Stressors and Problem-Solving: The Individual as Psychological Activist." *Journal of Health and Social Behavior*, 35, no. 2 (June 1994): 143–160.

Thomas, Melvin E., and Michael Hughes. "The Continuing Significance of Race: A Study of Race, Class and Quality of Life in America, 1972–1985." *American Sociological Review*, 50, no. 6 (December 1986): 830–841.

Tomaskovic-Devey, Donald. *Gender and Racial Inequality at Work: The Sources and Consequences of Job Segregation.* Ithaca, NY: ILR Press, 1993.

Torrey, E. F., S. M. Wolfe, and L. Flynn. *Care of the Seriously Mentally Ill: A Rating of State Programs*, 2nd ed. Washington, DC: Public Citizen Health Research Group, 1988.

Townsend, John Marshall. *Cultural Conceptions and Mental Illness: A Comparison of Germany and America.* Chicago, IL: University of Chicago Press, 1978.

Trent, Kim. "Postal Workers Union Tackles Violence on Job, Workers' Stress." *Detroit News* (August 16, 1994), sec. B, p. 1.

Turner, J. Blake. "Economic Context and the Health Effects of Unemployment." *Journal of Health and Social Behavior*, 36, no. 3 (September 1995): 213–229.

Turner, J. C., and W. J. Tenhoor. "The NIMH Community Support Program: Pilot Approach to a Needed Social Reform." *Schizophrenia Bulletin*, 12 (1978): 319–344.

Turner, R. Jay, and Donald A. Lloyd. "Lifetime Traumas and Mental Health: The Significance of Cumulative Adversity." *Journal of Health and Social Behavior*, 36, no. 4 (December 1995): 360–376.

Turner, R. Jay, and Franco Marino. "Social Support and Social Structure: A Descriptive Epidemiology." *Journal of Health and Social Behavior*, 35, no. 3 (September 1994): 193–212.

Turner, R. Jay, and Patricia Roszell. "Psychosocial Resources and the Stress Process," in *Stress and Mental Health: Contemporary Issues and Prospects for the Future*, ed. William R. Avison and Ian H. Gottlib. New York: Plenum Press, 1994.

Turner, R. Jay, Blair Wheaton, and Donald A. Lloyd. "The Epidemiology of Social Stress." *American Sociological Review*, 60, no. 1 (February 1995): 104–125.

Ulbrich, Patricia M., George J. Warheit, and Rick S. Zimmerman. "Race, Socioeconomic Status, and Psychological Disorder." *Journal of Health and Social Behavior*, 30, no. 1 (March 1989): 131–146.

U.S. Bureau of the Census. *Poverty in the United States: 1992*. Current Population Reports, Series P-60, no. 185. Washington, DC: U.S. Government Printing Office, 1993.

U.S. Bureau of the Census. *Current Populations Reports: Household and Family Characteristics, March 1996*. Washington, DC: U.S. Government Printing Office, 1997.

Vachon, Mary L. S., and Stanley K. Stylianos. "The Role of Social Support in Bereavement." *Journal of Social Issues*, 44 (Fall 1988): 175–190.

Vanfossen, Beth E. "Sex Differences in the Mental Health Effects of Spouse Support and Equity." *Journal of Health and Social Behavior*, 22 (1981): 130–143.

Vanfossen, Beth E. "Sex Differences in Depression: The Role of Spouse Support," in *Stress, Social Support, and Women*, ed. Stephen E. Hobfoll. Washington, DC: Hemisphere Publishing Corporation, 1986.

Veith, Ilza. "The Far East," in *World History of Psychiatry*, ed. John G. Howells. New York: Brunner/Mazel, 1975.

Veroff, Joseph, Elizabeth Douvan, and Richard Kulka. *The Inner American: A Self Portrait from 1957 to 1976*. New York: Basic Books, 1981.

Wallace, Meredith, Mary Levens, and George Singer. "Blue Collar Stress," in *Causes, Coping, and Consequences of Stress at Work*, ed. Cary L. Cooper and Roy Payne. New York: Wiley, 1988.

Wallerstein, Judith, and Joan Berlin Kelly. *Surviving the Breakup: How Children and Parents Cope with Divorce*. New York: Basic Books, 1980.

Wasow, Mona. "The Need for Asylum for the Chronically Mentally Ill." *Schizophrenia Bulletin*, 12, no. 2 (1986): 162–167.

Weiss, Carol H., and Michael J. Bucuvalas. "Truth Tests and Utility Tests: Decision Makers' Frames of Reference for Social Science Research." *American Sociological Review*, 45, no. 2 (April 1980): 302–313.

Weissman, Myrna M., and Gerald L. Klerman. "Sex Differences and the Epidemiology of Depression." *Archives of General Psychiatry*, 34 (1977): 98–111.

Willie, Charles V. *The Caste and Class Controversy*. Bayside, NY: General Hall Inc., 1979.

Wilson, Holly S., and Carol R. Kneisl. *Psychiatric Nursing*, 4th ed. Redwood City, CA: Addison-Wesley, 1992.

Winerip, Michael. *9 Highland Road*. New York: Pantheon Books, 1994.

Winhurst, J. A., F. H. Marcelissen, and R. J. Kleber. "Effects of Social Support in Stress-Strain Relationship: A Dutch Sample." *Social Sciences and Medicine*, 16, no. 4 (1982): 475–482.

Wolf, Wendy C., and Neil D. Fligstein. "Sexual Stratification: Differences in Power in the Work Setting." *Social Forces*, 58, no. 1 (September 1979): 94–107.

Yogev, Sara. "Do Professional Women Have Egalitarian Marital Relationships?" *Journal of Marriage and the Family*, 43 (1981): 865–871.

Young, Laura M., and Brian Powell. "The Effects of Obesity on the Clinical Judgements of Mental Health Professionals." *Journal of Health and Social Behavior*, 26, no. 3 (September 1985): 233–246.

Zipple, A. M., P. J. Carling, and J. McDonald. "A Rehabilitation Response to the Call for Asylum." *Schizophrenia Bulletin*, 13, no. 4 (1987): 539–546.

INDEX